CRADLE C

The Story of the Mag ⋅ːy and the Cradle of Humankind

Vincent Carruthers

WITH CONTRIBUTIONS BY MARINA ELLIOTT

Published by Struik Nature
(an imprint of Penguin Random House South Africa (Pty) Ltd)
Reg. No. 1953/000441/07
The Estuaries No. 4, Oxbow Crescent, Century City, 7441 South Africa
PO Box 1144, Cape Town, 8000 South Africa

Visit **www.penguinrandomhouse.co.za** and join the
Struik Nature Club for updates, news, events and special offers.

First published in 2019
1 3 5 7 9 10 8 6 4 2
Copyright © in text, 2019: Vincent Carruthers
Copyright © in photographs, 2019: Vincent Carruthers unless otherwise
indicated alongside images
Copyright © in illustrations, 2019: Vincent Carruthers &
Penguin Random House South Africa (Pty) Ltd unless
otherwise indicated alongside illustrations
Copyright © in maps, 2019: as indicated alongside maps
Copyright © in published edition, 2019:
Penguin Random House South Africa (Pty) Ltd

Publisher: Pippa Parker
Project manager: Helen de Villiers
Editor: Karen Press
Designer: Janice Evans
Illustrator: Sally MacLarty
Cartographers: Gerry Comninos, Lynda Whitfield & Sally MacLarty
Proofreader & indexer: Emsie du Plessis

Reproduction by Studio Repro and Hirt & Carter Cape (Pty) Ltd
Printed and bound by Novus Print Solutions, Cape Town, South Africa

MIX
Paper from
responsible sources
FSC
www.fsc.org   FSC® C022948

Print: 9781775845973
ePub: 9781775845881

PHOTO CREDITS

Front cover: Star formation in deep space – ESA/Hubble; 'Mrs Ples' – Marina Elliott;
Visitors leaving Sterkfontein Caves – Anthony van Tonder / Africa Media Online / AfriPics
Back cover: View from the Cradle to the Magaliesberg – Author;
Aerial view of the Maropeng Visitor Centre – Author;
Tswana subjects carrying tribute to Mzilikazi (by Charles Bell) – Museum Africa;
Author with students in the Magaliesberg – Eduard Stam
Title page: Magaliesberg waterfall – André Wedepohl
Pages 4–5: View of the author's Magaliesberg property – Author
Pages 20–21: Crocodile River flowing through Lion and Safari Park – Dane Bishop
Pages 88–89: The lofty main chamber in Sterkfontein Caves – Justin Lee Photography
Pages 152–153: Hartbeespoort Dam wall – Author

Author's note

For many years I have been intrigued by the area now known as the Magaliesberg Biosphere Reserve. Here, close to the throbbing cities of Johannesburg and Tshwane/Pretoria, lies the evidence of the long and complex story of the origins of life – not only the hominin fossil record for which it is most famous, but the entire evolution of our living environment. I have derived a life-long pleasure from hiking, observing, reading and working professionally in this rocky countryside and, from the generously shared expertise of others, I have learned to enjoy and respect its magnetic charm. Over the years, I have tried to convey some of that fascination in talks and in other publications about the Magaliesberg and I hope to do so further in this work by exploring the full evolutionary history revealed in this landscape.

Many people have helped to make my pursuit of the story of the Cradle-Magaliesberg such a rewarding experience. There have been adventurous field trips, interesting discussions over long Sunday lunches and hikes along winding paths with wonderful friends. Tim Partridge and Tony Brink introduced me to the unique geomorphology, and the ever-cheerful Phil Bonner shared his unequalled knowledge of the history of the people of the Cradle. Revil Mason was the first to show me the archaeological richness of the region in the 1970s, and Lee Berger fired my enthusiasm for palaeoanthropology a decade later. Kevin Gill taught me about the botany and Paul Fatti encouraged me to join the Mountain Club of South Africa as part of their dedicated defence of the environment. At the time of the centenary of the South African War, I accompanied John Pennefather and the Rustenburg Military History Group on some wonderfully informative field trips to the battlefields in the Magaliesberg area, and the history of that war has become an abiding interest of mine.

With the emergence of a new political dispensation in South Africa in the 1990s, opportunities arose to broaden the heritage estate of the country and make it more inclusive. I was privileged to participate in the consulting teams that prepared plans for the Cradle World Heritage Site and associated developments. On those projects I worked alongside and learned a great deal from colleagues who were archaeologists, palaeontologists and environmental lawyers with prodigious knowledge of the Cradle region. Other assignments brought me into contact with landowners of the area, and some favourite times were spent on the properties of Prospero Bailey, John Nash and his family, Mark and Christine Read, Hennie Joubert, and owners of the Rhenosterspruit Conservancy, all of whom were embracing the World Heritage Site concept in the early 2000s.

In 2004, Belinda Bozzoli, then Deputy Vice-Principal Research of the University of the Witwatersrand, invited me to work with Neville Passmore of the Skye Foundation to help develop plans for the newly established Institute for Human Evolution (IHE) and to define terms of reference for its director. Seven years later the university amalgamated the IHE with the Bernard Price Institute for Palaeontological Research and I was again asked to prepare plans for the emergent Evolutionary Studies Institute (ESI). These projects were among the most instructive assignments of my career and I benefitted enormously from the discussions I had with scientists, administrators and funders.

While serving on the North West Parks and Tourism Board during that time, I became increasingly concerned that the legislation intended to protect the Magaliesberg was often flouted and irreversible damage was being done. In 2006 I got together with a group of enthusiasts to have the entire Cradle-Magaliesberg region registered by UNESCO as a Biosphere Reserve. The group, which included Paul Fatti, Belinda Cooper, Kevin Gill, John Wesson, Mercia Komen, Anthony Duigan, Andrew Cauldwell and Paul Bartels, was backed by the Magaliesberg Protection Association, the Mountain Club of South Africa and the Wildlife and Environment Society of South Africa. For a decade we shared difficult but rewarding experiences and I greatly value their friendship and their perseverance, which ultimately resulted in the proclamation of the Magaliesberg Biosphere Reserve in Paris in June 2015.

The view from the author's property in the Magaliesberg where his lifelong interest in the region was first kindled.

Acknowledgements

I have drawn information from many sources, and I would like to express my appreciation to the many scholars and authors whose publications have been used and are listed at the end of the book.

I have also been particularly privileged to have had the assistance of some of the most authoritative experts in their respective disciplines. They have given their time and expertise most generously and I am deeply indebted to them for their substantial contributions:

Dr Marina Elliott, leader of the team that recovered the now famous *Homo naledi* fossils, provided extensive information for the palaeoanthropological chapters, and her unique experience, knowledge and many photographs are much appreciated.

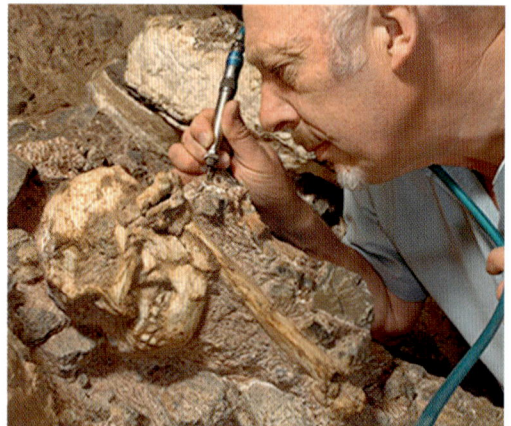

Professor Ron Clarke, discoverer of the famous 'Little Foot' skeleton, reviewed parts of the manuscript and added considerably to their accuracy. His assistance was particularly generous as it was given while he was at his busiest completing the publication of his own work.

Professor Kathleen Kuman, leading authority on the Early Stone Age in the Cradle-Magaliesberg, gave me a clearer understanding of that critically important tool-making phase of human evolution and provided excellent images.

Professor Tom Huffman greatly improved my knowledge of pre-colonial society and the Iron Age – his special field of expertise – and gave access to photographs held by the Wits Department of Archaeology.

Professors Morris Viljoen and **Richard Viljoen**, two of South Africa's most eminent geologists, gave invaluable advice and guidance that significantly enhanced the geology sections of the book.

Marion West introduced me to the remarkable world of radio astronomy and geodesy and the work being done at the Hartebeesthoek Radio Astronomy Observatory.

Many others have taken an interest in my work and provided advice and information. Dr Pierre Durand of the ESI at the University of Witwatersrand explained his work in molecular biology and early life, Professor Renzo Perissinotto of the Nelson Mandela University gave information on the stromatolites in the Eastern Cape, and Professor John Carter provided details about the Leiden telescopes. Professor Amanda Esterhuysen, Michael Worsnip and Lindsay Marshall gave me insights into developments at Maropeng.

I have been given considerable practical and technical help for which I am immensely grateful. Gerry Comninos drew most of the maps, and Lynda Whitfield of Bushveld Minerals drew the geology map. The work of artist Sally MacLarty is a wonderful asset. Dane Bishop took photographs of inaccessible places using his drone, and helicopter pilot Ed Couzyn helped me in a similar way. The following people generously allowed me to use their photographs: Amy L. Carter, Ron Clarke, Lynette Clennell, Peter Delmar, Marina Elliott, Kevin Gill, Kathleen Kuman, Justin Lee Photography, Rob Milne, L. Mulligan, Dirk van Rooyen, André Wedepohl and John Wesson. Images were also made available by Maropeng: The Official Visitor Centre of the Cradle of Humankind World Heritage Site, Museum Africa, Ditsong Museum of Natural History, the Department of Archaeology at the University of the Witwatersrand, the Trustees of the Natural History Museum, London, and South African National Parks. Lebogang Diale of the North West Provincial Government assisted me with the photograph of the Magaliesberg Biosphere Reserve certificate.

I am sincerely grateful to Terence McCarthy and Bruce Rubidge, the authors of *The Story of Earth and Life* (Struik, 2005), and to Jo van As, Johan du Preez, Leslie Brown and Nico Smit, the authors of *The Story of Life & The Environment: An African Perspective* (Struik Nature, 2012), who kindly allowed me to make use of illustrations from their books.

Pippa Parker, Helen de Villiers, Janice Evans and Belinda van der Merwe of the Struik Nature publishing team at Penguin Random House have been professional and delightful to work with, and I am grateful to Emsie du Plessis for her careful and constructive proofreading and indexing. In particular, I would like to thank Karen Press who skilfully edited my manuscript.

Professor Jane Carruthers, an internationally acclaimed environmental historian, has given me enormous support as well as researching, editing and providing scholarly comment – all priceless contributions for which no words of appreciation are adequate.

CONTENTS

INTRODUCTION

Human beings are innately curious, and few topics are more absorbing than those that relate to ourselves – who are we, where do we come from, and how did we become what we are? These questions have dominated religious and philosophical thinking throughout the ages. They have drawn scientists, historians, pioneers and explorers from a dozen different disciplines to seek answers in the caves and hillsides, cliffs and rivers of the Magaliesberg Biosphere Reserve and its core area, the Cradle of Humankind. In the course of more than a century of endeavour they have given rise to an enormous body of knowledge, and this book draws the threads of their expertise together into a single chronicle of an extraordinary landscape.

The Magaliesberg Biosphere Reserve is a remarkably small region to contain such a wealth of information about our past. In an area less than a fifth of the size of the Kruger National Park, we can see the evidence of the nuclear age at Pelindaba, where atomic weapons were once built and techniques using radioactivity are now developed for medical purposes, and we can find our heritage in the walled settlements of the Tswana, the stone tools of hunter-gatherers, and the fortifications of wars that once devastated our country. We can also explore the fossil evidence of that crucial phase of evolution when our ancestors gradually acquired the erect, large-brained anatomy of the human form. We can see the impacts of climate change on the landscape,

The view from the Cradle of Humankind towards the Magaliesberg. Few places in the world harbour such an extensive record of our origins.

and the consequent spread of savannah habitats that determined our evolutionary development as a species. We can look up at the Magaliesberg, its crests levelled by polar ice, and down into limestone caves made from fossils a thousand times older than the hominins – the members of the subfamily Hominini that includes humans and their ancestral relatives since they diverged from the ancestors of apes. We can inhale the oxygen produced by photosynthesis and touch the rocks of the first continental landmass on the planet. And we can see everywhere the life-giving consequences of a miraculous coincidence of the hydrosphere, lithosphere and atmosphere in the unique world that sustains us. This treasure lies not far from South Africa's largest urban region, where more than 10 million people live today.

This book traces the entire story of life on Earth by exploring the history of the Cradle-Magaliesberg landscape. Each chapter reveals an aspect of the past that has been recorded in the landscape, moving step-by-step from the beginnings of time up to the present. 'Interludes' between chapters offer some contextual details, or add background information to the chronicle. Each chapter can be read as a separate episode, a narrative about one aspect of the past, but the chapters are ordered in historical sequence so that the book can be read from beginning to end as a complete story of this region.

The three parts of the book each deal with a different period. Part 1, 'Life and Landscape', focuses on the emergence of the geomorphology (the structure, origins and development of the Earth's surface) and the living environment of the region before the time of the hominins. In this section, time is measured in billions of years, and scientific disciplines ranging from radio astronomy to microbiology are used to describe the origins and development of the landscape and the life that inhabited it. In Part 2, 'Human Evolution', the time scale narrows down from billions to millions of years, and we turn to the evolutionary sciences – palaeoanthropology, genetics, taphonomy (the study of how fossils form from dead organisms), and others – to explain the Cradle's remarkable fossil record and the evolution of humankind. Part 3, 'Archaeology and History', covers the 250,000 years of human existence and follows the history of our species, *Homo sapiens*, from the Stone Ages to the present. Archaeology gives insights into the lives of those who inhabited the region in the early millennia, while written sources and oral tradition guide the narrative through recent centuries up to the present day.

The Cradle-Magaliesberg

The geographical area covered in this book includes the Cradle of Humankind World Heritage Site and the Magaliesberg Biosphere Reserve in which it lies. Both of these sites have been designated by the United Nations Educational, Scientific and Cultural Organisation (UNESCO) as places of exceptional, worldwide interest, rich in biodiversity and evidence of the evolution of life. Throughout the book this area is referred to as the 'Cradle-Magaliesberg'.

Biosphere Reserves and World Heritage Sites have different legal status and management structures, and are created for different purposes, but the two designations complement each other. They are both responses by the international community to the Anthropocene – the modern age in which humans are having a profound influence on the core features of the Earth: its geomorphology, climate and evolution.

World Heritage Sites focus on the preservation of the outstanding universal value of a specific aspect of a locality (in this case, the fossil deposits in the Cradle of Humankind), while the purpose of a Biosphere Reserve is to combine the conservation of ecosystems and heritage with sustainable development. Biosphere Reserves are critically important institutions because they promote and support the better management of the world's natural resources. The Biosphere's twin objectives of economic development and environmental protection are especially significant in South Africa: the development of the natural environment is an important way to create economic opportunities for the people of the country and thereby help to reduce poverty, and at the same time South Africa's irreplaceable natural and cultural resources need to be preserved.

MAGALIESBERG BIOSPHERE RESERVE

Rustenburg

Marikana

Bapor

N4

Kroondal

Mooinooi

Buffelspoort
Dam

Olifantsnek
Dam

Sterkstroom

MAGALIESBERG PROTECTED ENVI

N4

Hekpoort

R30

Rooikloof

R24 Maanhaarrand

R560

Koster

Hex

Maropen

R509

Magaliesburg

R500

N14

MAGALIESBERG
BIOSPHERE

☐ **Transition Zone**

☐ **Buffer Zone**

☐ **Core Zone**

0   5   10   20km

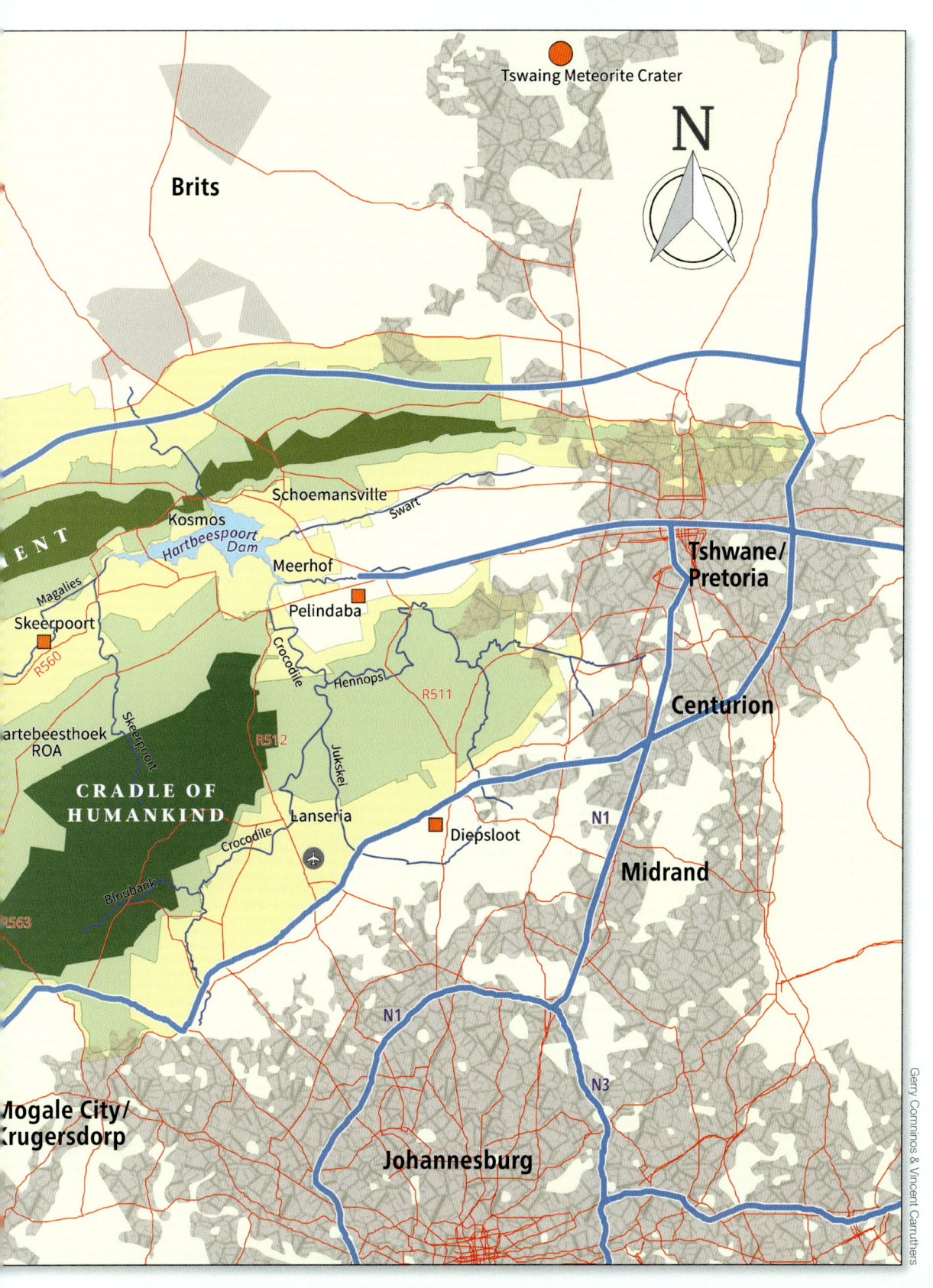

Tswaing Meteorite Crater

N

Brits

Schoemansville

Swart

Kosmos

Hartbeespoort Dam

Meerhof

Tshwane/
Pretoria

Magalies

Skeerpoort

R560

Pelindaba

Crocodile

Hennops

R511

Centurion

artebeesthoek
ROA

Skeerpoort

R512

Jukskei

CRADLE OF
HUMANKIND

Lanseria

Diepsloot

N1

Crocodile

Midrand

Broubank

R563

N1

N3

Mogale City/
Krugersdorp

Johannesburg

The Magaliesberg Biosphere Reserve

The word 'biosphere' is a scientific term that refers to the fragile layers of air, land and water covering the Earth and in which every known living organism exists or has ever existed. The biosphere provides all the resources these organisms need to stay alive.

By the mid-twentieth century there was a growing realisation amongst environmentalists and other scientists that the life-supporting resources of the biosphere were being consumed faster than they could replenish themselves. To help redress this depletion, in 1971 UNESCO initiated the Man and the Biosphere Programme (MAB) by establishing Biosphere Reserves worldwide. The World Network of Biosphere Reserves (WNBR) is an important component of the MAB Programme: it encourages dynamic and interactive Biosphere Reserves around the world to share their experiences, successes and failures, and to help one another achieve the combined goals of conservation and development. However, at the time of the first Biosphere Reserves in the 1970s, South Africa was prohibited from participating in UNESCO initiatives because of its apartheid policies; it was not until 1998 that the first South African Biosphere Reserve was registered, in the Western Cape.

Like all Biosphere Reserves, the Magaliesberg Biosphere Reserve does not restrict the rights of people living within it. Instead it encourages them to undertake research, education programmes and environmental planning to try to find solutions to the conflicting goals of conserving landscapes, ecosystems and culture on the one hand, while developing a sustainable economy on the other.

MBR LOGO

The logo of the Magaliesberg Biosphere Reserve was designed by Gerry Comninos. Its components have symbolic meanings:

- The shape of the logo represents the distinctive shape of the Magaliesberg ranges.
- The cavity in the mountain represents the cave system of the Cradle of Humankind.
- The circle represents the biosphere encapsulating the Earth.
- The overall green colour represents the natural environment.
- The human figure represents humanity and human endeavour.
- The three hills represent the three biomes that make up the biosphere: grassland, savannah and forest.

(Information from Gerry Comninos)

Biosphere Reserve proclamation

All Biosphere Reserves must have one or more legally protected core areas. The Magaliesberg has two: the Magaliesberg Protected Environment (the top of the mountain range) which is protected under the National Environmental Management: Protected Areas Act No. 57 of 2003, and the Cradle of Humankind World Heritage Site protected under the Heritage Resources Act No. 25 of 1999.

Various initiatives to safeguard the Magaliesberg from inappropriate development have been attempted over the past 50 years, but inadequate regulations and poor implementation of the law left the area vulnerable to illegal development. In 2006 a small group of concerned people banded together to form the Magaliesberg Biosphere Initiative Group (MBIG), under the auspices of the Magaliesberg Protection Association, and resolved to have the region proclaimed a Biosphere Reserve. They hoped that the spotlight of international recognition might secure a brighter future for this unique landscape.

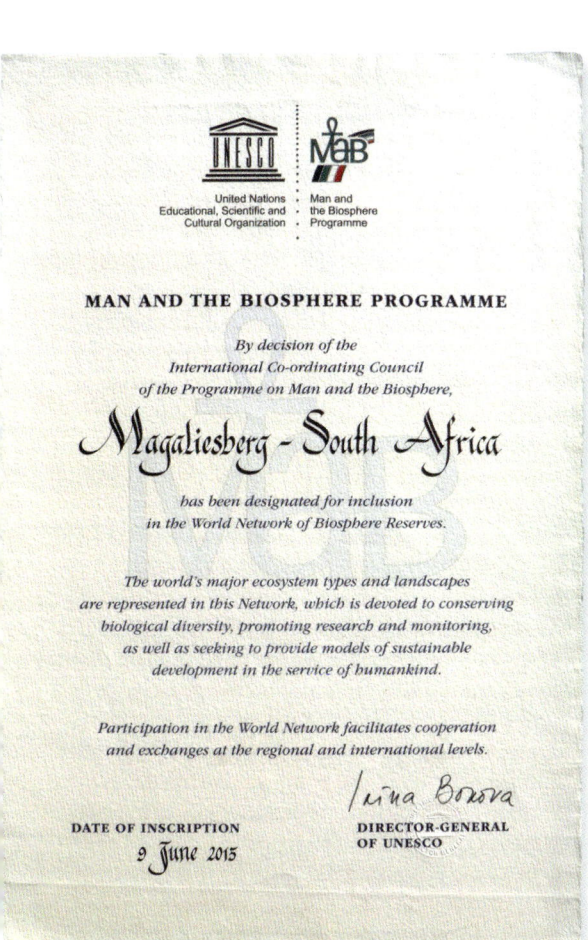

Cape vulture research combined with birding tourism is an example of Biosphere Reserve principles.

John Wesson

MAN AND THE BIOSPHERE PROGRAMME

By decision of the
International Co-ordinating Council
of the Programme on Man and the Biosphere,

Magaliesberg - South Africa

*has been designated for inclusion
in the World Network of Biosphere Reserves.*

*The world's major ecosystem types and landscapes
are represented in this Network, which is devoted to conserving
biological diversity, promoting research and monitoring,
as well as seeking to provide models of sustainable
development in the service of humankind.*

*Participation in the World Network facilitates cooperation
and exchanges at the regional and international levels.*

Irina Bokova

DATE OF INSCRIPTION
9 June 2015

DIRECTOR-GENERAL
OF UNESCO

The UNESCO certificate of registration for the Magaliesberg Biosphere Reserve was awarded on 9 June 2015.

Applications for the registration of Biosphere Reserves must be made by governments, not by individuals or private groups. The MBIG approached the Premier of North West Province, Edna Molewa, who subsequently became the national Minister of Environment Affairs, to support the application, and she gave an enthusiastic response. After a long process of setting up a government committee and appointing consultants to prepare the application, the Magaliesberg Biosphere Reserve was finally proclaimed under the UNESCO Man and the Biosphere Programme in June 2015.

Four aspects of the Magaliesberg make it exceptional, and justify its Biosphere Reserve status:

1. It lies at the interface between the grassland biome of the South African central plateau and the savannah biome, or bushveld, to the north. It draws species of fauna and flora from both biological regions and therefore has a particularly rich biodiversity.

2. The geology of the region is unique. In the south, the dolomitic fields of the Cradle of Humankind were created by the microscopic activity of cyanobacteria and contain the fossil-bearing caves. In the north, large-scale seismic activity uplifted the Magaliesberg mountain range and created the Bushveld Complex, with its enormous mineral wealth.

3. The water resources in the region are critically important. They derive from three separate sources: the dolomitic springs in the Cradle, the runoff from the Witwatersrand watershed, and the clear mountain sponges in the Magaliesberg.

4. The region has an extraordinarily rich history from the dawn of humankind to the present.

The Cradle of Humankind World Heritage Site

The Cradle of Humankind contains the world's largest assemblage of hominin fossils. The Cradle of Humankind World Heritage Site covers an area of about 47,000ha of undulating grassland and rocky outcrops interspersed with clear, natural springs and streams. The hills are honeycombed with dolomitic caves and sinkholes in which the world-famous fossils have been discovered. The private owners of the land have all entered into conservation agreements with the Cradle of Humankind Management Authority that oversees activities on the site, and most are enthusiastic supporters of the concept.

World Heritage Site proclamation

The palaeontological importance of the region now known as the Cradle of Humankind grew gradually over the decades after the identification of the first hominin fossil by Robert Broom in 1936. In 1996, Trish Hanekom, the head of the Gauteng Provincial Department of Agriculture,

Visitors entering the Sterkfontein Caves. Guided tours are one of the highlights of the Cradle of Humankind.

Conservation and Environment, initiated a project to have it proclaimed a World Heritage Site. Under her inspiration and leadership, the International Council on Monuments and Sites (ICOMOS) was consulted by Gauteng Province officials. South Africa became a signatory to the UNESCO World Heritage Convention in 1997, and in 1998 ICOMOS recommended that all 13 of the known fossil-bearing localities in the area and the surrounding countryside should be embraced into the proposed World Heritage Site. This has since been increased to 15 sites (see map on page 114). To give legal protection to this and other World Heritage Sites in South Africa, a new law was passed in South Africa, the World Heritage Convention Act No. 49 of 1999, and the site was listed on 2 December 1999 under the name 'The Fossil Hominid Sites of Sterkfontein, Swartkrans, Kromdraai and Environs', and recognised as a site of global scientific and natural value. It was not long before the now-familiar phrase, the 'Cradle of Humankind' came into use to refer to the site. Four years after the nomination of the Cradle of Humankind, the fossil sites at Taung in Northern Cape Province and Makopane in Limpopo Province were added as serial sites under the same World Heritage Site status – that is, parts of the World Heritage Site that are geographically separate from the main site. The priceless heritage of the Cradle of Humankind is rigorously protected under the World Heritage Convention, as well under as the South African World Heritage Convention Act and the Heritage Resources Act.

Since the successful proclamation of the Cradle of Humankind World Heritage Site, the Cradle of Humankind Management Authority, appointed by Gauteng Province, has developed and implemented an expansive master plan for the region, encompassing historical, cultural and environmental resources, tourism development, and economic benefits for local communities. The Management Authority is accountable to the South African government and to UNESCO.

Management plans have been compiled for each of the fossil sites in the area, and the Maropeng Visitor Centre was opened in 2005. The nomination document for World Heritage Site status recognised that these localities are of 'outstanding universal value because they

Grassland, trees and distinctive outcrops of dolomitic rock typify the Cradle landscape.

Most of the Maropeng Visitor Centre is underground. The building is modelled on a northern European Ice Age tumulus, and the interior simulates a subterranean environment.

Kathleen Kuman

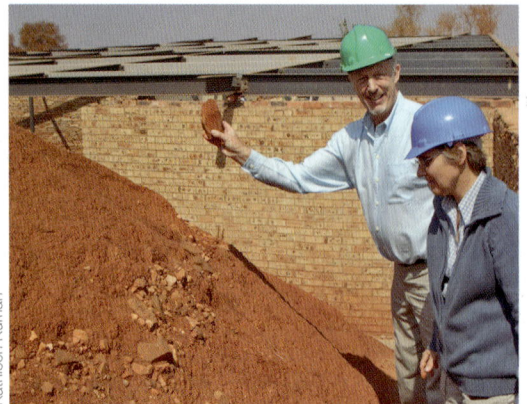

Ron Clarke and Kathy Kuman show one of the Acheulean tools discovered during the construction of the Maropeng Visitor Centre. The band of stones and artefacts is visible in the excavation.

encapsulate a superbly preserved record of the fauna, including the stages in the emergence and evolution of humanity, over the past 3.5 million years'. This makes the Cradle of Humankind one of the most important sites for evolutionary study and research, drawing scientists from all over the world. The fossils discovered in the Cradle belong to the people of South Africa, while the University of the Witwatersrand (Wits University) owns the intellectual property rights to the scientific discoveries and evolutionary research, and provides academic expertise for the management of the sites.

The UNESCO World Heritage Site status of the Cradle of Humankind demonstrates the international acknowledgement of its importance, and gives the assurance that these treasures and their provenance are protected and secured for future research, education and enjoyment.

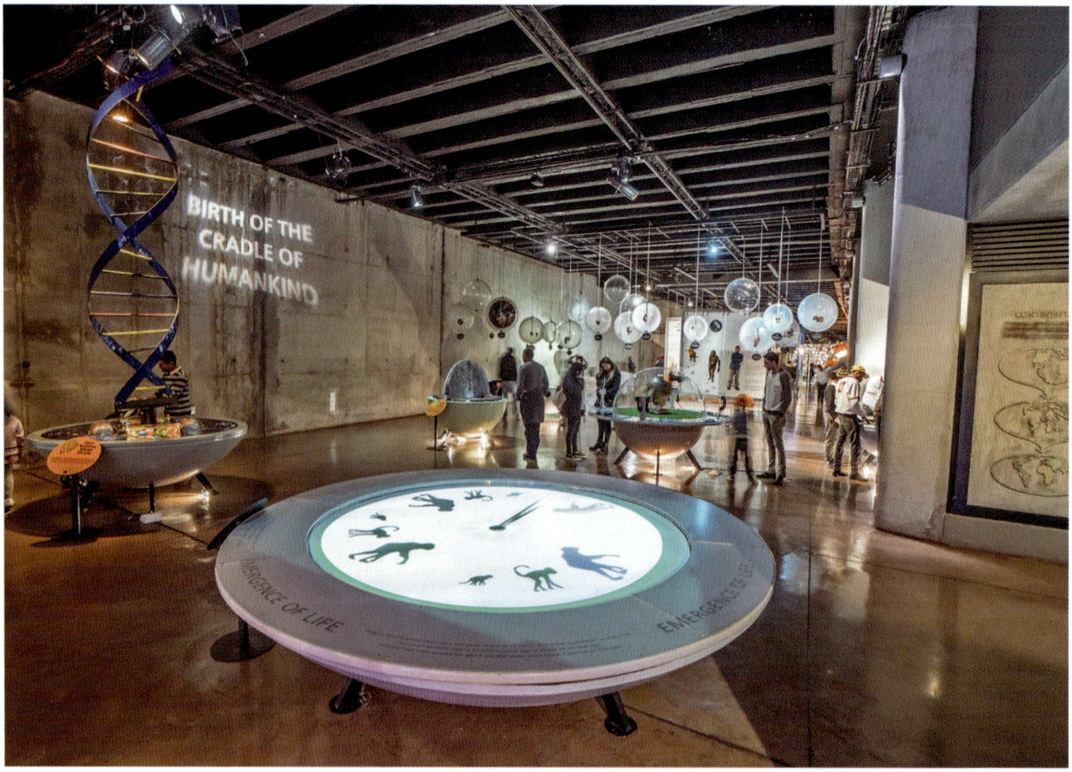

Maropeng Visitor Centre

Maropeng exhibits explain the origins of humankind and life on Earth and include some of the most famous fossils recovered from the Cradle.

The Maropeng Visitor Centre

Maropeng, which means 'return to the place of origins' in Setswana, is the official visitor centre for the Cradle of Humankind. It was opened in December 2005 by the then president of South Africa, Thabo Mbeki, and its interior is a vast semi-submerged exhibition hall. The exterior design of the building is modelled on a northern European Ice Age tumulus or ancient burial mound, although this type of burial structure is unrelated to the African fossil sites.

The sensitive dolomitic geology underlying most of the Cradle of Humankind is unsuitable for such a structure; it was therefore built in the quartzite hills to the west of the Cradle, on land donated by the Standard Bank of South Africa.

During the construction of Maropeng, a bed of early Acheulean artefacts (primitive tools made by proto-humans) was unearthed by earth-moving machinery and identified in the excavated rubble by Wits University archaeologist Kathleen Kuman and colleagues. The tools included hand axes and cleavers about 1.5 million years old, and provided the first evidence of Early Stone Age occupation of an open-air site from that period (other Acheulean tools in the Cradle have all been recovered from the interiors of caves into which they had been washed by rain or floods).

The exhibition at Maropeng includes interactive displays relating to human evolution, with an emphasis on our common African origins. An environmental education centre called 'Hominin House' is located nearby. Maropeng has further tourist facilities at the Sterkfontein Caves 12km away, where there is a small but very informative museum. Underground tours of the caves are conducted by trained guides.

Maropeng Visitor Centre

The fountain in the foyer at Maropeng represents the origins of life, and a symbolic boat ride takes visitors into the heart of the exhibition centre.

PART 1
LIFE AND
LANDSCAPE

Life and landscape		Millions of years ago	Events affecting the Cradle-Magaliesberg
The Universe		13,800	Time and matter begin from a singularity in the 'Big Bang'.
		13,400	Nucleosynthesis fuses subatomic particles into hydrogen and helium atoms.
Earth		4,600	The Solar System develops. The Earth acquires a unique collection of attributes that allow life to exist.
		4,540	The Moon deflects the axis of the Earth's rotation. Milankovitch cycles drive climatic change.
		4,500	A magnetic field is created and deflects lethal cosmic radiation.
		4,400	Gravity retains a gas atmosphere around the Earth.
		3,900	Water is retained on the Earth in liquid form.
		3,500	Early life forms in submarine greenstone rocks now found in the Cradle.
Kaapvaal		3,100	The Kaapvaal Craton becomes the first stable landmass on the Earth.
		2,714	The Cradle area subsided under water. Sediments consolidated into the Black Reef.
Cyanobacteria		2,700	Cyanobacteria photosynthesise in the waters covering the Cradle. Stromatolites form a calcified substrate.
		2,690	Oxygen from photosynthesis oxidises iron, forming banded iron deposits.
		2,350	Sediments swamp the cyanobacteria and build deposits on the seabed.
		2,250	Oxygen accumulates in the atmosphere. Ozone establishes a shield against ultraviolet radiation coming from the Sun.
Magaliesberg		2,060	The Bushveld Complex magma erupts, lifting the seabed which is eventually exposed by erosion to form the Magaliesberg.
		2,023	A meteor strikes at the Vredefort Dome, burying the Magaliesberg under debris.
		2,000	The Kaapvaal and Zimbabwe cratons unite with others to form the continent of Ur.
		2,000	Eukaryotic cells develop.
		1,400	The Pilanesberg volcano erupts. The continents of Ur, Nena and Atlantica consolidate into the supercontinent Rodinia.

Life and landscape	Millions of years ago	Events affecting the Cradle-Magaliesberg
Gondwana	1,100	All continents consolidate into Pangaea.
	500	The Cradle-Magaliesberg is located under the polar ice cap.
	350	The Cradle-Magaliesberg emerges. Gondwana splits from Pangaea.
	280	A mass extinction destroys most mammal-like reptiles and vascular plants.
	251	Dinosaurs evolve and inhabit the region.
	210	Desert sand dunes cover the Cradle area.
	190	Gondwana ruptures. Lava covers the Cradle-Magaliesberg.
Africa	180	The Indian Ocean separates Africa from India, Australia and Antarctica.
	140	Karoo sediments erode and expose the ancient Magaliesberg geology.
	130	South America splits from Africa. The Cradle-Magaliesberg lifts on a plateau. Rivers flow south-west into the Atlantic.
	120	Dinosaurs become extinct, thus vacating an ecological niche for mammals.
	65	The Transvaal-Griqualand Axis lifts, diverting the Cradle-Magaliesberg rivers northwards to the Limpopo.
	60	Primates evolve in Africa.
	55	The hot, wet climate begins to cool.
	35	Grasses spread across the central plateau, displacing woodland.
	30	The earliest apes evolve.
Cradle-Magaliesberg	25	Groundwater begins to leach caverns in the dolomitic substrate of the Cradle.
	20	A marked rainfall gradient from east to west spreads grasslands towards the Cradle-Magaliesberg.
	20	Cold Atlantic currents cause further cooling and drying of the climate.
	14	The hominin subfamily separates from a common ape ancestor.
	8	The interface between grassland and savannah reaches the Cradle-Magaliesberg.
	5	Erosion exposes the karst caves in the Cradle.

In the chronology of deep time, dating the features of the landscape is an essential part of reconstructing the past. The immensity of the time scale means that scientists have to use a number of specialised dating techniques. Most of the dates of the geological and evolutionary events in the following chapters were calibrated against the time elapsed in isotope decay or solar radiation, two phenomena that were set in motion by the events described in Chapter 1.

RADIOMETRIC DATING

Radiometric dating uses the calculation of the gradual decay of unstable radioactive isotopes, called 'parent' elements, as they break down into non-radioactive forms referred to as 'daughter' elements. The relative amounts of parent and daughter isotopes in a rock sample indicate its age measured in terms of the half-life of the isotope, i.e. the time it takes for 50 per cent of its mass to degenerate into the daughter form. Differences in decay rates make various elements suitable for dating rocks and artefacts in different situations.

Some examples of isotopes used to date fossils and rock are:

- **Uranium (^{238}U) to lead (^{206}Pb)** (half-life 4,500 million years) is suitable for some, but not all, sediments between 1 million and 4.5 billion years old.

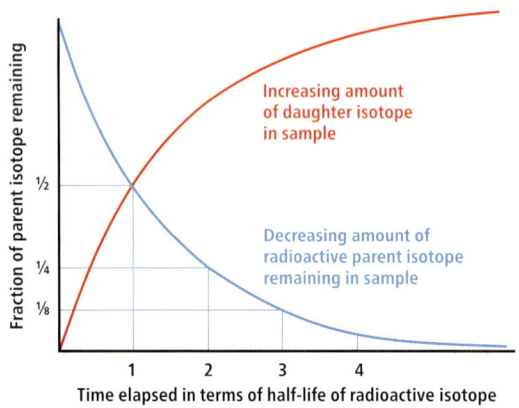

Radiometric dating: the half-life of a radioactive 'parent' isotope is the time it takes for 50 per cent of the atoms to decay into a stable 'daughter' isotope.

- **Potassium (^{40}K) to argon (^{40}Ar)** (half-life 1,260 million years) is particularly suitable for measuring lava tuffs and is used extensively to date fossils from the Great Rift Valley in East Africa.
- **Carbon 14 (^{14}C) to Carbon 12 (^{12}C)** (half-life 5,700 years). The relatively short half-life makes it suitable only for organic material up to 50,000 years after death.

COSMOGENIC OR ISOCHRONIC BURIAL DATING

The Earth is constantly exposed to cosmic radiation that creates minute amounts of radioactive isotopes, called cosmogenic nuclides, in quartzite. When quartzite gravel is washed into a cave it is shielded from further radiation, and the radioactivity in the nuclides begins to decay. The number of nuclides left after burial can be compared on what is called an isochronic scale with nuclide accumulation at the surface to indicate the period of time that the sediments have been buried.

This was one of the methods used to date the Little Foot fossil.

OPTICALLY STIMULATED LUMINESCENCE (OSL) DATING

Radiation from various background sources is absorbed by minerals such as quartz, and small amounts of electron energy can become trapped in imperfections in the molecular structure of quartzite crystals. The trapped energy soon escapes if exposed to sunlight, but if the quartzite is buried in cave deposits away from light the trapped radiation dosage accumulates. Exposure of samples to bright artificial light stimulates the trapped energy, which emits a luminescent signal, and the strength of this signal indicates the length of time it has been buried.

ELECTRON SPIN RESONANCE (ESR) DATING

When radioactive elements decay, negatively charged electrons are released and quickly pair once more with positively charged protons. However, in certain substances, such as tooth enamel, some unpaired, high-energy electrons become trapped in what are termed paramagnetic centres. These paramagnetic centres accumulate as radiation continues over time.

They can be detected by ESR spectrometry, and the number of trapped electrons indicates the age of the substance (e.g. the tooth) being measured.

ESR was one of the dating methods used to establish the age of *Homo naledi*.

PALAEOMAGNETIC DATING

The Earth's magnetic field is approximately aligned between the poles. At irregular intervals the polarity of the magnetic field flips, so that the north magnetic pole becomes the south pole, and vice versa – an event that has occurred many times in the history of the planet.

The Earth's crust is constantly renewed by the lava that erupts between tectonic plates as they separate. As the lava cools and solidifies, minute quantities of magnetite, a mineral prone to magnetisation, retain the polarisation of the Earth's magnetic field at the time of their formation: they carry the magnetic signature of the moment of their cooling. When the magnetic field flips,

new crust carries the reversed polarisation. The result is a series of parallel bands of oceanic crust, each bearing alternating magnetic polarisation. Sensitive instruments record the rate of tectonic spread and use the polarisation of each band. These bands become markers to create a long-term geological calendar, a time scale against which other magnetised rock anywhere in the world can be compared and dated. This was one of the methods used to date the *Australopithecus sediba* fossil.

STRATIFICATION

Sedimentary layers are deposited in a time sequence with newer strata overlying older ones in a process called stratification. The age of a fossil can sometimes be determined by using one of the methods described above to date the deposit in which it is located, or a deposit that is directly above or below it. However, the cave systems in the Cradle of Humankind have been subject to considerable geological disturbance – upper sections have collapsed, roofs have buckled, and geological formations have been disrupted. Stratigraphic dating has therefore been particularly complicated.

FAUNAL DATING

An older way of dating hominin fossils in the Cradle has been to use the known (or assumed) dates of fossils of other fauna in the same strata; these fossils were often cross-referenced to fauna in East Africa where dates were known. The method is unreliable, however, as South African fauna was not necessarily contemporary with animals elsewhere.

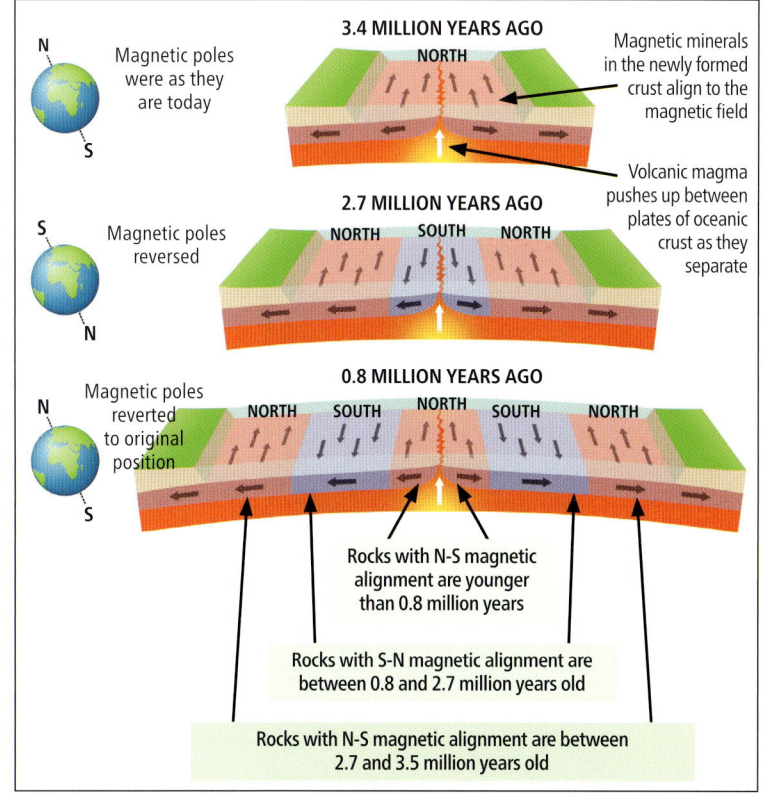

3.4 MILLION YEARS AGO

Magnetic poles were as they are today

NORTH

Magnetic minerals in the newly formed crust align to the magnetic field

Volcanic magma pushes up between plates of oceanic crust as they separate

2.7 MILLION YEARS AGO

Magnetic poles reversed

NORTH   SOUTH   NORTH

0.8 MILLION YEARS AGO

Magnetic poles reverted to original position

NORTH   SOUTH   NORTH   SOUTH   NORTH

Rocks with N-S magnetic alignment are younger than 0.8 million years

Rocks with S-N magnetic alignment are between 0.8 and 2.7 million years old

Rocks with N-S magnetic alignment are between 2.7 and 3.5 million years old

The magnetic polarity of bands of oceanic crust indicates their age as determined by the dates on which the alignment of the Earth's magnetic field reversed.

1 | THE BIRTH OF THE PLANET

The very beginning of the story of life in the Cradle-Magaliesberg is to be found not in the landscape itself, but in the stars above it. Before life could emerge, the elements that comprise all matter had to be synthesised, consolidated into stars and planets, and incorporated into the Earth and into living organisms.

Outer space is exceptionally hostile to any form of life. Temperatures range from absolute zero to millions of degrees Celsius. Lethal cosmic radiation streams from every star, black holes swallow starlight, and inter-stellar bodies collide with devastating violence. For any living organism to survive these hazards, a benign and protective environment was required – a planetary home with a wide range of defensive systems and life-nurturing processes. These conditions included a strong magnetic field to deflect solar wind, a large moon to stabilise its rotation, a deep atmospheric shield to protect it from assault by meteors, and abundant water in liquid form, which is essential to life. The remarkable coincidence of all these factors occurring on the same planet at the same time made the Earth unique, and allowed life to develop and flourish.

This chapter describes briefly how the Earth became the only planet we know of that provides all these conditions, and how the cosmic radiation and radioactive elements that help scientists to date rocks and fossils came about.

Pixabay.com

Above: The Earth is the only planet known to have a biosphere – layers of air, land and water that sustain all known forms of life.

Left: The Orion Nebula as seen from the Hubble Space Telescope. Gas and dust are condensing into stars. Our own Sun would have formed in a similar way.

ESA/Hubble

An array of radio telescope antennae being tested at HartRAO for the Hydrogen Intensity and Real-time Analysis Experiment (HIRAX). The project will investigate dark energy remnants of the Big Bang and will require 1,000 such antennae.

The Big Bang

The pursuit of our origins in the Cradle-Magaliesberg starts at the very beginning of time with the formation of the substances of which all matter is made. The stars that are visible on a clear night above the Cradle-Magaliesberg are situated within galaxies that are all moving away from one another at an accelerating velocity. Their origin is known as a 'singularity', and from it all energy and matter came into existence 13,800 million years ago. The notion that time and matter began with a 'Big Bang'

is almost beyond comprehension, but astronomical discoveries over the past century have consistently confirmed that all matter in the Universe originated at a particular moment, and alternative theories suggesting a cyclical process through eternal time have been whittled away. Within the Cradle area itself, scientists at Hartebeesthoek Radio Astronomy Observatory (HartRAO) are monitoring radiation from pulsars, supernovae and dark matter in the expanding galaxies, and contributing to a better understanding of the Big Bang phenomenon.

Stars are formed from the consolidation of nebula gases drawn together by their own gravity.

Stellar nucleosynthesis

The seemingly benign twinkling stars in the night sky are, in fact, a constant succession of powerful nuclear explosions. In the moments immediately after the Big Bang, subatomic protons, neutrons and electrons dispersed rapidly away from the singularity and began to fuse into atoms. Initially, only hydrogen was formed, with just one proton and one electron. As the atoms continued to scatter, their gravitational pull drew them together into nebulae – clouds of thinly distributed matter – and consolidated the gases further. The hydrogen atoms bonded in pairs to form molecules, and the centres of the nebulae compacted into increasingly dense hubs, heated by their own compression. Eventually, the intensity of heat

ignited explosive chain reactions of nuclear fusion. The protons and neutrons in the hydrogen nucleus fused together into helium, and the centres of the nebulae became super-heated, brilliantly lit stars like our own Sun, where the inner temperature is around 15 million degrees Celsius.

When a large star has converted its supply of hydrogen into helium, the helium atoms themselves fuse into elements of greater atomic mass, such as carbon, oxygen and eventually iron. Beyond that point the star shrinks, increasing the density and temperature further and creating elements heavier than iron. Finally the star either collapses into a neutron star or black hole or it explodes spectacularly in a supernova. By this means, a variety of elements is dispersed from the exploding star into inter-stellar space, where they reconsolidate into planetary nebulae that form new stars or consolidate into orbiting planets.

Increases in the atomic mass of elements through stellar nucleosynthesis eventually reach a point where the elements become unstable. More protons and neutrons cannot be added, and they begin to break away from the nucleus through radioactive decay or nuclear fission. The number of naturally occurring elements is therefore restricted, the heaviest being uranium, although nuclear scientists have created heavier artificial elements to generate nuclear energy. The rate of radioactive decay can be monitored to determine the date of fossils, rocks and artefacts containing traces of these elements, and is an important aspect of the evolutionary studies undertaken in the Cradle.

ESA/Hubble

Above: Towards the end of their lives, stars explode as supernovae, dispersing elements that will become future planets.

Below: The Solar System comprises eight planets. Those closest to the Sun consist of elements with high melting temperatures. The four outer planets are gas and remain very cold.

NASA/JPL

➤ 4,600 million years ago: Planet Earth

The Universe described in the previous section provided the elements needed to make up living organisms, but an extraordinary combination of circumstances was still required for life to evolve. In the Cradle-Magaliesberg these unusual conditions have a particularly distinctive presence.

New stars were regenerated from the debris of older ones; our Sun is one of these stars. It began to form about 9,000 million years ago in an outer arm of the spiralling galaxy we refer to as the 'Milky Way'. Like other stars of its size, the Sun began as the central hub of spiralling stellar gas and debris. As the clouds of elements spiralled into the hub, immensely high temperatures triggered nuclear fusion, converting hydrogen into helium and releasing the heat and light that we receive from the Sun every day.

The Sun is a third-generation star, i.e. the composition of the elements in the Sun indicates that they were first formed in a preceding star and subsequently dispersed into space, reconsolidated in a second-generation star, dispersed once more, and finally consolidated for a third time as our Sun. The debris orbiting around it contained a diversity of heavy elements from earlier iterations of stellar nucleosynthesis. As some of those fragments of interplanetary material spiralled around the Sun, centrifugal force that throws spinning objects apart counter-balanced the gravitational pull at the centre, and locked them into perpetual orbit. There, their own gravity flung them together in violent collisions

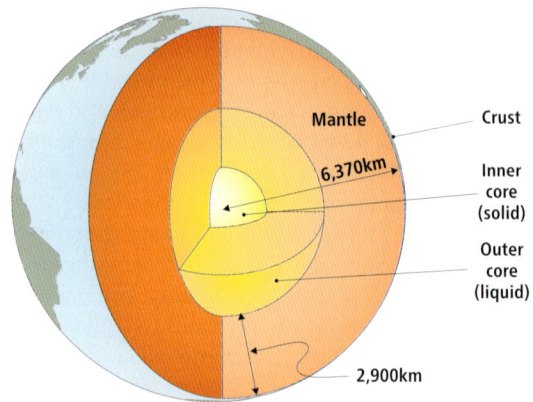

From *The Story of Earth & Life*, McCarthy & Rubidge (2005)

The Earth is made of many elements. In its hot molten state, heavy elements such as iron and nickel sank to the core while lighter ones floated near the surface.

as they consolidated into ever larger planetary bodies. Eight planets, one of which was the Earth, and three dwarf planets were formed in this way, and together with thousands of smaller bodies, they now orbit the Sun as part of our Solar System.

As the Earth grew in size through the accretion of constant bombardments by astral bodies, each meteor contributed to the diversity of chemical elements in its composition. Meteor impacts also generated sufficient heat to keep the component

4,540 million years ago a large astral body struck the Earth.

Large volumes of rock and debris were vaporised and ejected into space where gravity retained them in orbit around the Earth.

4,300 years ago the particles of debris had been drawn together by their own gravity and consolidated into the spherical Moon orbiting the Earth.

An astral body about the size of Mars struck the Earth 4,540 million years ago, tilting the Earth's axis and blasting debris into space, where it reconsolidated into the Moon.

Climates, habitats, tidal fluctuations and many evolutionary processes were influenced by both the tilt of the Earth and the presence of the Moon.

materials of the Earth in molten form. Heavier elements such as iron and nickel sank to the centre, while lighter elements like silicon remained in the mantle and outer crust near the surface. Four important elements that accumulated on the Earth were carbon, hydrogen, nitrogen and oxygen, and these eventually became the essential organic components present in all living organisms.

The presence of organic chemicals was not, however, sufficient for life to develop. Several other critical factors distinguished the emerging Earth from the other planets and made it unique.

➤ 4,540 million years ago: The Moon and climate change

The Moon has had a greater effect on the evolution of life than people realise. While the Earth was still molten and somewhat smaller than its present size, a large planetary body, probably about the size of Mars, collided with it and vaporised part of the outer mantle. Debris from this collision was hurled into space, where it slowly consolidated into the spherical Moon that now orbits the Earth 385,000km away.

The collision tilted the axis of the Earth by about 23°, giving us the annual summer and winter seasons as the Earth swings around the Sun each year. In addition, the large mass of the Moon acts as a gyroscopic anchor, stabilising the Earth on its tilted axis and effectively preventing the erratic oscillations that are experienced by other planets. Mars, for example, wobbles around its axis by about 60°. Without the stabilising effect

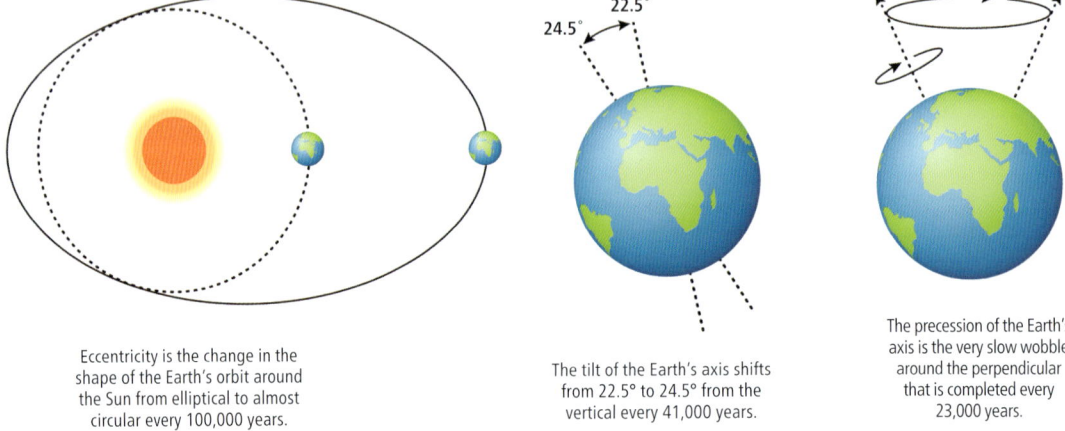

Climate change caused by the Milankovitch cycles altered the vegetation of southern Africa from forest to savannah, and triggered evolutionary changes in our hominin ancestors.

Eccentricity is the change in the shape of the Earth's orbit around the Sun from elliptical to almost circular every 100,000 years.

The tilt of the Earth's axis shifts from 22.5° to 24.5° from the vertical every 41,000 years.

The precession of the Earth's axis is the very slow wobble around the perpendicular that is completed every 23,000 years.

Climatic changes are affected by a combination of three cyclical changes in the Earth's rotational axis: eccentricity, tilt and precession, which are collectively known as the Milankovitch cycles.

of the Moon, the Earth's axis would also slew about arbitrarily. The frequency and duration of seasons would be violently irregular, and life would probably not have evolved beyond bacteria – if it had survived at all.

Even with the stabilising effect of the Moon, the tilt of the Earth's axis varies slightly in cycles of about 41,000 years. This, combined with the precession (very slow wobble) of the axis around the perpendicular every 23,000 years, and changes in the eccentricity of the Earth's orbit from elliptical to near-circular every 100,000 years, imposes long-term macro-climatic changes on the planet which are called the Milankovitch cycles. Over time these climatic cycles triggered an acceleration in the evolution of new species, as well as the extinction and migration of species in the Cradle, and this may have affected the evolutionary process of hominins.

Precession and tilt also reposition our view of the stars. Two thousand years ago the Greek astronomer Ptolemy could see and describe the Southern Cross, a constellation we think of as the symbol of the southern night sky, from where he lived in the northern hemisphere.

Another important effect of the Moon on life in the Cradle was its gravitational pull on the oceans. When the Cradle-Magaliesberg region was an inland sea some 3,000 million years ago, the inter-tidal zones provided a critically important environment for the development of cyanobacteria, and thus for the beginnings of mass life on Earth.

➤ 4,500 million years ago: The magnetic field

The most important evidence of the magnetic field in the Cradle-Magaliesberg is the presence of life itself. Without its protection no higher forms of plants and animals would have survived the intense cosmic radiation from the Sun. But the magnetic field has also been an important aid to the evolutionary scientists and archaeologists studying the region, by providing an accurate palaeomagnetic measurement of the age of rocks and, indirectly, fossils and other artefacts.

As well as radiating light and warmth, nuclear activity on the Sun discharges emissions of subatomic protons and electrons known as solar wind. Cumulatively, these emissions would be lethal to all living organisms. The magnetic field of the Earth intercepts these life-threatening particles and deflects them away from the planet, while allowing the beneficial sunlight and warmth to reach the surface unaffected.

The magnetic field can be thought of as a giant magnet aligned approximately with the axis of the rotation of the Earth, but subject to slight deflections at different points on the planet. The magnetised needle of a compass is drawn along this axis because the arrow of the compass is the south pole of the magnetised needle, and it is pulled towards the north pole of the Earth's field.

Scientists do not fully understand how the magnetic field is generated. The dynamo theory, published by German-born American physicist Walter Elsasser in 1940, remains the most widely accepted explanation. In its formative stages the Earth was molten, and elements settled at different depths according to their various densities. Iron and nickel sank to the centre, where they retain a temperature

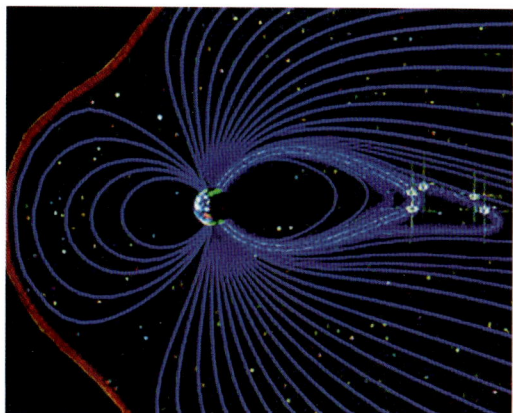

Solar wind (from the left in this diagram) distorts the protective magnetic field which would otherwise be distributed symmetrically for about 50,000km around the axis of the Earth.

of around 5,500°C even today. This is well above their melting point, but at the centre of the Earth the pressure is so great that they are compressed to a solid core with molten iron around it. According to Elsasser's theory convection currents, caused by hot material rising from the centre, drive the fluid outer iron around the central solid core and generate the magnetic field like a giant dynamo.

➤ 4,400 million years ago: The atmosphere

On clear nights in the Cradle-Magaliesberg you can often see 'shooting stars', as meteors from outer space enter our atmosphere and burn to destruction in fiery streaks across the sky. On rare occasions, the Earth's orbit carries our planet through the rocks and ice trailing behind a passing comet, and a spectacular shower of meteors lights up the sky. The atmospheric shield in which these meteors are incinerated is one of the most critical factors that have made Earth uniquely suitable for the development of life.

As the size of the emergent Earth increased through the constant accretion of meteorites and asteroids, the gravitational pull from its growing mass attracted increasing amounts of interplanetary material. At the same time, the greater force of gravity also prevented volatile gases from escaping into space and created an atmospheric envelope around the planet. As the atmosphere expanded, more meteors were incinerated before they could reach the Earth and the number of impacts diminished. Eventually, a balance was achieved when the mass of the Earth gave it enough gravity to retain an atmosphere that was large enough to prevent all but a few meteors penetrating the shield.

Occasionally this balance is disrupted. The Vredefort and Tswaing meteor impacts described in

Above: A meteor shower over the Cradle-Magaliesberg. If one of the larger meteors were to penetrate the protective shield of the atmosphere, its impact could have a devastating effect.

Left: Greenhouse gases moderate the global temperature by admitting short-wave radiation from the Sun by day and inhibiting long-wave reflection of heat by night.

Sun

Infrared (long-wave) heat is trapped by greenhouse gases

Greenhouse gases: carbon dioxide, methane, CFCs, nitrous oxide and water vapour

Short-wave radiation penetrates

Some heat escapes

Atmosphere

From The Story of Life & the Environment, Van As, et al. (2012)

Chapter 3 are reminders that without the protection of the atmosphere, incessant bombardment by meteorites would almost certainly have curtailed the evolution of life on Earth.

The atmosphere brought a second benefit for emerging primitive forms of life: it moderated the severity of climatic changes and insulated our world against heat loss. During the day about 50 per cent of the radiant heat of the Sun is dispersed by the atmosphere, or reflected back into space by cloud cover. The remainder warms the surface of the Earth and is absorbed into the land and oceans. At night the land cools and releases energy in the form of long-wave infrared heat. Greenhouse gases – carbon dioxide, water vapour and other gases – inhibit this infrared radiation and reflect it back to the Earth, retaining and even increasing its warmth. Without this moderating effect, the ambient temperature on the Earth would be 18°C colder. Humans and most other forms of life would freeze. By contrast, an increase in carbon dioxide would intensify the greenhouse effect and cause temperatures to rise. This is the reason for the international concern about artificial increases in carbon dioxide emissions: these increases are approaching levels that could change climates and significantly affect life.

➤ 3,900 million years ago: The hydrosphere

Water is the single most important substance in the story of life. Nowhere is there more spectacular evidence of its significance than in the Cradle-Magaliesberg. The cyanobacteria that created the Cradle landscape required water to photosynthesise and propagate. Water leached out the caves in the dolomite, and dripping water created the stalactites and flowstones. The lakes and reservoirs in the caves feed the streams of the area, and ripple marks on the face of Magaliesberg quartzite show that it was once a submerged sediment subject to the flow of water.

The hydrosphere is the total amount of water on the planet, and its presence and abundance are inseparable from the existence and evolution of life itself. Life began in water just under 4,000 million years ago, and all life remained aquatic for 3,500 million years after that. Water comprises more than 50 per cent of the body weight of living organisms (generally much more), and the metabolic functions of every living cell take place in a water-based fluid. No plant or animal, aquatic or terrestrial, can exist for long without it. The extraordinary properties of water also make it the single most important cause of land transformation. Despite its yielding, passive fluidity, water can erode mountains, build landscapes, and determine climates and ecosystems.

This vast and irreplaceable resource came from outer space during the period of bombardment by asteroids more than 4,000 million years ago.

Russell Achterburg

Ripple marks on Magaliesberg quartzite were made by tidal currents in an ancient seabed. They are exposed where rock strata separate along the plane where a new layer of sand was deposited onto an older one.

Much of the bombardment came from ice comets originating in the Kuiper Belt, a disc-shaped region of a trillion or more comets beyond the orbit of Neptune on the frozen outer fringes of the Solar System. Drawn by the Earth's gravity, these comets vaporised as they approached the molten planet Earth, dumping water vapour into the developing atmosphere. By about 3,900 million years ago the Earth began to cool sufficiently for the vapour to condense and precipitate, and immense downpours flooded the entire surface of the planet under one uninterrupted ocean.

The presence and abundance of this vital resource came about because of an extraordinary planetary coincidence. The orbit of the Earth lies about 150 million kilometres from the Sun. At that distance, the heat of the Sun, moderated by the greenhouse effect of the atmosphere, keeps the ambient surface temperature somewhere between the freezing and boiling points of water over most of the surface of the Earth. No other planet maintains its temperature within such slender margins, or at the precise level needed to keep water in its liquid form. The 100°C temperature range within which water remains liquid is minute compared with the extremes of high and low temperatures throughout the Universe. A relatively small orbital deviation would take the Earth either closer to the Sun and all its water would vaporise, as has happened on Venus, or further from the Sun where the water would freeze, as on Mars. In either situation, the essential liquid resource would be inaccessible, and life would not exist.

The water itself helps to stabilise this optimum temperature range. Water vapour acts as a greenhouse gas and traps the Sun's heat, while oceanic water distributes the heat evenly over the Earth.

Water leached out the subterranean caverns in the Cradle, and minerals in the water enabled fossilisation of skeletons to occur.

The Cradle-Magaliesberg is an important catchment for uncontaminated water from mountain springs and dolomitic caves.

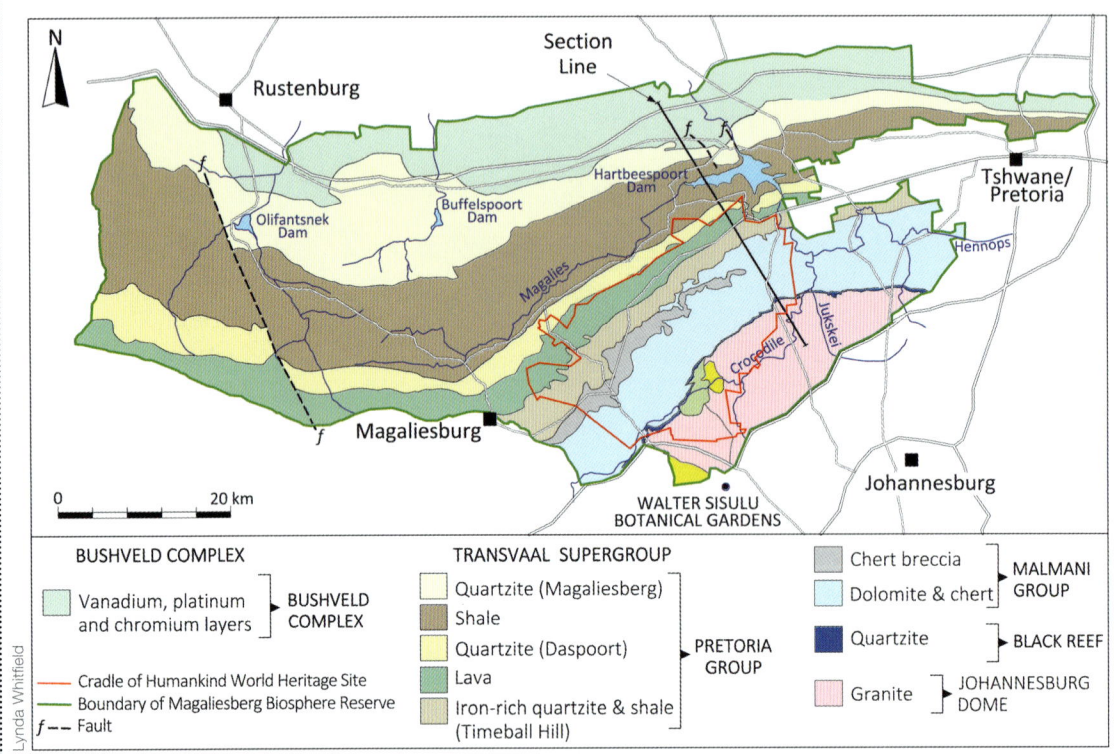

Geology of the Cradle-Magaliesberg.

The topography of the Cradle-Magaliesberg is characterised by a series of parallel mountain ridges running east-west between the modern towns of Tshwane/Pretoria and Rustenburg, and bounded by the Witwatersrand on the south and the Bushveld Complex on the north. When viewed from the air these ridges resemble waves breaking on a petrified sea. They are actually the tilted edges of an ancient seabed lifted at an angle about 2,060 million years ago. Each ridge has its own particular geomorphology. Chapter 2 describes how they were formed and what influence they had on the evolution of life. Botanists call them the Bankenveld – an old name given by early Dutch settlers who compared the ridges to rows of benches (banke). Geologists refer to them as the Transvaal Supergroup.

Viewed from the south (and showing the time sequence in which they were deposited), the five ridges that make up the Cradle-Magaliesberg landscape are:

● **First ridge**: The **Black Reef** is a narrow quartzite deposit that separates the Transvaal Supergroup from the granite dome and quartzite of the Witwatersrand.

● **Second ridge**: The **Malmani Dolomite** is the combination of dolomitic limestone and chert that gives rise to the karst landscape, in which the dolomite dissolves and forms the tunnels and caves for which the Cradle is famous. The northern edge of the Malmani dolomite is the elevated ridge of the Skurweberg, which is rich in chert and hence resilient to erosion.

● **Third ridge**: The **Timeball Hill** quartzite prominences on which Freedom Park and Unisa are built. The quartzite in this ridge is rich in iron ore that was oxidised by oxygen released by cyanobacteria.

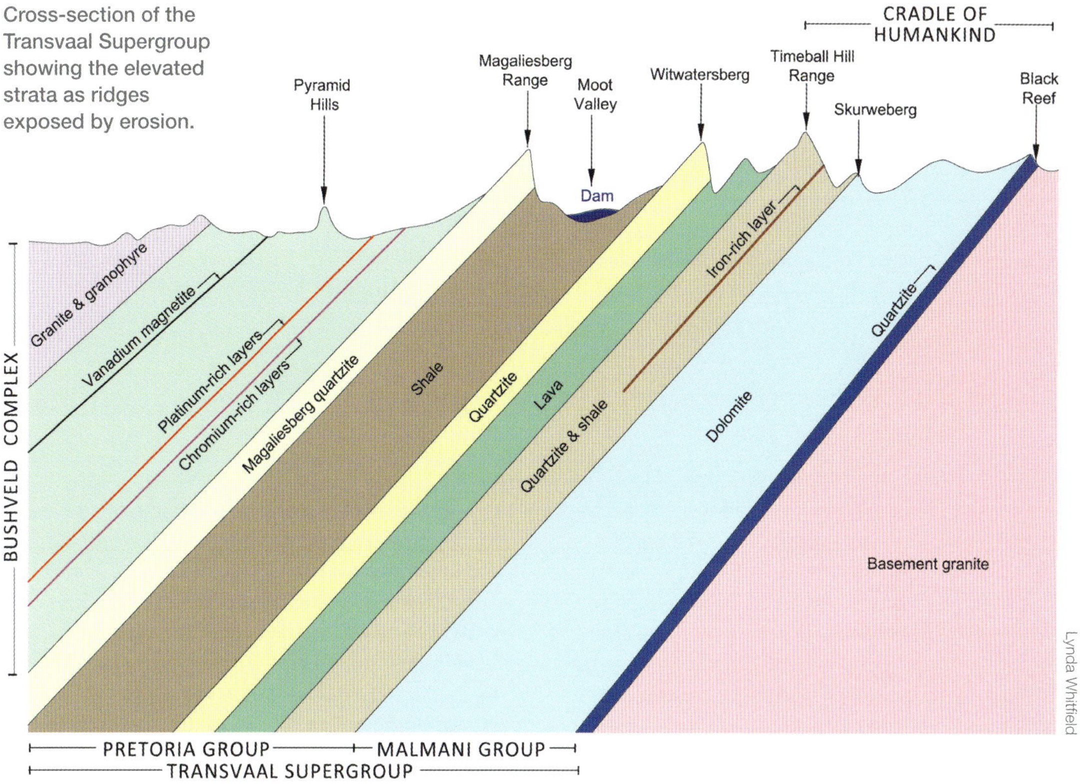

Cross-section of the Transvaal Supergroup showing the elevated strata as ridges exposed by erosion.

Diagram labels:

CRADLE OF HUMANKIND

Pyramid Hills — Magaliesberg Range — Moot Valley — Witwatersberg — Timeball Hill Range — Skurweberg — Black Reef

Dam

BUSHVELD COMPLEX

Granite & granophyre
Vanadium magnetite
Platinum-rich layers
Chromium-rich layers
Magaliesberg quartzite
Shale
Quartzite
Lava
Quartzite & shale
Iron-rich layer
Dolomite
Quartzite
Basement granite

|— PRETORIA GROUP —|— MALMANI GROUP —|
|———— TRANSVAAL SUPERGROUP ————|

- **Fourth ridge**: A bed of andesite lava separates Timeball Hill from the **Witwatersberg** (not to be confused with the Witwatersrand), a ridge of Daspoort quartzite into which sills of andesite lava have intruded.
- **Moot valley:** Between the Witwatersberg and the Magaliesberg lies a wide shale valley, called the **Moot**, part of which is flooded by the Hartbeespoort Dam.
- **Fifth ridge**: The **Magaliesberg** is the highest of the five ridges. It has a striking shape, with high cliffs of Magaliesberg quartzite on the south, and the sedimentary floor of the ancient seabed sloping gently down to the Bushveld Complex in the north. Heat from the magma intrusions has metamorphosed and recrystallised the face of the northern slope.
- **The Bushveld Complex** marks the northern limit of the Magaliesberg Biosphere Reserve. It comprises rocks created from the upwelling of molten magma and includes some of the richest mineral deposits in the world.

The northern face of the Magaliesberg metamorphosed by the heat of the Bushveld Complex.

2 | THE FIRST LANDMASS AND EARLY LIFE

In the depths of the hydrosphere described in the previous chapter, the surface of the planet had solidified into rocky crust. It was continuously ruptured by seismic disturbance and life is thought to have begun under these extreme conditions. This chapter describes how part of that life-bearing crust was elevated above the surface to become the Cradle-Magaliesberg landscape.

➤ 3,100 million years ago: Plate tectonics and the first continent

As the Earth cooled some 3,900 million years ago, a deluge of precipitation submerged the entire planet under water. The Kaapvaal Craton, which was thrust above the unbroken surface of the sea by plate tectonics more than 3,000 million years ago was the first continental landmass on the planet; and at its centre lies the Cradle-Magaliesberg. Over time and through fusion with other landmasses, this craton grew to be a full-sized continent.

Plate tectonics

Below the surface of the water covering the planet, the Earth's crust is like a cracked eggshell, with large plates floating on a hot, semi-fluid mantle. The plates move relentlessly, chafing against each other along boundary lines that are constantly disrupted by volcanoes, earthquakes and other seismic activity. Convection currents in the mantle beneath the oceanic crust draw the plates apart and, as they separate, volcanoes push molten magma into the widening gap, creating a mountain ridge on the ocean floor and forming new sheets of oceanic crust as they spread away from the ridge in both directions.

As new material is added along one edge of a plate underwater, the further edge is thrust up against its neighbour and forced to slide underneath it in a process known as subduction. The ancient crust from the lower plate melts back

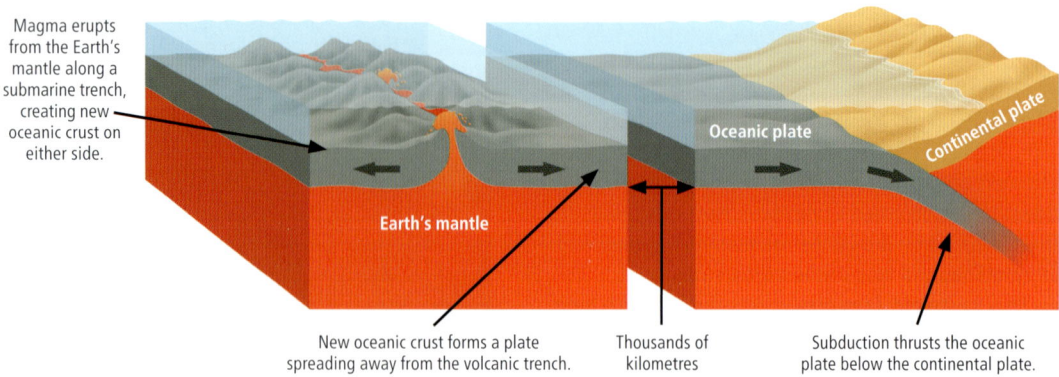

Magma erupts from the Earth's mantle along a submarine trench, creating new oceanic crust on either side.

Earth's mantle

Oceanic plate

Continental plate

New oceanic crust forms a plate spreading away from the volcanic trench.

Thousands of kilometres

Subduction thrusts the oceanic plate below the continental plate.

Plate tectonics: as plates separate under the sea, magma erupts into the gap, pushing them further apart to collide into the adjacent continent and slide below it into the molten mantle.

into the mantle, accompanied by frequent buckling, folding and volcanic eruption, while the upper plate is thickened and elevated as continental crust.

About 3,100 million years ago, as the subduction of one plate elevated another, parts of the latter plate emerged as volcanic islands above the surface around the subduction zone. Small landmasses (cratons) drifted together and collided violently. Many such islands probably appeared briefly, eroded, and subsided again, but eventually several of them consolidated and stabilised as the first permanent continental landmass above sea level. Known as the Kaapvaal Craton, it straddles what eventually became southern Africa between Mozambique and Botswana, with the Cradle-Magaliesberg region at its centre.

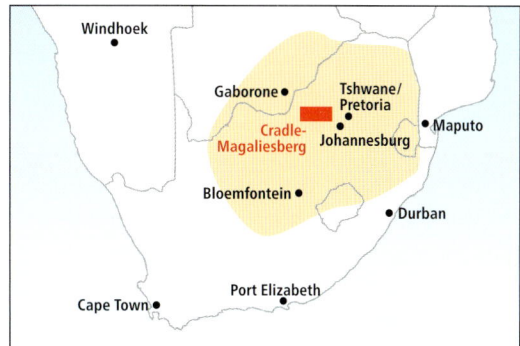

The Cradle-Magaliesberg lies at the centre of the Kaapvaal Craton, which gradually grew to a full-sized continent. The map shows the craton's position in relation to modern southern Africa.

DISCOVERING & MONITORING CONTINENTAL DRIFT

For many centuries, cartographers had observed that the African and South American coastlines mirrored each other across the Atlantic Ocean. However, it was not until 1915 that German geophysicist Alfred Wegener suggested that the two continents had once been united, and were slowly moving away from each other. He named the ancient supercontinent Pangaea, and described its subsequent division into Gondwanaland (now shortened to Gondwana) and Laurasia (see map on page 61). At the time, Wegener's theory of drifting continents was not well received by scientists working in the mainstream of geophysical research.

In 1991 a set of commemorative stamps was issued to honour notable scientists, two of whom feature prominently in the story of the Cradle-Magaliesberg: palaeontologist Robert Broom (see Chapter 7) and Alexander du Toit, who verified Alfred Wegener's theory of continental drift.

In the 1930s South African geologist Alexander du Toit traversed the entire southern African subcontinent, sometimes by donkey cart or bicycle, and compiled a meticulously accurate geological map. In the course of doing so, he gathered further compelling geological information that supported and expanded Wegener's theory of continental drift. However, geologists in the United States were particularly resistant to accepting any new thinking and his discoveries, like Wegener's, were disregarded.

Ironically, it was an American who finally validated Wegener's and Du Toit's theories. In 1964 Harry Hess, an oceanographer and Rear Admiral with submarine experience in the US navy, observed that the volcanically active Mid-Atlantic Ridge lying between Africa and America was constantly adding new material to an expanding seabed as continental plates pulled apart. His findings proved Wegener's and Du Toit's theory of plate tectonics but, regrettably, neither of them had lived to see their hypotheses confirmed.

Volcanic island arcs emerged above sea level and consolidated into the Kaapvaal Craton 3,100 million years ago.

Scientists think that life may have first evolved about 3,500 million years ago along the submarine volcanic ridges that cause plate tectonics and gave rise to the emergence of the Kaapvaal Craton. Fossilised evidence of these early life forms has been identified in the Kaapvaal greenstones where they are exposed near Barberton, and it is probable that these microscopic fossils, the oldest known signs of life on Earth, also exist in the greenstones in the Cradle area.

The first continent and evidence of life

A second landmass, the Zimbabwe Craton, emerged and drifted against the Kaapvaal, and the impact of their collision disrupted much of the original land surface. A high mountain range was thrown up along the impact zone in much the same way as the Himalayas were lifted thousands of millions of years later by the collision of India with Asia. At a point south of the Cradle-Magaliesberg, near present-day Ventersdorp in North West Province, the continental crust fractured and huge volumes of magma erupted, burying the entire region under lava and ash.

Other cratons developed and began to consolidate. Throughout its three billion-year existence, the Kaapvaal Craton has remained at the centre of the fusion and dispersal of several supercontinents in changing patterns across the planet. It has been subjected to volcanic eruption, meteor strikes, and submersion under ice and desert sand, but the basic geological region has remained intact. The basement rocks of the Kaapvaal Craton are known as greenstone, and are among the oldest rocks in the world. Most of them lie buried under layers of subsequent sedimentary and igneous deposits. However, on the southern boundary of the Cradle, from the Walter Sisulu National Botanical Garden to the Oaktree turnoff to the Sterkfontein Caves, some of the original surface of the first continent on Earth lies exposed.

Plate tectonics created the first continent on the planet, and have shaped and re-shaped the surface of the Earth throughout its existence. Scientists call this process 'continental drift'. The continental movement is imperceptible on a daily basis – geodesy programmes (studies of the precise measurement of the Earth) carried out at the HartRAO station show that South Africa is moving towards India at a rate of 2.5cm per year – but, in the immensity of geological time, the rearrangement of vast continents across the planet has profoundly influenced the landscape and climate of the Cradle-Magaliesberg.

An example of greenstone basement rock in the Walter Sisulu National Botanical Garden. Small outcrops are visible on the southern edges of the Cradle and may retain signs of the earliest life.

➤ 2,714 million years ago: The Black Reef

The oldest of the prominent ridges of the Cradle topography is the Black Reef.

The collision between the Kaapvaal and Zimbabwe cratons deformed the topography of the emerging continental landscape, and 2,714 million years ago caused part of the Kaapvaal Craton to subside. The ocean invaded that part of the landmass, and what is now the Cradle-Magaliesberg was submerged under a shallow sea. Rivers that had once flowed across the landscape were truncated, and mud and gravel sediments were deposited in estuaries along the new coastline. There they consolidated into a layer of quartzite called the Black Reef. This was the first of a series of sedimentary rock types that make up the formation known collectively as the Transvaal Supergroup, the geological system that underlies the Magaliesberg Biosphere Reserve. When the entire Transvaal Supergroup was later elevated and exposed as mountain ranges, the Black Reef became the most southerly ridge in the uplifted series.

More than 2,500 million years old, the Black Reef is clearly visible as a low quartzite outcrop running across the southern part of the Cradle. It separates the geology of the Cradle-Magaliesberg from the Johannesburg Granite Dome, and extends east and west for many kilometres beyond the Cradle.

For a relatively short period during the time when the alluvial sediments that became the Black Reef were being deposited, small quantities of gold were washed down among the gravel. These were compacted into a narrow seam of gold-bearing quartzite, sandwiched between the other strata in the Reef. Before the discovery of the huge Witwatersrand goldfields, gold was mined in the Black Reef, and productive mining continued into the twentieth century. Today, old adits (horizontal passages) still exist in the hillside and lead to the derelict narrow mining stopes underground.

Although the Black Reef is only a few metres wide, it is easily visible in many places in the Cradle. One of the best views is at the Cradle Restaurant, on the road from Lanseria to Kromdraai.

During the South African War, Boer commandos hid in these mines and built low-profile lookout points along the ridge. From these they were able to watch the movement of British soldiers to and from military bases in Krugersdorp and Johannesburg. The remnants of many of these observation posts can still be seen along the Black Reef today.

The narrow seam of gold-bearing reef is visible in the Blaauwbank Mine near Magaliesburg town. The mine remained in production until well into the twentieth century.

The most significant evolutionary event recorded in the Cradle-Magaliesberg landscape is not the fossilisation of human ancestry: it is the development of photosynthesis and the microbiology that preceded and followed it.

The essential property of living matter that distinguishes it from non-living matter is its ability to reproduce and sustain itself. No one yet understands how inert molecules acquired that capability, but pioneering work by evolutionary biologists Pierre Durand and Nisha Dhar at the Evolutionary Studies Institute at the University of the Witwatersrand has demonstrated that small, non-living RNA molecules have the capacity to join together and thus form into larger, more complex molecules. Such spontaneous random fusion of RNA molecules (called ligation) could have led to the emergence of a collection of molecules capable of self-replication, and thus to the beginning of elementary life.

The widely accepted hypothesis that such primitive life originated in hydrothermal vents in the ocean depths where the tectonic plates diverge has been mentioned earlier. Microorganisms called prokaryotes occur around such vents, and scientists think they are similar to the earliest living entity from which subsequent life has evolved – the so-called last universal common ancestor (LUCA).

During the first billion years of the existence of life on Earth, prokaryotes evolved into various types of bacteria and primitive archaea, which were sparsely distributed and dependent on external energy sources to survive. Signs of this early life are found in the greenstone of the Kaapvaal Craton, and

probably also occur in the outcrops in the Cradle. However, the tilting of the Kaapvaal Craton and the submergence of part of the Cradle-Magaliesberg under water provided an environment suitable for the development of a new life form. In the shallow tidal water that covered the rocks of the Black Reef, one bacterial group, the cyanobacteria, evolved the ability to photosynthesise about 2,700 million years ago. Using energy from the Sun, they extracted carbon dioxide from the atmosphere to manufacture their own hydrocarbons (compounds of hydrogen and carbon essential for life) and nutrient energy.

The impact of photosynthesis

Photosynthesis made it possible for cyanobacteria to flourish in a way that no life form on Earth had ever done before. Sunlight, water and carbon dioxide were abundant; and, without competitors or predators to inhibit development, cyanobacteria

Layers of calcium carbonate deposited by cyanobacteria billions of years ago are visible in a cross-section of a broken stromatolite in the Cradle.

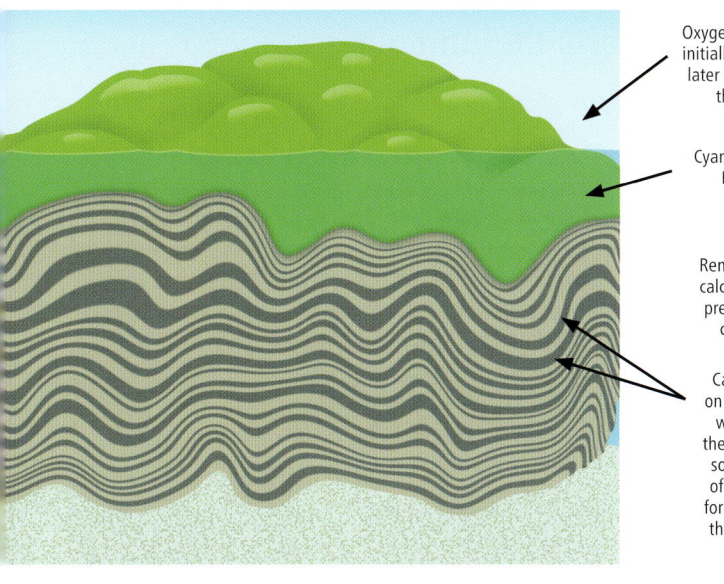

Oxygen was a by-product, initially oxidising iron and later being released into the atmosphere.

Cyanobacteria converted H_2O and CO_2 into carbohydrates.

Removal of H_2O caused calcium in the ocean to precipitate as calcium carbonate $CaCO_3$.

$CaCO_3$ accumulated on the cyanobacteria, which regrew over the calcium carbonate so that a succession of alternating layers formed, one on top of the other, over time.

Photosynthesis: cyanobacteria were the first life form to use sunlight to convert carbon dioxide and water into carbohydrates. The process precipitated calcium carbonate (limestone) and generated oxygen that changed the course of evolution.

spread prodigiously in a wide swathe of clusters along the shoreline that later became the Cradle-Magaliesberg. Not only did photosynthesis accelerate the growth and rapid reproduction of living bacteria, allowing them to diversify and eventually evolve into new organisms; it also produced two vital by-products: oxygen and calcium carbonate. These two substances changed the composition of the atmosphere and altered the basic geology of the Cradle-Magaliesberg environment.

Unlike most other bacteria, cyanobacteria consolidate into long filaments that mat together in large colonies. Their extraction of carbon dioxide for photosynthesis caused an imbalance in the primordial seawater, causing calcium carbonate to precipitate and adhere to the surface of the cyanobacterial colonies. This calciferous crust blocked out the sunlight and inhibited photosynthesis, but it also provided a platform on which new bacterial layers could grow; thus new alternating layers of bacteria and calcium carbonate were constantly being added onto a growing hemispherical dome. As the layers of bacteria died, the calcium carbonate crusts remained as onionskin-like structures called stromatolites.

Stromatolites are conspicuous fossilised features in the Cradle landscape, relics of one of the earliest forms of life on Earth that flourished more than 2,500 million years ago. They are the base material for dolomite and the karst geology of the region discussed in the following section. Stromatolites vary considerably in size. Tidal movement in the shallows restricted the size of the stromatolites there to marble-sized spheroids called oncolites. In deeper water, however, they grew into large domes a metre or more in diameter.

Lynette Clennell

Cyanobacteria still exist. This colony of living stromatolites is found in tidal pools on the Eastern Cape coast.

The dolomitic landscape underlying the Cradle of Humankind was built by cyanobacteria. For millions of years the exponential growth of cyanobacteria deposited calcified stromatolites that accumulated one on top of another to considerable depths along the south-western coastline of the Kaapvaal Craton. Over time the calcium carbonate content reacted with magnesium to become calcium magnesium carbonate – $MgCa(CO_3)_2$ – also called dolomite, a form of limestone. This is the rock formation that today underlies much of the area of the Cradle of Humankind.

Deposited on top of the Black Reef, dolomite is the second layer of sedimentary rocks that comprise the Transvaal Supergroup or Bankenveld. However, unlike the other ranges in the Supergroup, dolomite forms an elevated ridge only where it is blended with substantial deposits of resilient chert. On its own it is semi-soluble and any high ground is constantly weathered away. Undulating hills with outcrops of distinctive grey 'elephant skin' dolomitic rocks interspersed with bands of chert are the major visible landform. Being the by-product of living organisms, they are chemically and structurally unlike the other geological formations in the Transvaal Supergroup, which were all formed from inert sandy sediments or volcanic lava.

The subterranean topography is especially interesting, because the solubility of limestone resulted in the leaching out of subterranean caves that honeycomb the entire area. This is the unique karst landscape in which the hominin fossils are found. Sinkholes and avens open into the caves from the surface, and in some cases the entire roof has weathered away so that the cave is

Dolomitic rock is slightly soluble and aquires a distinctive 'elephant skin' texture as it weathers.

Dolomite deposits are sandwiched between blue-grey chert, which is more resilient and forms prominently exposed layers.

The spherical shape of stromatolites remains clear in the dolomitic rocks of the Cradle even after thousands of millions of years.

Where the Hennops River enters the chert-rich hills of the Skurweberg it cuts spectacular gorges through the rugged landscape.

essentially an open pit. Many caves extend below the water table and retain large underground lakes. These important natural reservoirs are constantly recharged by seepage from surrounding limestone that is strongly alkaline and calciferous.

Chert and the Skurweberg

While the stromatolites were transforming into dolomite, silicon silt from the surrounding high ground continued to be deposited in layers of fine-grained sedimentary rocks called chert. This formed a hard bluish-coloured rock, sandwiched between layers of dolomite. The chert strata are less susceptible to weathering, and they tend to protrude conspicuously from the dolomite. Many millions of years later, chert was to become one of the favoured materials for making stone tools in the Cradle-Magaliesberg area.

In parts of the submerged Cradle-Magaliesberg, silt from the incoming rivers appears to have been more plentiful, perhaps because weaker currents in the shallow waters allowed the fine-grained silt to settle. Chert deposits are thus more evident on the northern side of the dolomite beds, where

they form a line of rough, stony hills known as the Skurweberg (*skurwe* means 'rough' in Afrikaans). It is an extension of the dolomite deposits, but the chert intrusions make it more resistant to erosion and the uplifted substrate has survived as an elevated range of hills.

A recent sinkhole in the John Nash Nature Reserve demonstrates the instability of the subterranean cave formations.

➤ 2,350 million years ago: The Magaliesberg and the Pretoria Group

Within the Transvaal Supergroup or Bankenveld, the ridges north of the dolomite landscape of the Cradle are collectively referred to by geologists as the 'Pretoria Group'. They rise in ascending elevations from the Timeball Hill ridge in the south to the Magaliesberg, which is the highest, in the north.

The Pretoria Group is composed of sediments that were deposited in the shallow water of the submerged part of the Cradle-Magaliesberg after it had become carpeted with cyanobacteria. The surrounding shores were devoid of life, and were constantly eroded by violent storms. The atmosphere consisted mainly of carbon dioxide

André Wedepohl

and water vapour, with a toxic mix of sulphurous and acidic gases that etched away the barren rocks and washed vast quantities of sand and mud into the coastal waters. As the various sediments settled and solidified on the seabed, they swamped the cyanobacteria under alternating layers of sandstone and mudstone several kilometres thick.

Over millions of years, the topography and eroded material changed greatly. At times, the sediments comprised clean silicon gravel, rinsed by fast-moving mountain streams. At other times the landscape was flatter, and muddy residues were dumped from sluggish, meandering rivers. This resulted in a series of different layers of sediments, each with its own geological characteristics and mineral content.

The first sediments to swamp the cyanobacteria made up the Timeball Hill layer, rich in red iron oxide which has been exploited as iron ore for more than 1,500 years. The deposit takes its name from the early days of Pretoria when a gun was fired from the hilltop every day at noon.

The Timeball Hill sedimentation was covered by a sheet of andesite lava erupting from volcanic pipes that have long since disappeared. Andesite lava is a thick, viscous fluid that would have flowed slowly over the sedimentary layers and intruded between new sandy sediments as they were deposited. When the Pretoria Group was later elevated and exposed to erosion, the lava was more inclined to erode than the hard quartzite and it became the valley in which central Tshwane/Pretoria now lies.

The new layer of sand into which the andesite lava intruded was the Witwatersberg (or Daspoort Rand as it is called in central Pretoria). Now that the sediments have been elevated, the sills of lava have partially weathered away so that the Witwatersberg often has two or more false horizons where the cliffs are stepped in a series of terraces.

The climatic conditions that followed appear to have been particularly wet and severe, causing the next layer of sediment to be finely pulverised mud. It is particularly susceptible to weathering and has been eroded away in a wide valley called the Moot.

The final layer of sediments deposited on top of all the others was the Magaliesberg. Because it is much thicker than the other layers it has been the most resistant to erosion.

From the summit, the distinctive shape of the Magaliesberg is apparent, with sheer south-facing quartzite cliffs and the gentle slope of the tilted seabed to the north. The cliffs are the eroded remnants of an enormous dome of sedimentary rocks that was elevated by an up-thrust of the crust of the Earth under the Johannesburg area. The dome would have obscured the right-hand half of this photograph.

FORMATION OF THE BANKENVELD

A 2,350 million years ago sand and mud sediments consolidated into sandstone and mudstone deposits above the dolomitic rock that had been created by cyanobacteria on the bed of the shallow sea.

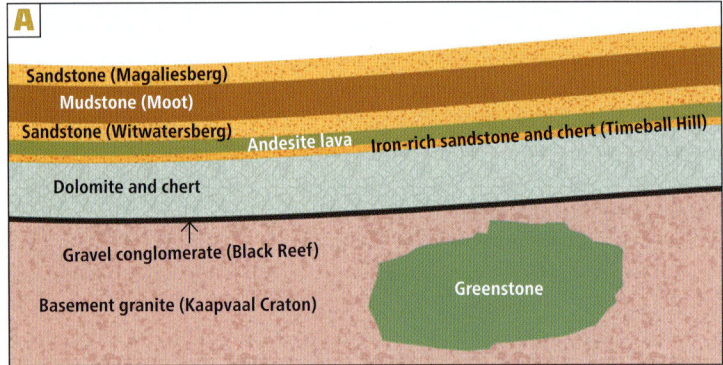

B 2,060 million years ago semi-liquid magma, known as the Bushveld Complex, surged up from the mantle of the Earth, settling above and intruding between the sedimentary rocks of the Pretoria Group. Heat and pressure converted the sandstone and mudstone into quartzite and shale. The weight of the Bushveld Complex depressed the centre of the system and elevated the edges. Rich deposits of platinum and other minerals were deposited at the periphery.

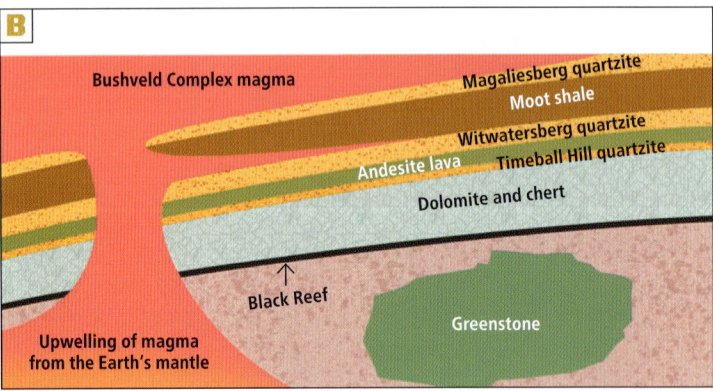

C Pressure from below the Earth's crust lifted the basement granite and greenstones of the original Kaapvaal Craton, together with the overlying strata of the Transvaal

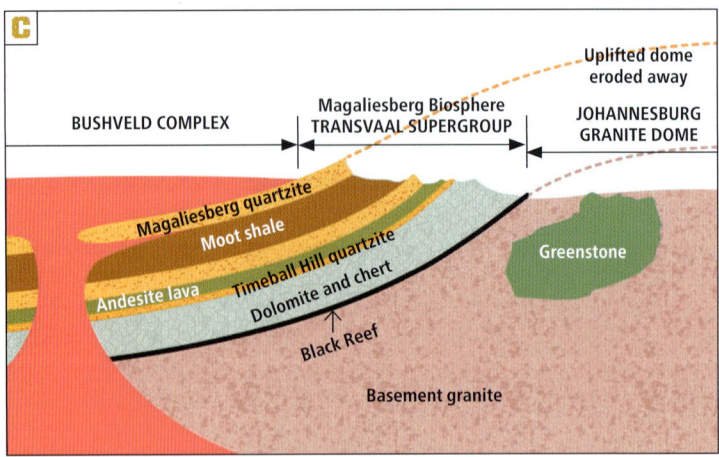

Supergroup, to form an elevated dome. The high parts eroded away to reveal the basement granite, now called the Johannesburg Granite Dome, and small outcrops of greenstone. The edges of the Pretoria Group strata were exposed as the Magaliesberg and adjacent ridges.

➤ 2,060 million years ago: The Bushveld Complex and the Johannesburg Granite Dome

More than 2,000 million years ago the seabed and its entire stratification of sediments that make up the Pretoria Group was elevated by the upwelling of the Bushveld Complex, an extraordinary phenomenon that scientists regard as one of the geological wonders of the world. The process began with massive volcanic eruptions of rhyolite that thrust molten lava above the level of the sedimentary seabed. These were followed by a more extensive series of ejections of basalt lava that cooled and solidified into granite at the surface, and capped any further rise of molten material. Successive pulses of rising magma were trapped under this granite ceiling and squeezed horizontally between the layers of the sedimentary rocks, splitting and expanding them. The high temperatures metamorphosed the sandstone and mudstone sediments into quartzite and shale. The intrusions of andesite lava sills carried small amounts of copper and silver that were later mined in the Cradle-Magaliesberg region.

The slope of the northern aspect of the Magaliesberg was recrystallised by exposure to the heat of the Bushveld Complex and has weathered into curiously sculpted shapes.

The view from the Black Reef to the Magaliesberg: the Cradle is in the foreground, then the flat-topped Skurweberg, the Witwatersberg and the Magaliesberg in the distance.

The upwelling north of the Magaliesberg persisted for a million years and solidified into one vast granite lopolith (an expanse of rock from a single igneous extrusion) called the Bushveld Complex. Shaped like a lens with a thick centre and thinner edges, it extends from Botswana to the Lydenburg escarpment, and from Tshwane/Pretoria to Polokwane – the largest formation of this type anywhere. Vast deposits of platinum, chrome and vanadium accumulated at the periphery, and two billion years later they are exploited in the world's richest platinum and chrome mines.

The weight of the granite layer of the Bushveld Complex pushed the quartzite rocks of the old seabed down at the centre, lifting the edges like the pages of a paperback book. These uplifted 'pages' eventually became the parallel ridges of the Magaliesberg Biosphere Reserve, with the erosion-resistant quartzite standing high above valleys of shale that weather more rapidly.

The thicker deposits of the Magaliesberg became the largest of the mountain ridges. When the Bushveld Complex welled up from below the Transvaal Supergroup, the Magaliesberg

Fractures in the quartzite seabed as it was uplifted left deeply incised kloofs across the northern face of the Magaliesberg.

The deep kloofs offer some of the finest scenery in the Cradle-Magaliesberg area.

sediments were exposed to the full heat of the rising magma and the upper surface (now the northern slope of the elevated ridge) melted and recrystallised into particularly large crystals. They crumble easily and have weathered into bizarre mushroom shapes and statuary on the exposed upper slopes of the mountain.

Below the sedimentary rocks of the Transvaal Supergroup lay the basement granite of the Kaapvaal Craton with its veins of greenstone, the oldest rocks in the world and possibly containing fossilised traces of the earliest life forms. After the upwelling of the Bushveld Complex these ancient rocks were themselves gradually thrust upwards by pressures deep in the mantle of the Earth: not by an outpouring of molten magma as in the Bushveld, but rather a gradual lifting of a subterranean granite dome. The layers of quartzite, lava and shale of the Transvaal Supergroup were lifted with the rising topography like a blanket drawn up over the elevated dome.

Over time the dome covering eroded away, exposing the Johannesburg Granite Dome and occasional outcrops of greenstone. The sedimentary strata of the Transvaal Group were truncated as the erosion cut them back and exposed their edges. The resilient quartzite of the Pretoria Group became prominent ridges while the softer rocks like dolomite, andesite lava and shale were weathered down to intervening valleys.

The distinctive wedge shape of the ridges clearly demonstrates the origin of their formation: the sheer quartzite cliffs are the broken-off edges of the earlier sedimentary strata, and the gradual slopes to the north are the tilted surface of the ancient seabed as it dips down into the Bushveld Complex.

As the sedimentary rock face of the old seabed was thrust upwards it fractured, and deep ravines cracked open along fault lines on the raised northern face. The most spectacular scenery in the Cradle-Magaliesberg is found in these narrow kloofs. Their sheer sides protect them from harsh, direct sun and severe weather, while their north-facing aspect guarantees a mild climate in all seasons. Water filters through fissures in the quartzite and collects along horizontal sills, spilling over in beautiful waterfalls. The perennial streams make it possible for a rich floral community to thrive, including some high-canopy Afrotemperate forest similar to that which existed in the region at the time of hominin evolution.

3 | EVOLUTION AND EXTINCTION

The cyanobacteria that produced calcium carbonate also released oxygen. The way in which this redirected the course of evolution, and the unrelated seismic disturbances that re-shaped the Cradle-Magaliesberg landscape, are the subjects of this chapter.

At the time that these changes took place, the Earth was little more than half its present age. Days and nights were shorter than they are now, because the planet rotated faster on its axis. The young Sun had not yet reached its full potential to generate nuclear power and was a third cooler than it is today, but greenhouse gases (carbon dioxide and water vapour) trapped heat within the Earth's atmosphere, and reduced the impact of the freezing temperatures. Over the next 2,000 million years continents drifted, collided and reunited into supercontinents, and volcanoes, meteor strikes and mass extinctions occurred.

A direct consequence of the release of oxygen through photosynthesis was the development of eukaryotic cells – cells that contain DNA in the nucleus and also mitochondrial DNA – and this enabled the processes of evolution to accelerate. The combination of nuclear DNA and mitochondrial DNA provided more opportunities for living organisms to adapt to their environment and to be selected naturally for survival in the changing world.

The release of oxygen into the atmosphere by photosynthesis redirected the course of evolution.

Evidence of these events can be seen in the Cradle-Magaliesberg region, and this makes it one of the most instructive places in which to discover how life came to occupy the narrow envelope of land, water and air that we call the biosphere.

Oxygen emissions from photosynthesis first oxidised the soluble isotopes of iron and manganese and formed red banded iron shales in the Timeball Hill formation close to Pretoria.

➤ 2,650–2,250 million years ago: Oxygen

Oxygen was the most important by-product of photosynthesis during the millions of years that cyanobacteria dominated the Cradle-Magaliesberg. It redirected the development of life on the planet.

The extensive cyanobacteria beds in the Cradle-Magaliesberg region released vast amounts of oxygen as a waste product from about 2,650 million years ago. At first, very little of it entered the atmosphere. Oxygen is highly reactive, and it burns, rusts and corrodes almost anything with which it comes into contact. The oxygen released by the cyanobacteria was initially used up by isotopes of iron and manganese that were dissolved in the sea; these isotopes combined with the oxygen in a process called oxidisation. Enormous quantities of iron and manganese oxide were precipitated from the ocean and formed sediments known as banded iron formations in the hills south of Pretoria. Early Iron Age smelters at Broederstroom exploited the ore from this source more than 1,500 years ago (see Chapter 8) and the Iron and Steel Industrial Corporation (Iscor) founded the South African steel industry in the iron-rich hills when it opened the first steel mill outside Pretoria in 1928. They are now being mined across the North West and Northern Cape provinces from Tshwane/Pretoria to Prieska.

100km	Thermosphere	Ultraviolet radiation
50km	Mesosphere / Stratosphere	Ozone layer O_3 → $O_2 + O$
10km	Troposphere	Commercial aircraft / Mount Everest

The composition of the atmosphere changes with altitude. Ozone lies above the stratosphere, about 50km above the Earth, where it intercepts harmful ultraviolet radiation. The ozone molecules, O_3, split and reunite, destroying the ultraviolet rays in the process.

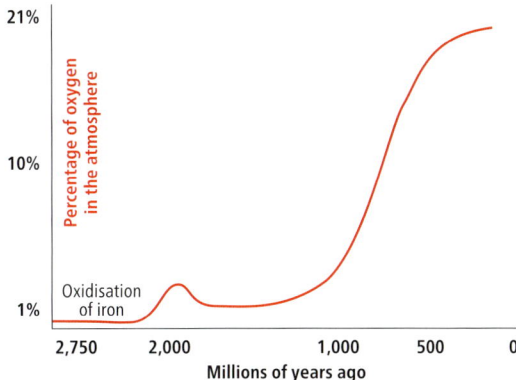

Free oxygen only began to be released into the atmosphere once the oxidisation of iron and manganese had been completed after about half a billion years.

It took 400 million years for this long process of oxidisation to be accomplished; only then was free oxygen gradually released into the atmosphere. Oxygen accumulated slowly, and its proportion of the atmosphere (currently about 21 per cent) has varied at different times in the past.

The presence of oxygen brought about an incidental benefit for life on Earth. A normal oxygen molecule, O_2, contains two oxygen atoms combined. However, in the stratosphere about 50km above sea level, the oxygen molecule O_2 bonds with a third atom to form ozone, O_3. When dangerous ultraviolet radiation from the Sun strikes an ozone molecule, it is absorbed by the molecule. The ozone temporarily splits into normal oxygen in the process, but quickly reverts to ozone after having prevented the ultraviolet rays from penetrating the atmosphere. The concentration of ozone at these very high altitudes is very low (20 parts per million), but it is sufficient to shield life on the planet from life-threatening radiation.

➤ 2,000 million years ago: Eukaryotic cells

For more than a billion years after the earliest life form (referred to as LUCA, the last universal common ancestor), bacteria were the only living organisms. They had evolved from primitive anaerobic prokaryotes (primitive microbes that exist without oxygen) and they derived their energy from sources other than the oxidisation of nutrients. When cyanobacteria began to photosynthesise, they released oxygen as an unwanted by-product and this created the opportunity for other microorganisms to evolve ways to generate their own metabolic energy, by using the oxygen to burn nutrients and expel carbon dioxide. A remarkable system of balanced symbiosis emerged, in which cyanobacteria used carbon dioxide and expelled oxygen, while the new type of bacteria used the oxygen and expelled carbon dioxide. Eventually the symbiotic relationship between these two types of bacteria flourished to a point where one of the partners was permanently absorbed into the other. An entirely new form of life emerged, in which the functions of both types of bacteria were enclosed within complex cells called eukaryotes.

Nuclear DNA and mitochondria

Eukaryotic cells have a nucleus in which the DNA of the original host partner is contained. In the fluid cytoplasm of the cell that surrounds the nucleus, the remnant of the energy-producing symbiotic partner is housed in separate structures; these structures are

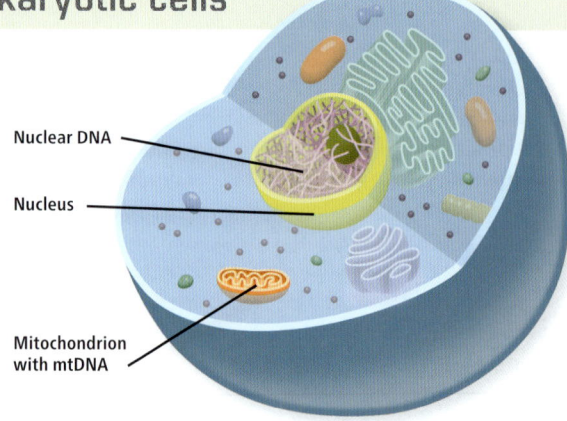

Nuclear DNA

Nucleus

Mitochondrion
with mtDNA

All living organisms are composed of eukaryotic cells, which contain two types of DNA. Nuclear DNA determines every function and feature of the organism. Mitochondrial DNA is contained separately in the mitochondria, and generates energy.

called mitochondria in animal cells, and chloroplasts in plant cells. The DNA in the nucleus carries the instructions for building the proteins that fulfil every feature and function of the organism. The mitochondria in animal cells produce metabolic energy by oxidising nutrients (this process is called respiration). They have their own small, circular loop of DNA which is quite distinct from the nuclear DNA of the main cells, and is a relict of their once independent state as separate organisms.

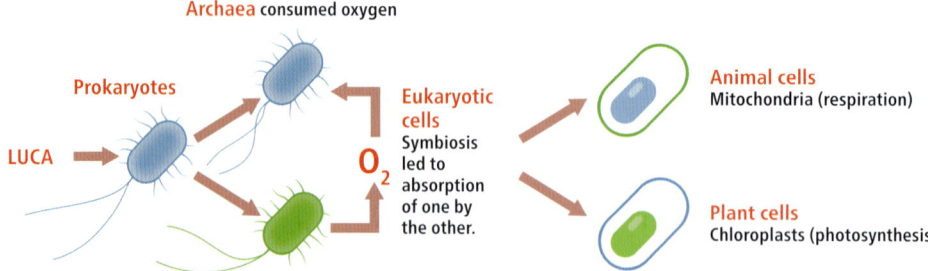

Archaea consumed oxygen

Prokaryotes

LUCA

O_2

Eukaryotic cells
Symbiosis led to absorption of one by the other.

Animal cells
Mitochondria (respiration)

Plant cells
Chloroplasts (photosynthesis)

Cyanobacteria released oxygen (photosynthesis)

A diagrammatic representation showing the development of eukaryotes from symbiosis between primitive oxygen-producing and oxygen-consuming organisms.

Organisms inherit their mitochondrial DNA (mtDNA) only through the female line, mother to daughter; males inherit mtDNA from their mother but never transfer it to the next generation. Mutations occur randomly in mtDNA, and the average number of mutations in two related organisms gives an indication of how long ago they shared a common ancestor. This, and its exclusively maternal inheritance, make mtDNA an important indicator of our evolutionary history.

Before the development of eukaryotes, all bacteria had reproduced by binary fission or mitosis – that is, they divided into two parts, each a near-perfect clone of its parent. Evolutionary processes were slow because of the absence of opportunities for natural adaptation and selection. Eukaryotes initiated the vitally important mode of inheritance through meiosis – the process in which the DNA of two reproductive parents combines. Random mutations and adaptations occasionally occur during this process, and the rate of evolution accelerated rapidly as natural selection favoured the advantageous adaptations. Eukaryotic cells became the basic unit in all plant and animal life that evolved thereafter.

➤ 2,023 million years ago: The Vredefort Dome

One reason why life exists on Earth is that the atmosphere shields us from cosmic bombardment. Occasionally, however, meteors are able to penetrate this atmospheric umbrella, and, if large enough, to cause serious damage to life and landscape. On five occasions a large proportion of existing life on Earth has been eliminated in mass extinctions, and scientists believe that meteor strikes are a probable cause of at least some of them.

The biggest meteor strike on record occurred 2,023 million years ago, 120km south of the Cradle of Humankind near the present-day town of Vredefort. It devastated the land for hundreds of kilometres around the impact site and helped to shape the landscape that is now the Cradle-Magaliesberg. The evolution of life was in its infancy. The beds of cyanobacteria in the Cradle were still dispersing oxygen into the atmosphere, and the size and devastation of the meteor strike would certainly have taken a toll on what remained of their existence. Geologists estimate that the meteor was either a rock or an ice block about 10km in diameter, probably travelling at 40,000km per hour. It penetrated more than 10km below the surface, where it exploded, releasing energy equivalent to several thousand atomic bombs. Rock at the point of impact was immediately vaporised, and thousands of cubic kilometres of debris were blown high into the air, leaving a circular crater some 5km to 10km deep and about 300km wide.

Distortion from the Vredefort Dome meteor impact can be seen in the rock face in the Walter Sisulu National Botanical Garden close to the Cradle-Magaliesberg.

220,000 YEARS AGO – THE TSWAING METEORITE

The Tswaing Crater 50km north of the Cradle was caused by a meteor impact, which would have had a devastating effect on the region and on the early human inhabitants. The crater was an important source of salt for neighbouring communities and, until recently, was known as Soutpan (Salt Pan).

Tswaing was a smaller and more recent meteor strike than the one at Vredefort, but it also had a major impact on the Cradle-Magaliesberg. It occurred about 60km to the north of the Magaliesberg, and the scientific details of the strike emerged in 1990 when Tim Partridge, a Wits University geologist, drilled a core into the crater. He and his colleague, Uwe Reimold, established that the meteor had struck about 220,000 years ago. It was probably about 50m in diameter, with an estimated impact speed of around 50,000km per hour. The fireball of the approaching meteor would have lit up the landscape for hundreds of kilometres and, at the moment of impact, observers would have seen an intense flash, brighter than the Sun, followed seconds later by a deafening explosion. The energy released would have been of the order of about a hundred atomic bombs detonated simultaneously. Hurricane-strength winds would have stripped away trees and driven fierce wildfires across the countryside. Darkness would have shrouded the area, perhaps for months, as dust and debris obscured the Sun, and massive unseasonal storms may have flooded the landscape.

The meteor strike occurred at the time when Early Stone Age humans and *Homo naledi* populated the area, and some of them would have witnessed the event and been victims of its devastation. They would have been exposed to flying debris and possibly suffered ear and lung damage from the concussion blast.

The Tswaing Crater is a closed system that receives rainwater runoff but is not filled or drained by streams or watercourses. A variety of minerals accumulate in the pan; one of these minerals is salt, and this was an important source for human use.

At the time of the meteor strike average rainfall was extremely low. It increased sharply during the next 50,000 years and has been declining ever since.

Regional rainfall in the Cradle-Magaliesberg over the past 200,000 years	
Years ago	**Average annual rainfall**
Present	635mm
50,000	720mm
100,000	800mm
150,000	880mm
200,000	440mm

Based on evidence from the Tswaing Meteor Crater

A compression wave radiated away from the point of impact and distorted geological formations as far away as the Cradle-Magaliesberg. The entire region was buried under several metres of super-heated rock and debris. Dust from the explosion was thrown into the stratosphere, shutting out sunlight and heat, and for many years the development of life was arrested everywhere on the planet.

Within seconds of the impact, the Earth's crust rebounded like a trampoline, pushing up an elevated dome which, during the ensuing millions of years, has been weathered away, leaving a rim of mountainous terrain around its base. Today a circular zone of hills and valleys about 90km in diameter is the visible evidence of this earth-shattering and unique event, and it is protected as a World Heritage Site, the Vredefort Dome.

➤ 1,400–1,200 million years ago: The Pilanesberg volcano

On the northern slopes of the Magaliesberg, beautiful kloofs are incised deep into the mountainside. They were created through the fracturing of the quartzite seabed when it was tilted by the Bushveld Complex; but a billion years later some of the kloofs were re-shaped by another titanic event, the eruption of the Pilanesberg volcano about 70km to the north-west.

The Pilanesberg may once have resembled the more typical cone-shaped volcanoes, such as Kilimanjaro, but the volcanic cone has now been eroded away and only the outer ring of its base remains. Its eruption was obstructed by a surface layer of brittle rock that had been laid down at the time of the Bushveld Complex. Geologist Terence McCarthy likens its formation to a stone hitting a motor-car windscreen: the force of the

erupting lava cracked the surface rock in a series of concentric rings at the point of impact. The lava was carried along a series of parallel channels, called dykes, running approximately from north-west to south-east. The rings of volcanic ridges gave the Pilanesberg National Park its distinctive circular shape, while molten lava consisting mainly of alkaline syenite flowed through the dykes and created rivers of lava that radiated away from the volcano for more than 100km.

Several of the lava dykes intruded into the Magaliesberg, and in one or two places they sliced right through fault lines and continued to flow south into the Cradle area and beyond. The igneous rocks were more subject to weathering than the hard Magaliesberg quartzite and they

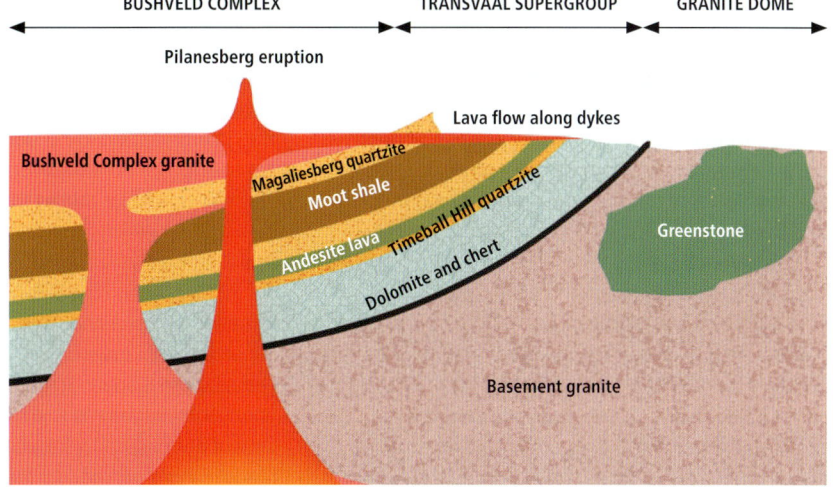

Between 1,400 and 1,200 million years ago the Pilanesberg volcano erupted on the edge of the Bushveld Complex. Lava flowed into the Magaliesberg, occasionally flowing directly through the range and beyond.

At the village of Maanhaarrand a syenite dyke from the Pilanesberg volcano forms an elevated cliff across the valley.

gradually eroded out of the kloofs, leaving them wider and less precipitous than their neighbours. However, where the lava flowed through the softer shales and clay of the valley, it was these intrusive dykes that were more resistant to erosion, and today they remain as elevated ridges. The most obvious instance of this is at Maanhaarrand, where a sheer ridge of Pilanesberg syenite stands up above the valley like a hogsback and gives the village its name.[1] Where the syenite flowed through the quartzite, however, it has weathered away to form the Breedtsnek Pass.

➤ 500 million years ago: The Cradle-Magaliesberg at the South Pole

The Cradle-Magaliesberg region lay under the South Pole 500 million years ago. While the landscape was being shaped by seismic upheavals, plate tectonics were shifting the Kaapvaal Craton up against other newer cratons and fusing them into large continents. Using extensive geological databases and computer modelling techniques, geologists have reconstructed the possible shapes and positions of several supercontinents that have formed and disintegrated over long periods of time.

At about the time of the Vredefort Dome meteor strike 2,000 million years ago, four cratons – the Kaapvaal, Zimbabwe, Congo and Pilbara (now part of Australia) – began to fuse into a single large continent called Ur. The Kaapvaal Craton, which included the elevated Magaliesberg mountain range, was positioned on the outer edge of this greater continent. The consolidation was complete 400,000 years later, and Ur drifted towards two other huge landmasses which have been named Nena and Atlantica that were forming elsewhere on the planet.

At some time after the eruption of the Pilanesberg volcano, Ur, Nena and Atlantica combined into a supercontinent called Rodinia. Rodinia lasted 400,000 years before it began to break up into separate continental fragments that rotated gradually over the face of the Earth. The fragment containing the Cradle-Magaliesberg moved into the southern hemisphere.

1 *Maanhaar* = the Afrikaans word for a mane of horse's hair or a hogsback; *rand* = ridge

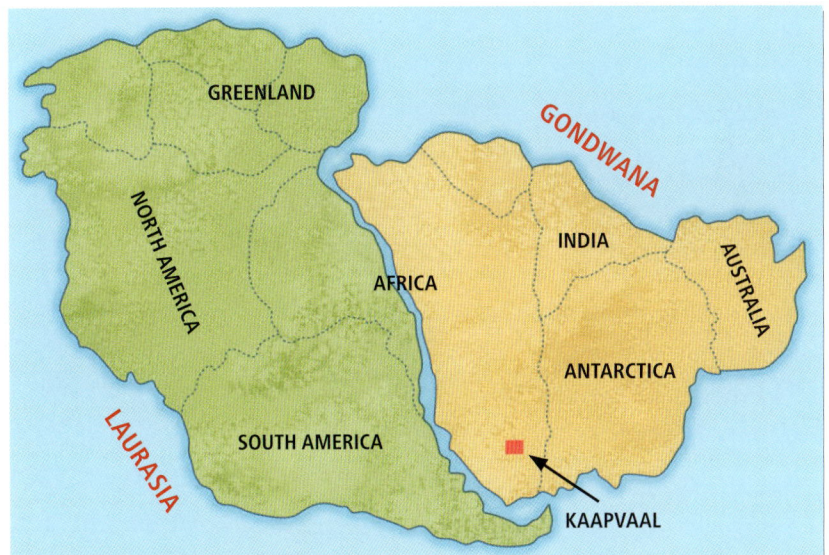

The supercontinent of Pangaea separated into Laurasia and Gondwana.

Between 700 and 500 million years ago the continental fragments reassembled into the supercontinent that Alfred Wegener named Pangaea in his theory of continental drift. Pangaea combined almost all of the continental landmass on Earth in two massive sections, Laurasia in the north and Gondwana in the south.

The Cradle-Magaliesberg region lay in the southern quarter of Gondwana, buried under polar ice several kilometres thick. As tectonic movement shifted the massive continent, the high ground scraped under the polar ice and the peaks of the Magaliesberg were scoured away. Debris from the scraping became frozen into the ice cap, where it remained for millions of years. As the continent later inched gradually northwards into warmer latitudes, these suspended rocks were dumped from the melting ice and consolidated into a conglomerate called tillite which was distributed across southern Africa from the Magaliesberg to the Cape.

As Gondwana drifted under the South Pole, the summit of the Magaliesberg was shaved by the polar ice cap to a constant altitude along its entire length.

Abrasion from the rough till in the ice cap bevelled the edges of the Magaliesberg into rounded slopes.

The effect of the polar crossing left the Magaliesberg landscape a scarred remnant of its former self. The high quartzite crests had been greatly reduced and planed off to a constant altitude along the entire length of the range. The sharp lip of the truncated crest had been smoothed to a rounded curve, and where geological faults and lava flows had cut through the mountains, the abrasive till-laden ice had scoured wide channels and bevelled the edges into sloping shoulders that later inhabitants were to name 'neks' or passes: the topography of the area had begun to take on the appearance it has today.

➤ 280–180 million years ago: The Cradle-Magaliesberg in Gondwana

As Gondwana began to emerge from under the ice about 280 million years ago, the climate became warmer, and terrestrial plants and animals began to develop and spread. However, on the Cargonian Highlands, the elevated land in southern Gondwana, ice remained, at least seasonally. Glaciers and rivers of melt water drained southwards from the Highlands across the Cradle-Magaliesberg area into what was then the Karoo Sea. Shallow deltas fanned out at the river mouths and provided ideal conditions for fossilisation to occur. Over the next 100 million years, the Karoo Sea gradually filled with sediments in a succession of deposits known as the Karoo Supergroup, and the sedimentary layers eventually covered the Cradle-Magaliesberg. These layers have subsequently been stripped away from the higher ground, leaving no trace of life in this region, but they still cover much of Free State Province and the Karoo, where fossils in the sediments offer us some insight into the biodiversity that might have inhabited the Cradle-Magaliesberg region during Gondwanan times.

Grasses and other flowering plants had not evolved at this time, and the floral landscape would have appeared very alien to modern eyes. Clubmosses and ferns were abundant, and *Glossopteris* was a particularly successful genus of seed fern, or Pteridosperm, throughout Gondwana. The dense forests of *Glossopteris* that flourished along the shores of the Karoo Sea were destined to become the coalfields of present-day Mpumalanga.

About 280 million years ago primitive reptiles were prolific in this region. Later, the therapsids (mammal-like reptiles) dominated the megafauna in southern Africa until about 251 million years ago, when they and almost all other species were eliminated in a mass extinction. The cause of that mass extinction is unknown, but it may have been the result of an event similar to the Vredefort Dome meteor impact.

The ecological niches that had been vacated by the therapsids were eventually filled by the dinosaurs about 210 million years ago. There were various species of dinosaur that dominated the landscape and roamed the hills of the Cradle-Magaliesberg region. The plant kingdom was also radically affected by the mass extinction. *Glossopteris* disappeared across all of Gondwana, to be replaced by newly evolved cycads and conifers.

By about 190 million years ago Gondwana had become more arid as it drifted further northwards, and desert sand dunes swept over the landscape. The desert phase of the history of Gondwana ended abruptly 10 million years later when the Earth's crust ruptured and sheets of lava flooded across most of what is now South Africa. Gondwana had begun the long process of fragmentation into the continents with which we are familiar today.

Marina Elliott

Glossopteris trees dominated the Gondwana landscape. They had tongue-shaped leaves to which seed pods were attached.

Marina Elliott

Species of mammal-like reptiles similar to *Diictodon*, a fossil found in Karoo sediments, may once have inhabited the Cradle-Magaliesberg area.

Interlude 3 Vegetation and habitats

N
Brits
Rustenburg
Tshwane/
Pretoria
Magaliesburg
Mogale City/
Krugersdorp
Johannesburg
0 5 10 20km

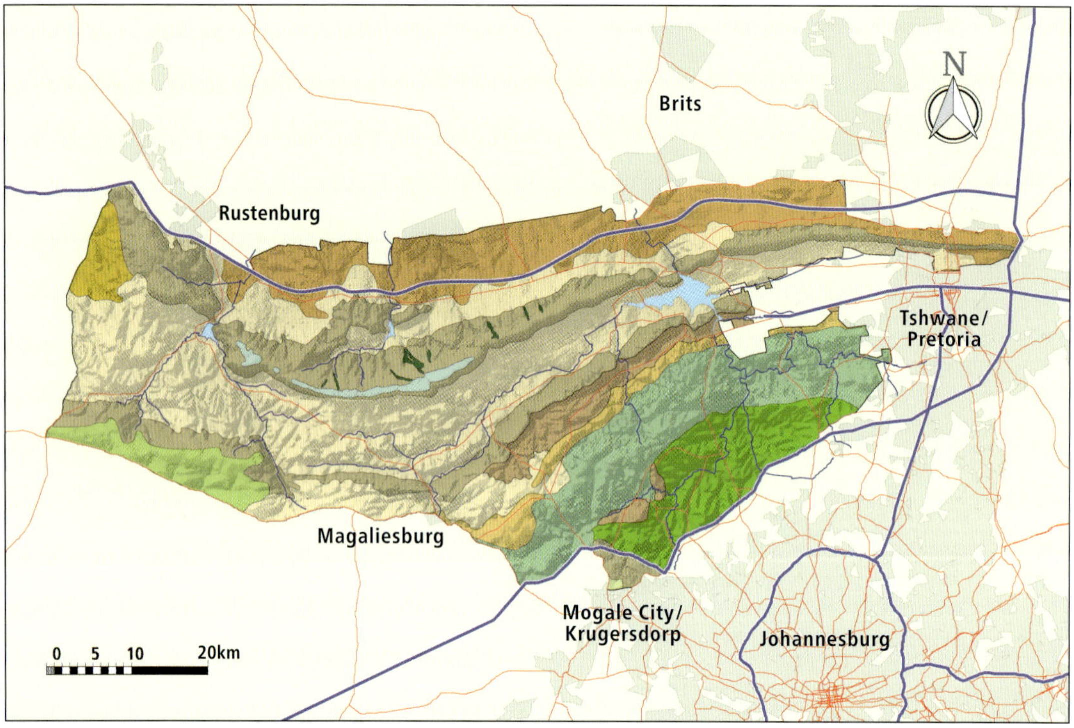

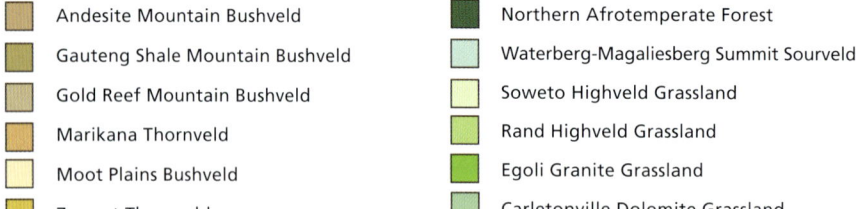

Gerry Comninos & Vincent Carruthers

VEGETATION TYPES

- Andesite Mountain Bushveld
- Gauteng Shale Mountain Bushveld
- Gold Reef Mountain Bushveld
- Marikana Thornveld
- Moot Plains Bushveld
- Zeerust Thornveld
- Northern Afrotemperate Forest
- Waterberg-Magaliesberg Summit Sourveld
- Soweto Highveld Grassland
- Rand Highveld Grassland
- Egoli Granite Grassland
- Carletonville Dolomite Grassland

The Cradle-Magaliesberg lies at the interface between two great biomes: the grassland of the central Highveld plateau, shown in shades of green on the map, and the African savannah, shown in browns and grey. Each biome has its particular plant, animal and climatic associations, but the boundaries are not precise and the vegetation in the Cradle-Magaliesberg is enriched by species drawn from both biomes. In the south, the dolomitic hills in the Cradle of Humankind provide examples of four types of grassland. A fifth grassland type, Waterberg-Magaliesberg Summit Sourveld, occurs on the windswept crest of the Magaliesberg.

Urbanisation and agriculture have transformed 60 per cent of the grassland biome in South Africa, making it one of the most threatened vegetation types in the country. Conservation legislation relating to the Cradle World Heritage Site and the Magaliesberg Protected Environment provides a valuable safeguard for this vulnerable biome.

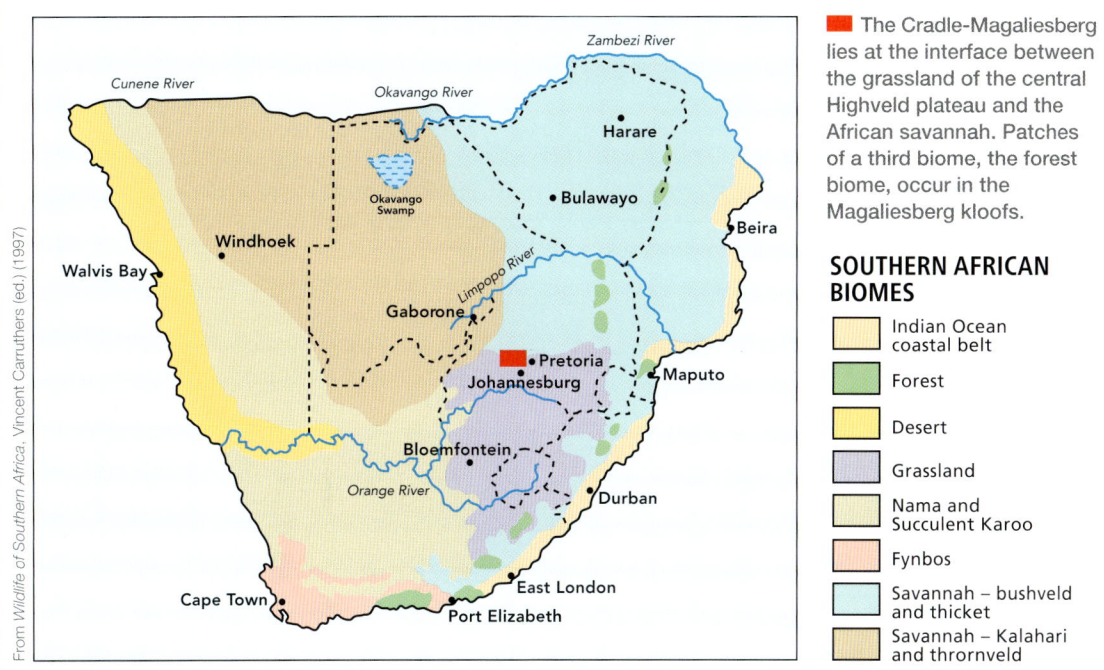

From *Wildlife of Southern Africa*, Vincent Carruthers (ed.) (1997)

■ The Cradle-Magaliesberg lies at the interface between the grassland of the central Highveld plateau and the African savannah. Patches of a third biome, the forest biome, occur in the Magaliesberg kloofs.

SOUTHERN AFRICAN BIOMES

- Indian Ocean coastal belt
- Forest
- Desert
- Grassland
- Nama and Succulent Karoo
- Fynbos
- Savannah – bushveld and thicket
- Savannah – Kalahari and thrornveld

GRASSLAND

Because many grass species thrive in areas prone to fire and frost, grassland offers a protective habitat for herbaceous plants so that, although grasses are visually the most noticeable type of vegetation, herbs account for more than half the species diversity in the grassland in the Cradle.

Grassland covers much of the Cradle of Humankind, where it is protected from the destruction that has so reduced it in other parts of southern Africa.

Trees are rare in grassland but some species do occur. The cabbage tree *Cussonia paniculata* has a thick, corky bark that insulates and protects its sensitive vascular system from being burnt in veld fires. Sinkholes are common in the karst topography of the Cradle and they offer a protective and moist microclimate in which a number of tree species are able to survive.

In the Skurweberg, grassland begins to give way to more woody plants, and the area is particularly conducive to the growth of the giant mountain aloe *Aloe marlothii*, which can be seen in profusion on many of the slopes.

SAVANNAH

The vegetation changes noticeably as you approach the Witwatersberg, the fourth of the Cradle-Magaliesberg ridges, and the most southerly area in the Cradle-Magaliesberg region to be formally classified as savannah. Savannah is a complex biome with patches of different types of open woodland. It has a great variety of tree species, and birdlife is abundant.

Between the Witwatersberg and the Magaliesberg lies the wide valley of the Moot. Here the deep alluvial soils are heavily cultivated and have supported agricultural communities for thousands of years. The

Forests of giant mountain aloes reaching up to 4m grow on the slopes of the Skurweberg.

most noticeable feature of the modern landscape, however, is the lake of Hartbeespoort Dam that floods the entire width of the valley.

The southern approach to the cliffs of the Magaliesberg is a mosaic of woodland and open areas. On the slopes below the cliffs, the south-facing aspect faces away from the Sun and the shade restricts the rate of evaporation. Moisture is retained in the soil and sustains extensive patches of woodland. Leopards and brown hyenas still hunt in this area and antelope, baboons and monkeys abound.

FORESTED KLOOFS

In sharp contrast, the barren summit of the Magaliesberg is windswept and exposed. Shallow soils and grassland are once again prevalent. However, an extremely benign climate prevails in the deep, well-watered and sheltered kloofs that were incised into the northern slopes by lava flows. Remnants of the Afrotemperate forests that once dominated the region can still be found in these secluded places and it constitutes the third important biome in the area.

The cabbage tree *Cussonia paniculata* is one of the few trees that survive in grassland because their corky bark insulates them from fire.

Isolated clusters of trees on the Cradle landscape invariably indicate the existence of a sinkhole or aven.

Grassland flowers	Savannah flowers	Woodland flowers
Cat's whiskers *Becium obovatum*	Crossberry *Grewia occidentalis*	Royal paintbrush *Scadoxus puniceus*
Veld violet *Ruellia cordata*	Canary nettle *Sphedamnocarpus pruriens*	Crimson flag *Hesperantha coccinea*
Gladiolus *Gladiolus elliottii*	Wild pear *Dombeya rotundifolia*	Wild gardenia *Rothmannia capensis*

A selection of the many wild flowers growing in the transition from grassland to woodland in the Cradle-Magaliesberg region.

Woodland covers parts of the southern slopes of the Magaliesberg and offers solitude and cover to many species of wildlife, including leopards.

High-canopy Afrotemperate forest still occurs in the protected kloofs of the Magaliesberg, a relict of the forest biome that once dominated the region.

Peter Delmar

4 | AFRICA

As the supercontinental complex of Pangaea drifted northwards, the southern part, Gondwana, split from Laurasia and began to subdivide into the continents we are familiar with today. This chapter describes the changes in the Cradle-Magaliesberg landscape as the continent of Africa emerged, and as the sedimentary layers that had been deposited in Gondwanan times were gradually stripped away to reveal the ancient topography that had formed some 2,000 million years earlier.

The process took place over a period of almost 200 million years during which a chain of events set the stage for new directions in evolution. The southern subcontinent lifted and this initiated changes in climate. Grassland spread, creating new habitats that affected the distribution and evolution of animal species, favouring adaptations to open countryside. At the same time, the old dolomitic substrate was eroded away to expose the caves in the karst landscape, and the process of fossilisation began.

Pixabay.com

The birth of Africa began 180 million years ago when subterranean pressure violently ruptured the Gondwana supercontinent and buried the Cradle-Magaliesberg under volcanic lava.

➤ 180 million years ago: The break-up of Gondwana

The separation of the African continent from Gondwana began about 180 million years ago with the rise of a mantle plume deep below the southern part of Gondwana, where the Cradle-Magaliesberg was located in a landscape built up on successive layers of sediments. The subterranean pressure lifted the entire subcontinent and magma erupted from rifts in the Earth's crust, spreading sheets of basalt lava over the Karoo sediments.

A rift in the crust 500km east of the Cradle broadened into a deep valley similar to the present-day Great Rift Valley of East Africa. By about 140 million years ago, this valley had become a widening Indian Ocean and the supercontinent had been torn into two halves. The eastern half was made up of what would

The split of Gondwana into its component continents over the past 140 million years.

The Cradle-Magaliesberg landscape of today was preceded by a series of continental and climatic changes that followed the break-up of Gondwana.

Sandstone cliffs at Golden Gate Highlands National Park are remnants of the sand dunes that covered Gondwana and the Cradle-Magaliesberg 190 million years ago, and the lava eruptions that ripped the supercontinent apart now form the basalt summit of the Drakensberg.

eventually become Australia, India and Antarctica, while the western half comprised the future Africa and South America.

The centre of what was to become southern Africa lifted again about 20 million years later. Another rift opened up 1,200km west of the Cradle-Magaliesberg. The continent of South America began to drift away, opening the Atlantic Ocean and leaving Africa, the central core of Gondwana, with the Cradle-Magaliesberg situated near its southern end.

As the continents separated, the elevated interior of Africa began to erode. The recently laid sheet of basalt lava was the first to disappear,

and today remnants of it form the summit of the Drakensberg; no evidence of it remains in the Cradle-Magaliesberg region. Next to erode were the layers of sandstone that had been deposited when the Cradle-Magaliesberg had been covered by desert dunes. The sandstone cliffs that characterise the eastern Free State are relicts of those dunes. As each successive layer of Karoo sediments was stripped away, more of the 2,000 million-year-old Magaliesberg landscape became visible. Gradually, the montane topography of the deep past began to re-emerge after millions of years of being buried.

120 million years ago

60 million years ago

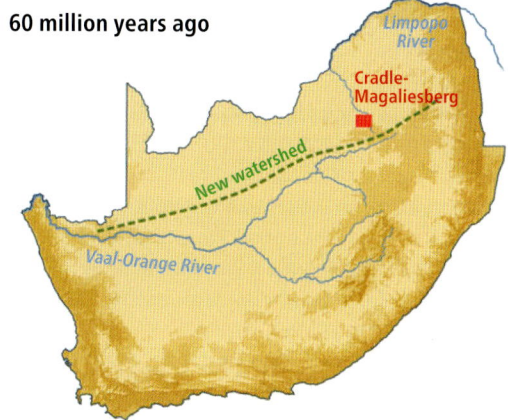

Rivers draining the Cradle-Magaliesberg 120 million years ago flowed south-west from the remnants of the Cargonian Highlands into the ancient Karoo river system.

About 60 million years ago the Transvaal-Griqualand Axis lifted and created a new watershed that deflected the Cradle-Magaliesberg rivers northwards into the Limpopo basin.

The Cradle-Magaliesberg region is an important freshwater catchment and much of its scenic charm comes from the network of streams and waterfalls that tumble down the valleys and gorges, draining northwards through the rocky landscape. But this has not always been the case. Before the break-up of Gondwana, the rivers in the Cradle-Magaliesberg area flowed south.

As Africa began to separate from the other continental segments of Gondwana, the hinterland of southern Africa lifted, and an extensive central tableland formed, sloping slightly westwards. Waters from this inland plateau, including the Cradle-Magaliesberg, flowed to the Atlantic via two great rivers, the Karoo and the Kalahari, and

RIVER PASSAGE

60 MILLION YEARS AGO: The Transvaal-Griqualand Axis lifted and created a watershed along the Witwatersrand. Rivers that had previously flowed south-west to the Atlantic Ocean were deflected northwards over the Karoo sediments covering the Cradle-Magaliesberg landscape.

40 MILLION YEARS AGO: The Karoo sediments had eroded away to reveal the upper surfaces of the Magaliesberg. Rivers flowed across the Cradle and found passages through fault lines in the emerging mountains to continue their northward flow to the Limpopo basin.

10 MILLION YEARS AGO: From about 10 million years ago to the present, the Karoo sediments have been stripped away. Most passages through the Magaliesberg became impassable. Rivers such as the Jukskei, Hennops, Magalies and Crocodile had to flow laterally along the face of the mountains until they could converge and penetrate the barrier through one of the few remaining passages such as Hartbeespoort.

the Cradle-Magaliesberg was part of the Karoo River catchment. A third large river system, the Limpopo, looped around the north of the plateau and drained from what is now Botswana and Angola into the Indian Ocean on the east.

This pattern was disrupted 60 million years ago by further partial uplift. An elevated axis called the Transvaal-Griqualand Axis rose diagonally across the subcontinent, creating a watershed, part of which was the Witwatersrand ridge on the southern edge of the Cradle. The Karoo and Kalahari rivers joined to become the modern Vaal-Orange river system, and runoff from south of the Witwatersrand continued to flow towards the Vaal River and thence into the Atlantic. Water rising on the northern side of the ridge, however, was deflected northwards and flowed through the Cradle-Magaliesberg towards the Limpopo River and the Indian Ocean, as it still does today.

At the same time, another elevation cut the Limpopo off from its central African headwaters and left it more dependent on its Cradle-Magaliesberg source.

The north-flowing rivers were hampered by the ancient ridges of the Magaliesberg, as the underlying topography was gradually re-exposed and became more prominent above the eroding sedimentary Karoo landscape. Initially, the streams found gaps in the emerging ridges, but as the landscape eroded further, the exposed height of the cliffs increased and the gaps became inaccessible. Streams were forced to meander along the southern face of the cliffs, converging into fewer, more powerful watercourses that cut gorges through fault lines in the mountains. Only five rivers in the Magaliesberg Biosphere Reserve breach the range today. The Crocodile River is the largest of these, and the gorge it created is now impounded by the Hartbeespoort Dam. The others are the Pienaars River, the Moreleta and the Apies, both in Pretoria, and the Hex River which is dammed at Olifantsnek.

A bend in the Crocodile River shows how it was deflected through the mountain ridges.

Thickly vegetated sponges on the summit of the Magaliesberg collect precipitation and deliver a constant supply of clear water.

The Crocodile River rises above the Walter Sisulu National Botanical Garden and becomes the main watercourse through the Cradle-Magaliesberg region.

The current river system

The Cradle-Magaliesberg is an important catchment area, drawing its water from three distinctly different sources.

The larger rivers, such as the Crocodile and Jukskei, rise in a network of tributary streams flowing northwards from the Witwatersrand watershed. The source of the Crocodile River plunges spectacularly over the waterfall in the Water Sisulu National Botanical Garden a few kilometres south of the Cradle, and is soon joined by other streams from the Witwatersrand. Many stretches of these rivers are very beautiful, and are rich in birdlife and riverine woodland. However, they are also contaminated by runoff from urban areas and effluent from numerous waste-water works.

The second significant water source is the clear alkaline water that bubbles up from the dolomitic caves of the Cradle. Its importance and consistent abundance in all seasons was known to hunter-gatherer communities and cattle herders for thousands of years.

The third water source lies high in the Magaliesberg. Precipitation from summer thunderstorms collects in thickly vegetated sponges near the summit of the mountain. From there, it gradually percolates over waterfalls and into the kloofs, and ranks as some of the purest water to be found in South Africa's natural systems.

➤ 65 million years ago: Mammal and primate evolution

While the topography and climate of Africa were undergoing post-Gondwana changes, other developments were occurring in the evolution of life. During the fragmentation of Gondwana dinosaurs dominated the megafauna of the planet, but about 65 million years ago they, and many other forms of life, suddenly became extinct. The cause of this was probably a massive meteor strike in the Yucatan Peninsula in Mexico, which ejected dust into the atmosphere that obscured the Sun and disrupted global ecosystems for a long period of time.

The mass extinction of dinosaurs allowed smaller surviving animals to gain access to ecological resources previously dominated by other megafauna.

Mammals, which had until then been limited to insignificant shrew-like species, were foremost in taking advantage of the new lack of competition. Within 10 million years of the extinction of the dinosaurs, mammals had diversified into the 19 orders we know today, 12 of which exist (or representative species have existed) in the Cradle-Magaliesberg.

One of these orders is the primates, to which humans belong. They share a collection of traits including a relatively large brain, binocular vision, reliance on sight more than smell, nails rather than claws, single offspring or occasionally twins, slower rates of maturation, and a highly developed social organisation.

Primate evolution over the past 55 million years.

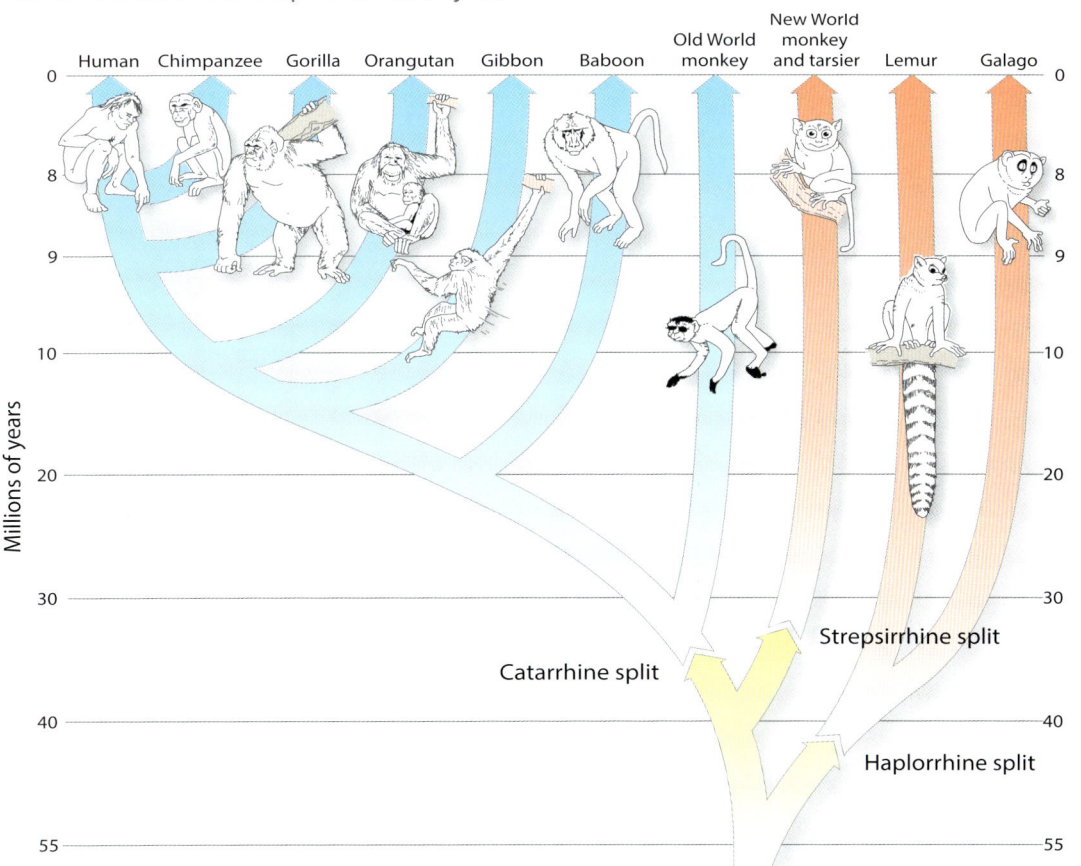

Modified from diagram by Adrienne Zihman from *The Story of Earth & Life*, McCarthy & Rubidge (2005)

Mammal orders in the Cradle-Magaliesberg

Mammal orders	Natural representatives in the Cradle-Magaliesberg
Aardvarks	Aardvarks
Artiodactyls (Even-toed ungulates)	Antelope, hippo, buffalo
Carnivores	Jackal, hyena, leopard, caracal, etc.
Chiroptera	Bats
Hyraxes	Dassies
Insectivores	Hedgehogs, shrews and moles
Lagomorphs	Rabbits and hares
Perissodactyls (Odd-toed ungulates)	Rhinoceros, zebra
Pholidots	Pangolins
Primates	Humans, monkeys, baboons, galagos
Proboscids (Elephants)	Elephants
Rodents	Rats, mice, porcupines

Of the 19 orders of mammal, 12 occur, or have occurred, in the Cradle-Magaliesberg region.

These characteristics began to emerge about 55 million years ago, and early in their evolution the primates divided into two sub-orders: the 'wet-nosed' Strepsirrhines (including the lemurs and galagos of Africa and Madagascar), and the 'dry-nosed' Haplorrhines (the tarsiers, monkeys and apes). Tarsiers and South American monkeys followed their own line of evolution on other continents 40 million years ago, leaving the subgroup Catarrhines, which includes the old-world monkeys, apes and humans that occurred in Africa, and specifically in the Cradle-Magaliesberg region. The Catarrhines developed diurnal habits, their diet became more omnivorous, and they showed more pronounced sexual dimorphism (males being larger than females), indicating possible social structures and courtship.

Apes (Hominoidea) are native to Africa and Southeast Asia, and the first ape-like primates appeared around 25 to 20 million years ago. One of the earliest was an East African species of the genus *Proconsul*, which retained many monkey-like features but also had some traits that placed it close to apes. Apes are distinguished from other primates by having no tail, and exhibiting some freedom of motion at the shoulder which allows them to swing through trees using only their arms. The widespread woodland environment of 20 million years ago favoured their emergence, and forests remain the preferred habitat for most modern species of ape.

The mandible of an extinct species of the baboon-like *Parapapio* from the Cradle.

Marina Elliott

About 18 million years ago, gibbons seem to have diverged from the great ape lineage, while orangutans probably split from African apes around 14 million years ago. The gorilla line separated next, around eight million years ago, with the chimpanzee lineage separating from hominins about seven million years ago. The bipedal hominin line (i.e. those walking naturally on two legs rather than four) is the one from which humans are descended. Natural selection probably favoured bipedalism in the open woodland savannah that was developing in parts of Africa at the time, while the chimpanzee lineage remained in the evergreen forests.

Several extinct primate fossils have been recovered from sites in the Cradle. These include baboon-like primates such as *Parapapio, Dinopithecus* and *Theropithecus,* as well as a species of colobine monkey, but none of the ape species besides hominins have been found.

➤ 50–20 million years ago: Climate change and the spread of grassland

After Gondwana had split and Africa had become a continent on its own, conditions in the Cradle-Magaliesberg were relatively warm and wet. The expanding oceans surrounding the southern part of Africa were warm, and inflows of humid air brought high rainfall that replaced the arid conditions that had typified central Gondwana previously. Dense evergreen forests spread across the region.

From about 50 million years ago temperatures began to fall from their high levels. At the same time pressure from subterranean mantle plumes lifted the centre of southern Africa, including the Cradle-Magaliesberg, so that it became the high, inland plateau we now call the Highveld.

Cold winter air carried less moisture to the high lands and seasonal weather patterns began to change from winter to summer rainfall. Further lifting of the plateau about 20 million years ago tilted the subcontinent to the west with a high escarpment, the Drakensberg, on the east. Sea breezes precipitated moisture on the escarpment, casting the central plateau in a partial rain shadow.

The climate was affected again about 14 million years ago when cold Antarctic waters flowed into the Atlantic and up the west coast of southern Africa, cooling and drying the atmosphere over the hinterland. A marked climatic gradient developed between the warm, rain-filled air from the east coast and the arid desert in the west. As these conditions developed, they favoured a vast and significant shift in vegetation across the continent and the spread of grassland.

Grass species had evolved before the fragmentation of Gondwana, but they remained

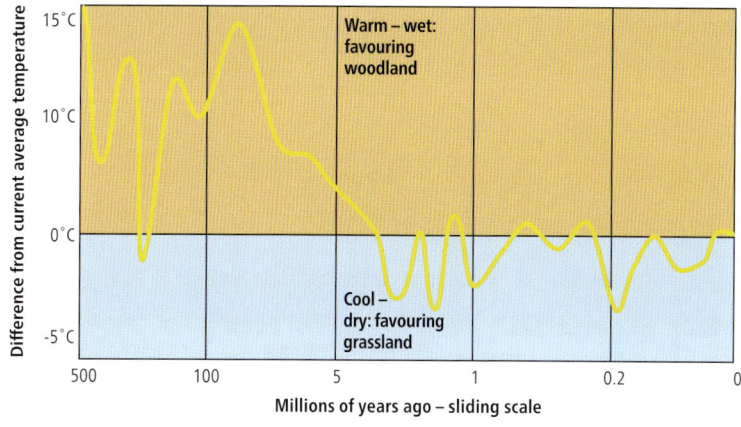

Temperatures rose substantially after the break-up of Gondwana, bringing warmer and more humid conditions, and from 50 million years ago they began cooling to their present levels.

Marina Elliott

The summer-rainfall pattern benefitted the spread of grass at the expense of forest, and created a mosaic of grassland, savannah and woodland habitats in the Cradle-Magaliesberg.

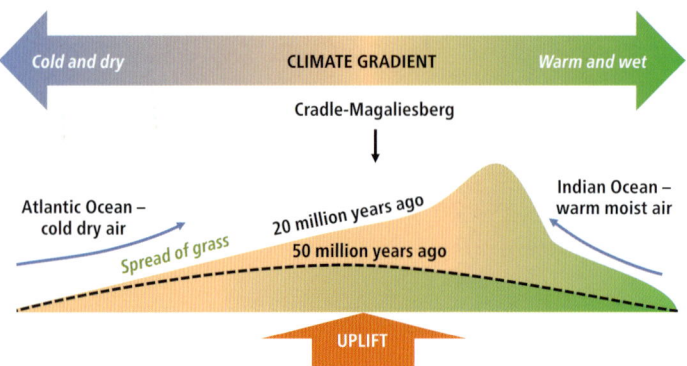

Southern Africa lifted about 50 million years ago. Temperatures fell and seasonal weather changed from winter to summer rainfall. Further lifting occurred 20 million years ago and created a westward slope with declining rainfall from east to west. Cold air from the Atlantic intensified the climate gradient 14 million years ago and favoured the spread of grassland.

an insignificant component of African flora until about 30 million years ago. The main growth points in grass are the stolons or rhizomes that are found at or below ground level. This gives grass great resilience against fire, frost and drought, from which it quickly recovers with regrowth from an unharmed base. These characteristics made it particularly well adapted for the increasingly harsh conditions on the central plateau. Grass spread widely at the expense of trees and shrubs

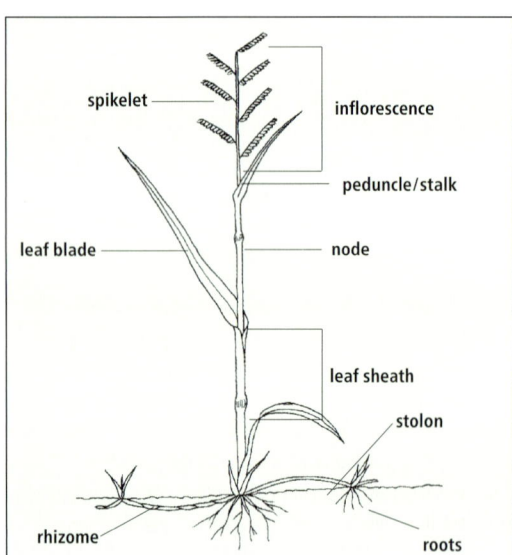

spikelet

inflorescence

peduncle/stalk

leaf blade

node

leaf sheath

stolon

rhizome

roots

The growth points in grass (rhizomes, roots and stolons) are at or below ground level, where they survive fire and frost better than those of most other plant types.

which, with their elevated branches and leafy growth, were vulnerable to dry frosty winters and spontaneous wildfires ignited by lightning.

At first, tough, semi-desert grasses developed in the west, but as they spread eastwards, taller, more luxuriant species evolved, benefitting from the moisture they received as they crossed the rainfall gradient while surviving winter frosts and drought.

Grassland did not advance across southern Africa in a simple progression. As forest areas shrank in cooler, drier climates, a grassy understorey encroached into clearings. When climatic cycles brought warmer, wetter conditions, the forests temporarily revived. The result was a constantly changing mosaic of sparsely wooded savannah, open plains and remnants of gallery forest along streambeds and in protected kloofs. Elisabeth Vrba, a leading evolutionary scientist who worked for many years in the Cradle, developed a theory known as the 'turnover pulse hypothesis', which states that these erratic ecological changes stimulated speciation and extinction, as natural selection favoured adaptations suited to the changing conditions. At the same time, open-habitat grazing species and large predators began to migrate onto the fluctuating landscape, putting competitive pressure on local species and accelerating evolutionary processes.

Where winter Highveld conditions were most extreme, the grassland became a treeless biome – an ecological region where grass and fire-resistant forbs (herbaceous flowering plants) dominated the vegetation and created an environment in which different species of grazing animals could prosper

Grassland interfaces with savannah and woodland in the Cradle-Magaliesberg. Natural selection favoured adaptations that suited this mosaic and stimulated the evolution of hominins and other species.

and diversify. Grass is an abundant food resource, but its high cellulose content makes it difficult to digest. Ungulates developed ruminant digestive systems to extract nutrients from the grass: partly digested food is regurgitated from one chamber of the stomach, re-masticated (chewing the cud), and passed to a second chamber for further digestion. Grasslands could thus support greater numbers of animals than woodland, and large herds moved over the plains while carnivores developed hunting and scavenging techniques to exploit the grazing herds.

Five or six million years ago, the spread of the grassland biome reached the Cradle-Magaliesberg.

In all but the most secluded kloofs forest began to be replaced by grassland or patches of savannah. Savannah is an extremely diverse biome both in fauna and flora, but it can generally be described as open woodland with an understorey of grass and sparse shrubs. Today various forms of savannah cover more than half the surface of sub-Saharan Africa, and for the past five million years the frontier between the grassland and savannah biomes has fluctuated back and forth across the Cradle-Magaliesberg region. The interface between them gives the region an unusually rich biodiversity, with species drawn from all three biomes – grassland, savannah and remnant gallery forest in the Magaliesberg kloofs.

The hominin fossils for which the Cradle has become famous occur in such abundance, not because there were more hominins in this locality than elsewhere, but because the unique features of the karst landscape that covers most of the Cradle area made the preservation of fossils more possible here than in other types of landscape. The Cradle's geology is characterised by subterranean caverns and drainage lines created when the semi-soluble bedrock dissolved. The original dolomitic substrate was created more than 2,000 million years ago and remained buried under Karoo sediments. The dissolution process in the Cradle-Magaliesberg probably began only about 20 million years ago, when the erosion of the Karoo sediments was almost complete and the dolomitic substrate, the last of the ancient landforms of the Transvaal Supergroup, was re-exposed. Like the other sedimentary layers in the Supergroup, the dolomitic strata were tilted upwards by the intrusion of the Bushveld Complex

Marina Elliott

Slowly dripping calciferous water evaporates and deposits calcium carbonate. This process formed the karst landscape and cave formations such as flowstone, stalagmites and stalactites.

Clear water from a karst aquifer surges up from a dolomitic spring and is constantly recharged by water levels in the cave systems.

Lee Berger points to a tiny stalactite that has regrown less than a centimetre since miners removed all the multimillion-year-old stalactites and flowstones a century ago.

but, unlike the quartzite ridges of the Magaliesberg and Witwatersberg, the comparatively soft dolomitic rocks were constantly weathered away before they could emerge as elevated ridges.

Dolomite, which is composed mainly of calcium magnesium carbonate $MgCa(CO_3)_2$, is slightly soluble in water. As erosion of the overburden of Karoo sediments brought the dolomitic bedrock closer to the surface, groundwater percolated into fissures in the rock and started to leach out cavities and crevices. Carbon dioxide in the atmosphere formed very dilute carbolic acid, H_2CO_3, in rainwater and this mildly acidic rain accelerated the leaching process.

Initially, the dolomite lay below the water table, and as seepage dissolved cavities in it they remained full of water as they developed. Water intrusions also opened subterranean dykes and fissures and created a network of underwater rivers, known as karst aquifers. Several times during its long geological history, the dolomite was warped and fractured so that the flow of underground water in the Cradle became complex and fragmented. The water-filled caves were compartmentalised into partially isolated subterranean networks that varied from a few hectares in size to several square kilometres. Today, the water table in the separate compartments stands in subterranean lakes at

different levels in different caves. It is gradually recharged by infiltrating rainwater, and the water level is controlled by springs at low points in the dip slope of the dolomitic strata. Some of the water that enters the system takes years to re-emerge as springs or seepage.

The formation of the cave system in the Cradle took place over hundreds of thousands of years. The process was caused by a unique series of circumstances described in the diagram on pages 86–87.

The development of the dolomitic karst landscape and the exposure of the caves to the land surface provided the unique conditions necessary for fossilisation, and thus for the preservation of evidence of a significant period in human evolution. It is a remarkable coincidence that these caves were exposed to the surface at exactly the same time as hominins were evolving critically important adaptations, such as bipedalism and growth in brain size, that eventually led to the development of human anatomy.

The cave systems lie at varying depths and have different points of access. Some may still be sealed below ground level, awaiting discovery. If so, we must hope that their irreplaceable splendour will be preserved.

CAVE FORMATION

Stage 1

Mildly acidic rainwater percolated into fissures along the dip slope of the dolomite and leached out water-filled chambers in the phreatic zone – the subterranean region below the water table. Chert, which is less soluble, accumulated at the bottom of the chambers.

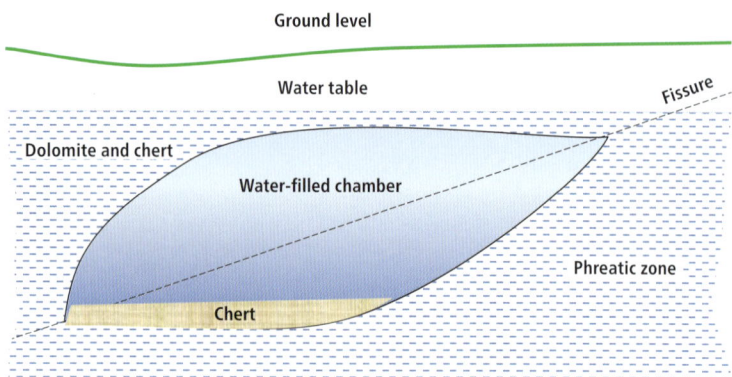

Ground level

Water table

Fissure

Dolomite and chert

Water-filled chamber

Phreatic zone

Chert

Stage 2

As the water table dropped, the chambers became situated in the vadose zone – the subterranean region above the water table – where they drained and became aerated caverns. Water, enriched with lime from the dolomite substrate, dripped into the caverns and created stalactites, stalagmites and flowstones from the lime as the water evaporated.

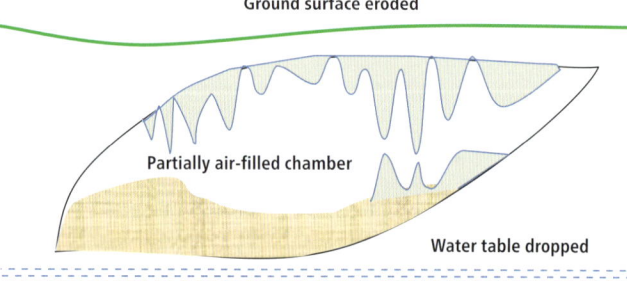

Ground surface eroded

Partially air-filled chamber

Water table dropped

Actively growing stalactites and stalagmites from dripping calciferous water on a breccia floor in Wonder Cave in the Cradle.

Stage 3

Ground levels were eroded, and the caverns were exposed to the surface. Debris, including hominins and other animals, fell through openings in the cave roof and accumulated on the floor. More organic debris may have been added from discarded predator meals and other sources. Calciferous water cemented the piles of debris into a concrete-like matrix known as breccia.

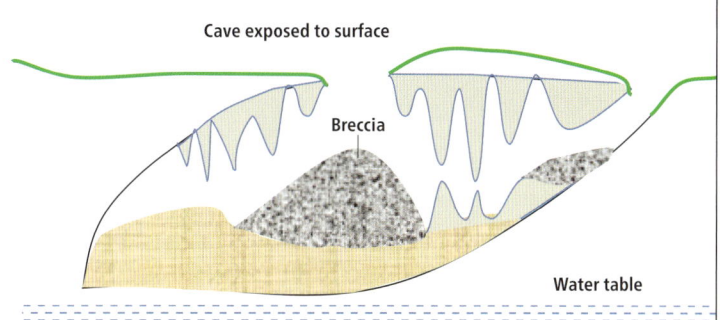

Cave exposed to surface

Breccia

Water table

Stage 4

The roof of the cave collapsed into a sinkhole and the breccia was exposed to the surface, where it began to decalcify. Limestone stalactites, stalagmites and flowstones were mined and removed.

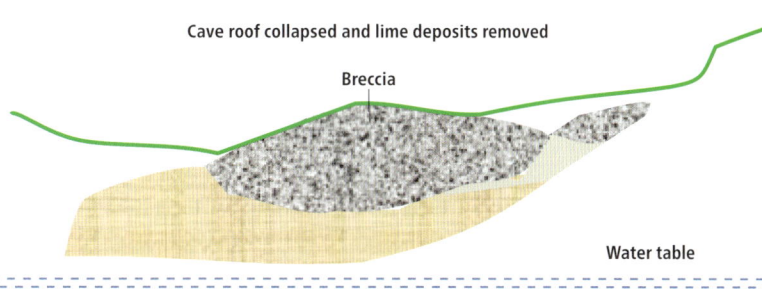

Cave roof collapsed and lime deposits removed

Breccia

Water table

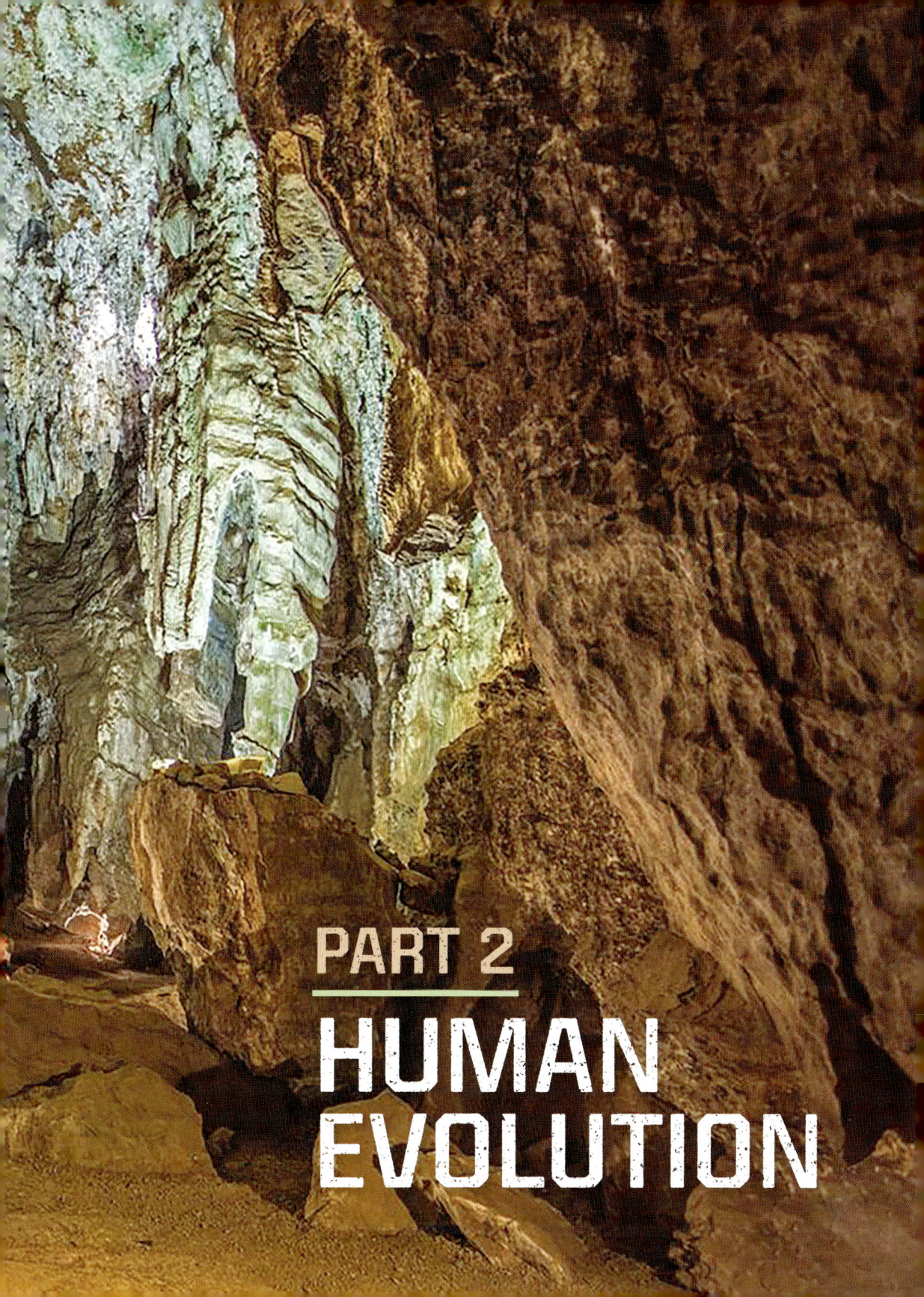

PART 2
HUMAN EVOLUTION

Climatic and ecological conditions	Hominin species	Million years ago	Evolutionary features
Warm, moist climate. Dense forest with open clearings.	*Sahelanthropus tchadensis*	7	Small brain. Heavy brow ridge. Prominent canines. Head on semi-vertical spinal column.
	Orrorin tugenensis	6	Curved fingers for arboreal climbing. Leg-hip joint indicating partial bipedalism.
Gradual cooling. Limited open savannah woodland replacing some high-canopy forest.	*Ardipithecus* species	5	Brain size of 350cc. Prognathic face – prominent lower face and jaws. Fairly long canine teeth. Long arms – possibly still knuckle-walking. Knees widely separated – unsuitable for walking upright on hind legs. Big toe splayed out from foot for climbing.
	Australopithecus anamensis *Australopithecus afarensis*	4	Palate still narrow – ape-like. Canine teeth reduced but still prominent. Thick dental enamel for diet of coarse material. Valgus knees (slight knock-knees) for habitual bipedal walking.
Cool, dry climate. Grassland and open savannah encroach. Gallery forest and woodland become patchy.	*Australopithecus prometheus*	3	Brain size of 380–450cc. Face still prognathic. Large, thickly enamelled teeth. Canines reduced but still obvious in males. Slightly splayed big toe but cannot grip. Arms longer than legs. Heel suitable for bipedal walking. Palms flat with elongated thumb.
Cold and dry climate. Grassland and open savannah, gallery forest and woodland.	*Australopithecus africanus*	2.8	Brain size of 400–500cc. Small canines. Gracile mandible (slender jawbone) with small teeth. Probably omnivorous with better protein diet.

Climatic and ecological conditions	Hominin species	Million years ago	Evolutionary features
Warmer, wet climate returns. Some recovery of forest.	*Paranthropus robustus*	2	At least three contemporary hominin species. Brain size up to 500cc in some species. Others have smaller brains but may be more cognitively competent. Some species with robust jaws and arboreal features (tree-climbing capability). Others with gracile jaws and smaller teeth. Arched foot, bearing weight on outer edge as in humans.
	Australopithecus sediba	1.8	Brain size of 600–650cc. Hands articulated for tool-making. Early Oldowan tool-making.
Slight cooling. Further encroachment of grassland and savannah.	*Homo habilis* / *Homo ergaster*	1	Brain size of 850cc Sides of head flat or tapering. Flattened face with short lower jaw and chin. Human-like teeth. Arms shorter than legs. No special arboreal features. Acheulean tools. Use of fire.
Temperate climate similar to the present. Grassland–savannah mosaic with gallery forest patches.	*Homo naledi* / *Homo sapiens*	0.5	Brain size of 1,500cc. High-domed cranium. Spatulate (flat, chisel-shaped) incisors and short canines. Thick dental enamel. Parabola-shaped palate.

The caves in the Cradle of Humankind open a window onto human origins that goes back almost four million years. Discoveries in East Africa take the process even further back in time. That complex path of human evolution is the subject of Part 2. Chapters in Part 1 traced the evolution of life and the development of the physical environment in the Cradle-Magaliesberg region to the point where a unique karst landscape had formed in which the fossilisation of early human ancestors could take place. This Interlude explains the historical background to the palaeoanthropology research in the Cradle and describes some of the techniques that scientists have used to study what they have found there.

Reliance on fossils as evidence of the past is hampered by several limitations, one of which is their scarcity. Fossilisation takes place under very specific conditions, and only an infinitesimal percentage of organisms ever becomes fossilised. Of those that do, we can only speculate how few come to the attention of scientists who can identify and interpret them. Even in the well-studied caves of the Cradle, the discovery of fossils with evolutionary significance happens very rarely, and there are enormous gaps in the fossil record. The hypotheses proposed by scientists are therefore constantly subject to controversy, revision and reinterpretation, as new discoveries are made and gaps are gradually filled or clarified.

A fossil is a record of one moment in time in a constantly changing process of evolution, and the ancestors or descendants of a fossil specimen can seldom be identified with absolute certainty. Many palaeoanthropologists are therefore reluctant to draw conclusions about the hereditary links between fossil specimens, or to compile family trees or genealogies.

STERKFONTEIN AND KROMDRAAI

Sterkfontein Cave is the best-known fossil site in the Cradle of Humankind. In 1895 David Draper, the Secretary of the Geological Society of South Africa, visited the Sterkfontein area and noticed fossil fragments embedded in the rocks at the surface. They were studied at subsequent meetings of the Geological Society and he and other members speculated about their origins.

A monument in the Buxton Limeworks commemorates the finding of the Taung Child skull in 1924. The discovery brought the science of palaeoanthropology to South Africa.

Stalagmites and stalactites as they might have appeared in Sterkfontein when it was first discovered.

Later that year, Guglielmo Martinaglia, a lime prospector, blasted through the wall of an old lime quarry in the area, and revealed a cavern of remarkable beauty. Shimmering stalactites and stalagmites encrusted with translucent crystals reflected the light of the quarrymen's lamps. News of the natural wonder of the caves spread rapidly and souvenir hunters soon began to strip the caves of their magnificent formations. In his history of Sterkfontein, Phillip Tobias relates that Gustav Molengraaff, the newly appointed Government Geologist of the Zuid-Afrikaansche Republiek and director of the Geological Survey, attempted to protect them from damage but in 1897 he wrote that 'the numerous visitors who arrived from Johannesburg destroyed this marvel in a few weeks and as the grotto is on private property the government unfortunately could not interfere.'[2]

The mining of lime from the caves, however, had a far more destructive impact than the visitors from Johannesburg. In the decades that followed, all the speleothems were blasted out of Sterkfontein and every other accessible cave in the Cradle area and burnt in the kilns. In *The Hunters or the Hunted?* Bob Brain tells the disturbing story of how, between 1918 and 1920, Sterkfontein was leased by the landowner, E.P. Binnet, to a lime miner named H.G. Nolan, brother of M.G. Nolan who owned the Buxton Limeworks quarry at Taung. Apparently, Binnet refused to renew the lease on its expiry, and this so infuriated Nolan that he dynamited everything he could of the remaining formations.

Scientific interest in Sterkfontein revived after the discovery of the first South African hominin fossil, *Australopithecus africanus*,[3] in the Buxton lime quarry at Taung, 500km away. Taung is now a serial site of the World Heritage Site of the Cradle of Humankind.

2 Phillip Tobias, 'The Story of Sterkfontein since 1895', in Bonner, *et al.* (2007: 225)

3 *Austral* = southern; *pithecus* = ape; *africanus* = from Africa

Raymond Dart's discovery of the 'Taung Child' in 1924 is described on pages 130–131. His belief that it was an ancestor of *Homo sapiens* was rejected by the scientific community of the day, partly because the specimen was a juvenile, but mainly because a decade previously a large-brained fossil skull had been 'discovered' in the Piltdown quarry in Sussex, England, by two reputable palaeontologists, Charles Dawson and Sir Arthur Smith Woodward. This 'discovery' was later revealed to be a fraud, but at the time the Piltdown Man presented seemingly irrefutable proof that humans had evolved in the northern hemisphere, and that therefore the South African fossils could not have been ancestral humans.

Despite this rejection, Dart had a powerful ally in Jan Smuts, twice prime minister of South Africa, and a strong supporter of the development of science in the country. The year after Dart's discovery Smuts gave a prophetic presidential address to the British Association for the Advancement of Science in London:

'Who knows,' he asked, 'whether South Africa may not become the Mecca of human palaeontology? … Discoveries already made point to the possibility that South Africa may yet figure as the cradle of mankind.'[4]

The phrase 'cradle of mankind' (or humankind) has been widely used to describe the South African fossil sites ever since.

THE DISCOVERIES OF ROBERT BROOM

Jan Smuts also befriended and supported Robert Broom, an eccentric Scottish medical doctor who held unorthodox views, a self-made palaeontologist, and an avid supporter of Raymond Dart's contentious claims. In 1903 Broom had joined the staff of Victoria College (later the University of Stellenbosch) as Professor of Zoology and Geology, but he was forced to resign in 1910 because he taught Darwin's theory of evolution. He returned to medicine and to fossil-hunting, but fell foul of his professional colleagues by selling valuable fossils to fund his collecting obsession. In 1934, thanks to the intervention of Smuts, the 67-year-old Broom was employed in Pretoria as Curator of Palaeontology at the Transvaal Museum (now the Ditsong National Museum of Natural

History). Broom's original fossil interest had been in therapsids (mammal-like reptiles), but Dart's discovery at Taung shifted his attention to hominins – called man-apes at the time – and he was determined to find additional fossils to support Dart's claim that *Australopithecus* was an ancestor of *Homo sapiens*.

The karst landscape in the Cradle area is geologically similar to the landscape at Taung, and several scientists hunted for fossils around Sterkfontein in the late 1920s and 1930s. These activities alerted Broom to the possibilities of finding hominins in the area. He began his search at Gladysvale (now lying within the John Nash Nature Reserve) but shifted his attention to Sterkfontein in August 1936. Within a few days, the Sterkfontein mine manager, George Barlow, showed him a fossil cranium. It was badly crushed,

Robert Broom with George Barlow, manager of Sterkfontein, and members of the Transvaal Museum staff. Broom is indicating the spot where he discovered an *Australopithecus* cranium.

Ditsong National Museum of Natural History

4 J.C. Smuts, 'Science from the South African point of view', in Dawson & Robertson (eds) (1940: 158)

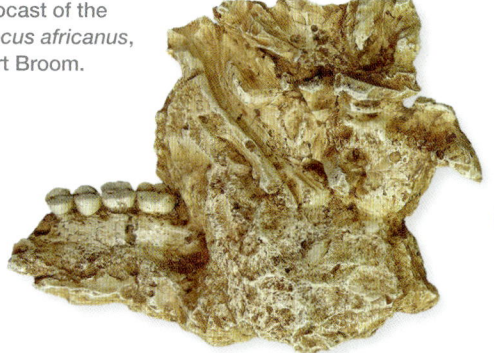

The crushed cranium and endocast of the first specimen of *Australopithecus africanus*, found at Sterkfontein by Robert Broom.

but it included an endocast (a cast of the interior of the cranium), and Broom recognised it as an ancestral hominin. He named it *Plesianthropus transvaalensis*[5] but it was later categorised as *Australopithecus africanus*. This was the adult specimen needed to demonstrate that Dart's claim was correct, but it was to be another 17 years before the Piltdown Man was exposed as a fraud.

Broom continued to excavate the Sterkfontein area. In 1938 he identified a new fossil at Kromdraai, a cave site two kilometres east of Sterkfontein. He placed it in a new genus because of its distinctly different jaw structure and robust dentition, and he named it *Paranthropus robustus*.[6] It was an important find because it demonstrated that human evolution had not been a progressive development within one species, but a complexity of similar, sometimes contemporary, species, some of which had prospered while others had become extinct. In 1947 his efforts were rewarded with a perfect, well-preserved cranium of *Australopithecus africanus*. He was still using the old generic name *Plesianthropus*, and the press soon abbreviated that to 'Mrs Ples'. The nickname stuck, even after the specimen had been reassigned to the genus *Australopithecus*, and it is probably the best-known fossil of that species yet unearthed.

However, the scientific community abroad continued to remain sceptical of the South African finds. Broom himself believed that the deposits in Sterkfontein were younger than those at Taung, and therefore possibly not ancestral to humans.

In 1946 a primitive hyena fossil was discovered by Dr Helmut K. Silberberg, a Johannesburg art collector and speleologist, in what is now known as the Silberberg Grotto (where, coincidentally, the famous Little Foot skeleton was discovered almost 50 years later). The presence of this very ancient species showed that the Sterkfontein deposits were much older than palaeontologists had originally thought, and Broom immediately revised his dating of the Sterkfontein strata. That same year he and G.W.H. Schepers, one of Dart's post-graduate students, published formal descriptions of all his fossil discoveries in a monograph entitled *The South African Fossil Ape-Men: The Australopithecinae* (Transvaal Museum Memoir No. 2), with a preface by Jan Smuts. The publication earned Broom the 1946 Daniel Giraud Gold Medal and Honorarium from the United States National Academy of Sciences, and elevated the stature of this contribution in international scientific circles. But the evidence of Piltdown Man still prevented the significance of his and Dart's discoveries from receiving unequivocal acceptance.

In 1946, Robert Broom and G.W.H. Schepers published a monograph that helped to establish the importance of South African palaeoanthropology in international circles.

---

5 *Plesi* = near, similar to; *anthropus* = human; *transvaalensis* = of the Transvaal

6 *Para* = adjacent to or parallel with; *anthropus* = human; *robustus* = strongly built or robust

Broom died in 1951, and two years later Piltdown Man was revealed to be a complete fraud. Examination by scientists using improved chemical testing and dating showed that someone, perhaps even Dawson and Woodward themselves, had cobbled together bits of modern human and orangutan skeletal material, and stained and stressed them in order to make their construction look like a fossil. For almost 40 years the hoax had deceived some of the greatest palaeontologists of the time, and hindered the advance of evolutionary science.

The exposure of the Piltdown hoax cleared the way for scientific recognition of the South African discoveries and placed the Sterkfontein and Kromdraai sites on the international map. But palaeoanthropology in the country was entering a difficult time. The Smuts government, which had been very supportive of the science, was replaced in 1948 by the National Party whose members held conservative views on evolution and race. The idea that all humans had a common ancestor could not be reconciled with apartheid dogma, and the teaching of human evolution was discouraged in some schools. Government funding for hosting the Pan African Archaeological Association Congress in 1951 was cancelled and the venue for the congress was moved to Algiers. South African academics were increasingly discouraged from attending palaeontological events overseas, and world interest in the southern African region dwindled as local scientists became increasingly isolated.

A painting by John Cooke in 1915 shows leading scientists examining the Piltdown Man *Eoanthropus dawsoni*[7]: Sir Arthur Keith (centre) was the leading palaeontologist of the day; Charles Dawson and Arthur Smith Woodward (standing on right) claimed to have discovered the 'fossil'. Charles Darwin looks down from the portrait behind them.

7 *Eo* = dawn; *anthropus* = human; *robustus* = strongly built or robust

THE EAST AFRICAN FOSSILS

While South African researchers tried to deal with political and religious obstacles to their work, important discoveries were being made in East Africa. The rise and fall of ancient lakes and the regular flooding of rivers in the Great Rift Valley were ideal conditions for the burial and preservation of fossil bones. Erosion of the arid soils in modern times had re-exposed the sedimentary strata and revealed a wealth of fossils, including several species of hominin. This region has the added advantage that repeated volcanic activity has laid down volcanic ash that can be dated using the potassium-argon method, and correlated with the fossil-bearing strata to give accurate dates for the fossils. In the early days of palaeoanthropology, fossils from the caves in the Cradle, which were at the time much more difficult to date, were compared with East African species to establish roughly comparable dates. However, incorrect assumptions often led palaeoanthropologists to draw inaccurate conclusions about the South African material.

Throughout the second half of the twentieth century scientists from around the world hunted fossils in Kenya, Ethiopia and Tanzania. At least 10 new hominin species were described from the region. Some of them, perhaps, were the result of palaeoanthropologists' penchant for naming new species to generate publicity and funding, but all the new discoveries were nonetheless valuable contributions to the understanding of human evolution. The names of the Leakey family (most famously, Louis

Marina Elliott

Homo habilis, found near Lake Turkana in Kenya in the 1970s, contributed to the debate around the definition of the genus *Homo*.

and Mary and their son Richard), together with Donald Johanson, Tim White, Michel Brunet, Brigitte Senut, Martin Pickford, Yves Coppens and others became familiar to the world of palaeoanthropology as each of their discoveries appeared prominently in scientific journals and the popular media.

THE APARTHEID YEARS

Despite the political and ideological setbacks being experienced in South Africa, researchers continued to undertake palaeontological work. In 1958 the Stegman family, owners of the Sterkfontein Caves, donated that portion of their farm to the University of the Witwatersrand. The following year Phillip Tobias replaced Raymond Dart as head of the Department of Anatomy at the university. He not only retained Dart's interest in palaeoanthropology but took it to new scientific levels. In 1966 he re-opened full-time excavation at Sterkfontein, with Alun Hughes as the principal palaeontologist on the site. Hughes continued this work for the next 25 years until Ron Clarke succeeded him in 1990, and excavations have been continuous at Sterkfontein throughout this time.

At the same time scientists from the Transvaal Museum (now part of Ditsong Museums of South Africa) were active at Swartkrans, close to Sterkfontein, where Bob Brain pioneered the science of taphonomy – the study of the processes that occur from the moment of death to the formation of a fossil – in South Africa. His research covered a wide range of fields, including cave stratigraphy, classification of faunal fossils, the discovery of the use of fire and stone tools by early hominins, and the scientific repudiation of Raymond Dart's widely accepted hypothesis of an osteodontokeratic culture (see page 133). Brain identified cycles of deposition within the Swartkrans cave, and linked habitat changes to global variability in temperature; he was the first to correlate these changes with hominid evolutionary events in Africa. For this multifaceted research he was awarded a DSc by the University of the Witwatersrand in 1981.

Working with Brain in the Cradle at that time was a colleague at the Transvaal Museum, Elisabeth Vrba. She was a graduate of the University of Cape Town, and she collaborated with Stephen Jay Gould from Yale University on theories of 'punctuated evolution'

Above: A small sign at the Sterkfontein Caves acknowledges the donation of the site to the University of the Witwatersrand.

Right: A bronze bust of Phillip Tobias at Sterkfontein commemorates his contribution to palaeoanthropology in South Africa, particularly during the difficult years of apartheid.

and 'exaptation' (changes in the functionality of evolutionary adaptations.) She later moved to Yale University herself, where she developed the 'turnover pulse hypothesis' based on the bursts of evolutionary adaptation, speciation and extinction she had observed in the Cradle fossil assemblages.

It was becoming increasingly difficult, however, to fund the growing interest in palaeoanthropology in South Africa, and by the early 1990s it seemed probable that the work of the Palaeoanthropology Research Unit (PARU) at Wits University would have to be discontinued for financial reasons. Lee Berger, a young and enthusiastic scientist in the unit, discussed the difficulty with Mark Read, one of the landowners in the Cradle. Together with two leading businessmen and philanthropists, Harry Oppenheimer and Gavin Relly, they launched the Palaeontological

Scientific Trust (PAST) in 1994. PARU was financially rescued and PAST has continued to fund research and educational programmes ever since.

REVIVAL OF WORLD INTEREST

South Africa's emergence from the apartheid era led the Gauteng Provincial Government to initiate the process of having the wider locality around Sterkfontein declared a World Heritage Site. It was inscribed by UNESCO in 1999 and has since become one of South Africa's most important tourism destinations. Besides creating unprecedented public awareness and the dissemination of information, the World Heritage Site inscription gives formal national and international protection to the fossil sites and the work being done there.

8 *Prometheus* = a mythological Greek Titan

The declaration of the Cradle of Humankind as a World Heritage Site took place at the same time that a series of remarkable discoveries were made which placed the region unequivocally at the forefront of evolutionary science. In 1998, shortly before the World Heritage Site nomination, Ron Clarke announced the discovery of a fossil nicknamed Little Foot and later identified as *Australopithecus prometheus*.[8] It was the most complete hominin fossil discovered at the time, and the oldest from the Cradle. Once again world attention focused on the caves of the Cradle.

On the retirement of Phillip Tobias in 1998, the Wits University management authorities decided to split PARU into two research units: the Sterkfontein Research Unit under Ron Clarke, and the Palaeoanthropology Unit for Research and Exploration under Lee Berger. The arrangement continued for some years, but it was an unsatisfactory compromise that fragmented palaeoscientific research in the university. In 2004 the two units were amalgamated to form the Institute of Human Evolution (IHE) and seven years later the IHE, the Bernard Price Institute for Palaeontological Research, part of the Department of Archaeology and other disciplines were merged into the Evolutionary Studies Institute (ESI).

In the meantime, two significant discoveries were made in the newly proclaimed World Heritage Site. Lee Berger found a new species, *Australopithecus sediba*, in 2008 and five years later he and his research team discovered *Homo naledi*, an extraordinary assemblage of fossils that demonstrated further the complexity of the human evolutionary line.[9]

Evolutionary science today embraces many complementary fields of research, and the ESI provides an academic base for the multidisciplinary studies that scientists are undertaking in the Cradle of Humankind and elsewhere. In its relatively short existence, researchers at the institute have made significant changes to the way in which the palaeosciences are conducted. Research is often carried out by large multidisciplinary teams who increasingly make use of rapidly advancing technologies across a wide range of scientific disciplines. Young PhD or post-doctoral students in their early careers are able to work on major projects at the ESI, and to co-author publications with senior scientists in the discipline. Often they can contribute greater familiarity with the latest technologies to the research than their older colleagues.

These changes have resulted in better public awareness of the prominence of Wits University and South Africa on the world palaeoscientific stage. Not since the days of Jan Smuts have the evolutionary sciences enjoyed such strong support from the South African government as they do now. In 2013, the Department of Science and Technology established the DST-NRF Centre of Excellence in Palaeosciences (hosted by Wits University) to acknowledge the worldwide importance of South African research in the various disciplines involved, while the South African Strategy for the Palaeosciences was established by the Department of Science and Technology to provide a framework for the development and coordination of the discipline in universities, museums and government departments, and helps to fund research in these fields.

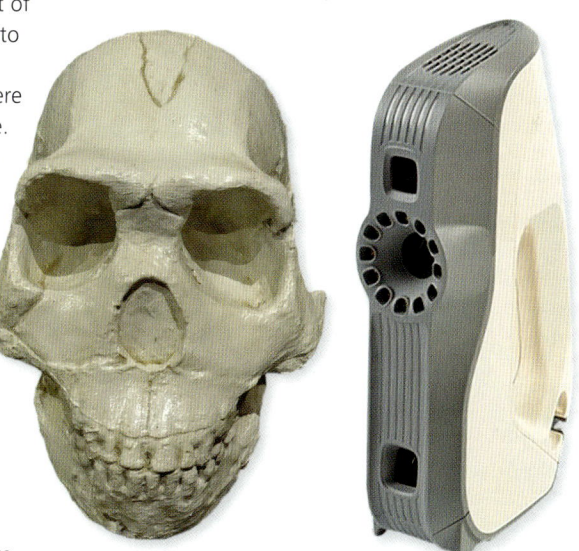

Scientists at the ESI use 3D scanning and printing to make precise fossil casts available to universities and museums throughout the world (see page 101).

9 *Sediba* = the Setswana word for a fountain or well; *naledi* = 'star' in Setswana – the fossil was discovered in the Rising Star cave system

TECHNOLOGY IN THE PALAEOSCIENCES

In the days of Robert Broom, it was common practice to search for fossils by rummaging through the debris left from lime mining or using dynamite to blast promising-looking rock deposits. Finding a fossil was largely serendipitous, and crucial information was inevitably lost through use of these crude techniques. (Broom attributed his extraordinary fossil-finding ability to supernatural powers.)

Scientists probably began to recognise the need for more precise methods when the new science of taphonomy was developed in the 1980s, and auxiliary disciplines such as palaeoclimatology, ecology, stratigraphy and accurate dating techniques began to be included in their research. These new disciplines introduced increasingly advanced technology, and the most recent discoveries in the Cradle have been characterised by very high-tech operations.

During recovery of *Homo naledi* fossils from an almost inaccessible cave, technological systems were used to allow scientists at the surface to participate in the excavation process. Here, a team monitors the laser scanning of the cave.

Marina Elliott

A copy of a 3D map of the Rising Star cave compiled from laser scans.

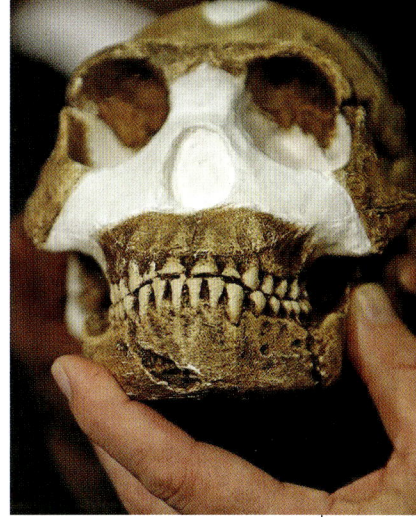

Fossil reconstruction using 3D printing.

PHOTOGRAMMETRY

One of the most important aspects of a fossil is its physical position before its removal, and much valuable taphonomic information was lost in the past when this was not recorded. Photogrammetry 'sweeps' a working area with a series of strobe-lit scans before and after recovery of fossils. The scans are then digitally compiled into three-dimensional (3D) images and archived for later analysis. The locality of each of the 3,000 fossils recovered from the *Homo naledi* site has been documented in this way. Besides providing permanent high-resolution records, the images can be transmitted to scientists above the ground who can monitor and direct the excavators in the cave in real time.

LASER SCANNING

Larger areas of a site can be mapped using laser beams to scan the interior of a cave. Special spheres or discs are placed strategically around the cave so that the scans can be accurately geo-referenced and consolidated into 3D maps.

COMPUTED TOMOGRAPHIC SCANS (CT SCANS)

Technological advances have also been made in laboratories sited away from the excavation areas. Fossils embedded in breccia need to be painstakingly prepared by using machines to remove the matrix rock – the rock in which the fossil is embedded – with air scribes (pencil-shaped precision tools with a sharp tip vibrating at high speed and driven by compressed air). In some cases, this can now be avoided by using CT scanners similar to those used in medical practice. A series of cross-section X-rays are scanned through the fossil-bearing rock to give a perfect image of the fossil within. Detailed casts can then be produced on a 3D printer. Not only is the fossil protected from inadvertent damage during preparation, but the image can be digitally transmitted for printing and examination by researchers or museums around the world.

5 | THE HUMAN EVOLUTIONARY LINE

Comparison between the mitochondrial DNA (mtDNA) in modern humans and modern chimpanzees shows that the two species are genetically very similar and that they diverged from a common ancestor between eight and six million years ago (mtDNA is discussed on pages 56–57). Descendants of that common ancestor followed two independent evolutionary paths to become the two separate species that exist today, and both are distinctly different from their original progenitor.

The evolution of a separate human family began about seven million years ago, but fossils only started to accumulate in the Cradle once erosion of the landscape had exposed the subterranean caves to the surface. The oldest hominin fossil recovered from the caves is 3.7 million years old, so the caves probably began to be exposed shortly before that time.

This chapter deals with early hominin evolution in the period between their divergence from other apes seven million years ago and the first fossils in the Cradle. The fossil record from that early period is extremely sparse and there are no examples from South Africa, but the hominins themselves, or other possible divergent branches on the evolutionary tree that have since become extinct, may well have lived in the Cradle-Magaliesberg region before the caves became exposed.

The five fossil discoveries described in this chapter are presented chronologically, to show how features of human evolution emerged over time. Chronology, however, does not imply genealogy: gaps in the fossil record make it difficult to assess whether a species that lived at a certain time may have been a direct ancestor of another species that lived later on. The timeline simply indicates the complex manner in which our human anatomy developed.

The spread of grassland placed the forest fauna under increasing environmental pressure. Ancestors of the great African apes managed to avoid extinction by migrating with their shrinking habitats and continuing to evolve into modern species in the forests of central Africa. However, the encroachment of grassland was sporadic. During times of drought or cold, patches of grassland intruded and fragmented the forests while in warmer, wetter climates, the woodland flourished and regained lost ground. Natural

Caves began to be exposed to the surface about 4 million years ago.

selection in human ancestors favoured adaptations that were suitable for existence in the transitional zone between forest and savannah. Among hominins the important anatomical developments for these habitats were bipedalism, changes in dentition (the size, shape, arrangement and function of the teeth) to suit new diets, and increased brain size and intellect. However, these new adaptations did not simply replace the original morphological characteristics. Bipedalism, for example, appears to have evolved while hominins were still predominantly forest dwellers, but their limbs retained some climbing faculties such as splayed toes and a strong grip so that they had access to arboreal fruits and safe roosts in trees. Modifications of habitat that took place over time

and in different regions resulted in a complex combination of new adaptations together with the retention of old ones as evolution proceeded.

Until the late twentieth century most researchers believed that East Africa, particularly the Rift Valley, held the key to understanding the origins of modern humans, and that South Africa was a quiet evolutionary backwater. Since then, numerous species have been discovered in southern Africa that challenge these ideas. At least a dozen different species of early hominins may have existed on the African continent, many of them at the same time. Some of these may have roamed over extensive territories, while others may have been regional variants of the same species or distinct species occupying restricted ecological niches.

Fossils of early hominins are from localities that used to be partially forested like this one, which indicates that human traits began to develop when our ancestors were still largely arboreal.

FOSSIL TAXONOMY

Species of living plants and animals are evident everywhere. Dogs, donkeys and daisies are all obviously specific entities, each with its own morphological characteristics that are carried through to its offspring. Species of extinct fossils, however, are less easy to define. Taxonomy – the science of classifying and naming organisms in an ordered system based on their natural evolutionary relationships – has developed over time to take account of new knowledge about how life on Earth evolved.

The Swedish naturalist Carl Linnaeus (1706–1778) introduced the species classification system we still use today. Each species is allocated a binomial (two-part) name indicating its genus (plural: genera) – the group of similar species to which it belongs – and its individual species name. The two parts of the name are usually based on Latin or Greek and are always italicised, with the first name, the genus, written with a capital letter. The system was based on the belief held by the Church at the time that each species had been individually created in its existing form, and could be defined in terms of the morphological characteristics of an immutable type specimen.

The principles of evolution introduced by Charles Darwin a century later showed that species *do* change and become new species through natural selection. Today, the concept of an immutable species is no longer valid, but scientists continue to use Linnaeus's binomial naming system. They have developed a plethora of innovative definitions of a species as they grapple with the complexity of natural selection, and the one most widely accepted is the Biological Species Concept (BSC) proposed by Ernst Mayr in the 1940s: *A species is a reproductively isolated population whose members can breed among themselves, but not with others, to produce viable offspring.*

However, the BSC is obviously not applicable to extinct fossils that no longer breed and produce offspring, viable or otherwise.

The emergence of genetics as a method for understanding evolutionary change has led scientists to develop the cladistic species model. This model defines a species as a group of organisms that share a common genetic lineage from a single ancestor. Cladistics makes use of DNA to create a cladogram, in which each clade represents the lineal descendants from a common evolutionary ancestor and collectively they show an evolutionary family tree on which each species is a terminal branch.

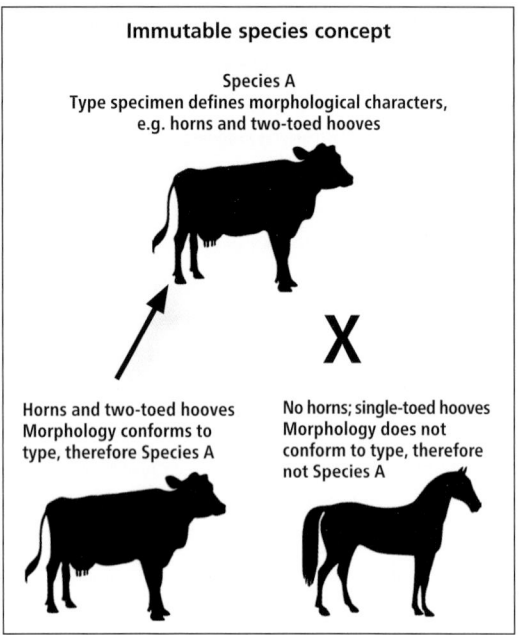

Immutable species concept

Species A
Type specimen defines morphological characters, e.g. horns and two-toed hooves

X

Horns and two-toed hooves
Morphology conforms to type, therefore Species A

No horns; single-toed hooves
Morphology does not conform to type, therefore not Species A

Pixabay.com

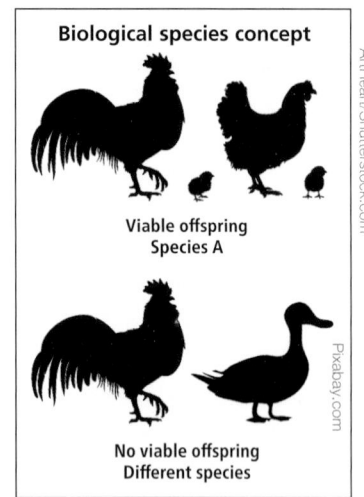

Biological species concept

Viable offspring
Species A

No viable offspring
Different species

ArtHeart/Shutterstock.com

Pixabay.com

Palaeontology recognises the concept of a common ancestor, but since there is no DNA in fossils it is not possible for palaeontologists to use the cladistic model to categorise different species.

Palaeontological taxonomy must deal with a further complication: each fossil found by palaeontologists represents a single moment in the process of evolution – it is one screenshot from a full-length film. Any two screenshots may be separated by hundreds of thousands of years. Two different species of hominin fossils may therefore represent an antecedent and its descendant in the phylogeny (the evolutionary development) of the same species; in this case the descendant is called a chronospecies of the earlier hominin species. Or one of the fossils

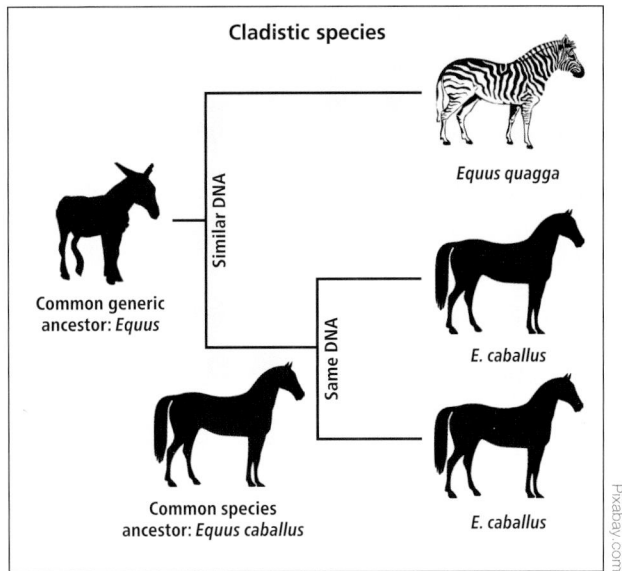

Cladistic species

Common generic ancestor: *Equus*

Similar DNA

Equus quagga

Same DNA

E. caballus

Common species ancestor: *Equus caballus*

E. caballus

Pixabay.com

may be a member of a different evolutionary line that ended in extinction. The fossil species that are discussed in the following chapters are therefore possibly, but not necessarily, descendants of one another and antecedents of humans.

Fossils can only be assigned to a species based on the anatomical attributes preserved in the fossil – usually only its skeletal anatomy. As far as possible, palaeontologists do this by comparing a new fossil find with other species. Accurate dating can help with the classification of the fossil, but it may be misleading in cases where two fossils of similar dates may have different anatomical features which would make them different but contemporary species. Inevitably, the classification and naming of fossils relies heavily on the judgement of the palaeontologists and their colleagues, and the taxonomy of the fossils described in the following chapters is subject to constant debate and possible review.

The term 'hominin' is also confusing. It is a term used in palaeoanthropology but is not a strictly defined taxonomic category. It is used to describe a group of species from several different genera which together are often loosely defined as

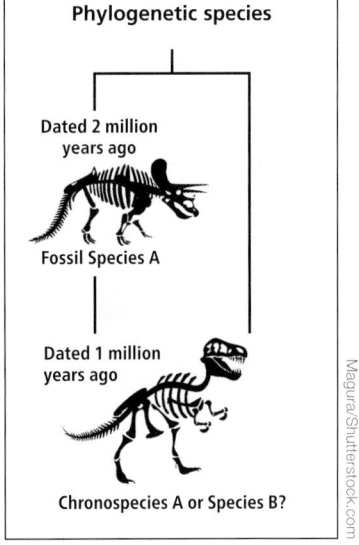

Phylogenetic species

Dated 2 million years ago

Fossil Species A

Dated 1 million years ago

Chronospecies A or Species B?

Magura/Shutterstock.com

'humans and their fossil ancestors'. However, many species that are included in the hominin category, such as *Paranthropus robustus* and *Homo naledi*, are clearly not human ancestors – their descendants no longer exist. Other species, such as *Australopithecus africanus*, may or may not be human ancestors – no one knows. To avoid this confusion it may be better to consider hominins as those species that diverged genetically from other apes, some of which may be ancestral to *Homo sapiens*.

➤ 7 million years ago: An upright posture – *Sahelanthropus tchadensis*

Age and significance

The oldest known human ancestor may have been a species named *Sahelanthropus tchadensis*.[10] Fragments of several crania were discovered by French palaeontologist Michel Brunet and his colleagues in 2001 and re-assembled by computer simulation. The cranium appears to have been supported on a vertical spinal column, a critically important development in the evolution of the human family. The fossil fragments were dated between 7.2 and 6.8 million years ago, which places them very close to the approximate date of divergence between hominins and apes.

Anatomy

The cranium has several distinctive features that indicate that this creature may have stood upright and walked on its hind legs. The position of the *foramen magnum* (the aperture where the spinal cord enters the skull) shows that the head was carried on a vertical spine. This indicates an upright posture, but the fossil includes no lower parts of the skeleton to confirm any bipedalism. The canine teeth, while not as small as human canines, are smaller than those of apes and they are not as sharply pointed. At the same time, the computer-generated reconstruction of the cranium fragments shows a very large brow ridge and almost no forehead or elevated brain case. The combination of these features suggests that the species had not evolved far from a common ape ancestor.

The desert region of Sahel was once well forested, and bipedalism in *Sahelanthropus* would have developed in tandem with arboreal features.

The cranium of the *Sahelanthropus tchadensis* was severely crushed and had to be digitally reconstructed. It showed an interesting combination of human and ape-like features.

Habitat

The fossils were found in the inhospitable deserts of Chad but, at the time that *Sahelanthropus tchadensis* existed, the region was well wooded alongside an ancient lake. This would indicate that, if bipedalism had evolved at this early date, it would have done so in a wooded environment.

Of particular interest from the point of view of the Cradle is that, if this is indeed a hominin fossil, it disproves earlier theories that human evolution occurred only to the east of the Rift Valley. Hominins, it seems, may have been dispersed elsewhere in Africa from fairly early on in their existence.

Tortsen Pursche/Shutterstock.com

10 Sahel = from the Sahel region; *anthropus* = human; *tchadensis* = from Chad

➤ 6 million years ago: Possible facultative bipedalism – *Orrorin tugenensis*

Age and significance

About 20 fossil fragments from several individuals named *Orrorin tugenensis*[1] were discovered in the Tugen Hills in Kenya in 2000 by French palaeontologists Brigitte Senut and Martin Pickford and dated between 6.2 and 5.6 million years ago. The limb morphology suggests that *Orrorin* may have been a very early bipedal hominin that was also adept at climbing.

Anatomy

The fragments found by Senut and Pickford include several femoral (thigh) bones, part of a humerus (arm bone) and two finger bones. The femurs have large ball joints with long necks, which indicate probable bipedalism. This may, however, have been only facultative bipedalism, meaning the animal *could* walk on two legs, but did not normally do so. The knee structure and the pelvis might have helped to resolve the question of bipedalism, but these are missing from the fossils that have been collected to date. The fingers are curved and there are strong muscle attachments in the elbow, both of which are associated with tree-climbing abilities.

Marina Elliott

The long neck and ball joint at the top of the femurs indicate that *Orrorin tugenensis* might have been semi-bipedal.

Habitat

Palaeoecological evidence for the Tugen Hills indicates that the region was thickly wooded in *Orrorin* times. The structure of the femur suggests some form of bipedalism and, if this was the case, then it may have been largely to facilitate moving along branches of trees, as is done by some of the modern apes such as chimpanzees, as well as walking on the ground.

nimuisabel/Shutterstock.com

Six million years ago the Tugen Hills were thickly forested and *Orrorin tugensis* would have been predominantly arboreal.

➤ 5 million years ago: Adaptations to a complex environment – *Ardipithecus*

Age and significance

Two species of *Ardipithecus* (*Ardipithecus ramidus* and *Ardipithecus kadabba*) have recently been described from a number of fossils, including one partially complete skeleton from the Middle Awash and Gona areas of Ethiopia.[11] They were first discovered in 1992 by Californian scientist Tim White, but difficulties in extracting and preparing them delayed detailed description until 2015. They are dated from about five million years ago, but they were found in open habitats where the taphonomy has probably been severely disturbed, so that the estimated dating is uncertain, with very wide margins of possible error.

White has suggested that this species lies on the evolutionary tree somewhere between *Australopithecus* and the common ancestor of apes and humans. He also suggests that many of the ape characteristics found in chimpanzees developed *after* the split with hominins, and never occurred in our early common ancestor.

Anatomy

The pelvis, limbs and feet of *Ardipithecus* are dissimilar to those of other primates and seem to suit both facultative bipedalism and tree-climbing; the *foramen magnum* is situated well forward under the cranium, suggesting a more-or-less erect stance. The presence of slightly elongated canines in males might have meant some degree of sexual dimorphism (males being larger than females) and male dominance. The foot is neither ape-like nor human-like; the big toe is divergent and opposed, but it would not have had a power grasp like that of a chimpanzee. The knees are placed well apart, suitable for climbing, but not for obligate bipedal walking (habitually walking upright on the hind legs). The arms are long and *Ardipithecus* may have occasionally made use of quadrupedal (four-legged) knuckle-walking.

Habitat

Ardipithecus has a mix of primitive features that appear in earlier fossil species and derived features (those that have evolved subsequently) which, combined, are unlike those of other primates. The differences demonstrate that human evolution probably took place as grass encroachment fragmented the habitat into a constantly changing mosaic of woodland, wooded savannah, riverine forest and open grassland. Hominins seem to have developed an advantage over other competing species by being able to search and find suitable nourishment in a wide variety of different habitats, possibly gathering food on the ground and carrying it to arboreal refuges.

Ardipithecus has a distinctively narrow face, long arms, widely separated legs and opposable toes.

11 *Ardi* = ground or floor; *pithecus* = ape; *ramidus* = 'root' in the Afar language; *kadabba* = from the Afar word for 'basal family ancestor'

A U-shaped palate with parallel rows of teeth on either side of the jaw are ape-like features of *Australopithecus anamensis*.

Age and significance

Australopithecus anamensis[12] is known from a four-million-year-old arm bone from south of Lake Turkana in Kenya collected by Bryan Patterson of Harvard University in 1965. Other scattered fragments, including palates, lower mandibles, teeth and a partial tibia bone, were collected by Kenyan palaeoanthropologist Mary Leakey in 1994. Since then almost 100 fragments from about 20 specimens of the species have been found in Kenya and Ethiopia, and dated between 4.3 and 3.8 million years ago. Clear indications of bipedalism are the primary reason why the species is allocated to the genus *Australopithecus* – it was originally thought that this was the earliest group of hominins to adopt a permanently upright posture. This has since been shown to be an oversimplification, as degrees of bipedalism are now known to occur in other genera as well. However, *Australopithecus anamensis* is the oldest known specimen of the genus.

Several scientists, including Louis and Mary Leakey, suggested that *Australopithecus anamensis* had evolved from *Ardipithecus* and directly into *Australopithecus afarensis*. While this may be the case, we can only speculate about simple linear evolutionary scenarios of this kind.

Anatomy

The tibia shows the distinctively angled (valgus) knee of an obligate biped and the thick, shock-absorbing ankle bone that are adaptations for bipedal locomotion. Reduced canines and relatively thick dental enamel also show that evolutionary traits towards an omnivorous diet were well established. However, the long forearms indicate tree-climbing capability, and the protruding lower face with a narrow palate and parallel rows of teeth are all reminiscent of apes.

Habitat

The majority of the fossil fragments of *Australopithecus anamensis* have been found in western Kenya. Today the region is a windswept desert, but four million years ago it lay on the shores of an ancient lake and was probably open savannah.

Australopithecus anamensis was probably the first hominid to habitually walk on its hind legs.

12 *Anamensis* = derived from the word 'anam', meaning a lake in the Turkana language

Peter Delmar

The Cradle of Humankind as it is today may look similar to how the western Kenyan landscape would have appeared millions of years ago, where many of the early hominins evolved.

One of the many reconstructions of *Australopithecus afarensis* made famous by the near-complete fossil skeleton nicknamed 'Lucy'.

➤ 3.5 million years ago: East African fossils contemporary with the Cradle – *Australopithecus afarensis*

Age and significance

Australopithecus afarensis is best known from the near-complete skeleton found by Donald Johanson in Hadar, Ethiopia, in 1975 and nicknamed Lucy. During the 50 years since its discovery, Lucy has become one of the most important fossil hominins ever found and it has been referred to in many comparative investigations. It is dated at 3.2 million years ago, but specimens found later at sites in Ethiopia and Tanzania are dated from 3.9 to 2.9 million years ago. This extended period of existence overlaps the dates of the first hominin fossils from the Cradle of Humankind described in the following chapter.

Because *Australopithecus afarensis* was believed to have existed for almost a million years with no other contemporary hominin species, palaeontologists have long considered it to be a certain ancestor to all subsequent hominin species. However, the discovery of *Australopithecus prometheus* in the Cradle from a similar period may have altered that hypothesis.

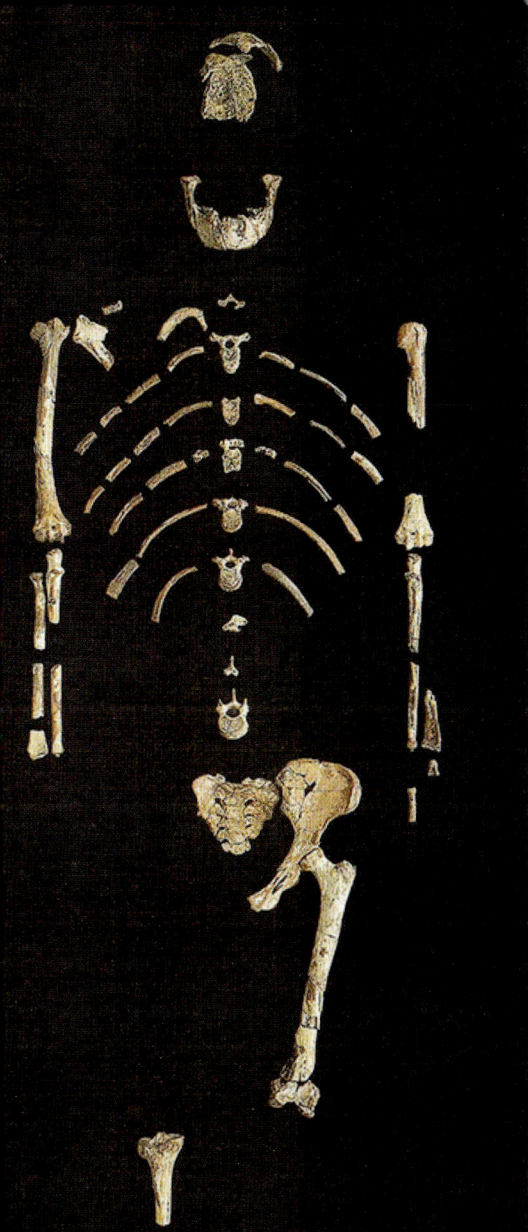

Anatomy

Lucy is an almost 40 per cent complete female skeleton, which includes a variety of elements such as ribs, not commonly found in the fossil record. She is estimated to have stood approximately 1.1m tall and to have weighed around 30kg, but males of the species were considerably larger. The face was prognathic (protruding forward as in the apes) with a low, sloping forehead, and a strong ridge over the eyes. The brain capacity varied between 380cc and 430cc. The canines and molars were relatively larger than in modern humans. Powerful chewing muscles were attached to a sagittal crest towards the back of the skull and acted horizontally across the jaw to pull and rip at items of tough food.

Taphonomy and habitat

In 1975 a group of about 17 *Australopithecus afarensis* fossils were discovered together. They had evidently died simultaneously in some catastrophic event. The assemblage included males, females, adolescents and juveniles; it demonstrated that there was considerable sexual dimorphism and that they evidently moved in groups of mixed age and gender.

The species is also known from fossilised footprints that were made in volcanic mud as a group of individuals made its way across the Tanzanian landscape. The style of the tracks shows that this was a striding biped, and confirms that the species was social – at least three individuals walked together across the 3.6 million-year-old surface. The tracks also indicate that during the million years of its existence *Australopithecus afarensis* gradually expanded its habitat to include open country and was no longer confined to the wooded savannah as it had been in the early stages of its evolution.

Above: The almost 40 per cent complete *Australopithecus* skeleton called Lucy caused a sensation at the time of its discovery, and its status remained unchallenged until recent finds in the Cradle of Humankind.

Right: The 3.6 million-year-old footprints of *Australopithecus afarensis* show a divergent big toe and a strong bipedal stride.

Fossil sites in the Cradle

The listing of the Cradle of Humankind as a UNESCO World Heritage Site in 1999 was based on twelve registered fossil-bearing sites plus Wonder Cave which has no hominin fossils – thirteen in all. Since then, two more sites have been discovered and more may yet be added. Each site, with the exception of Wonder Cave, is registered with the South African Heritage Resources Agency, which grants excavation permits to qualified scientists subject to strict regulation. Only one scientific team may excavate a site at any time.

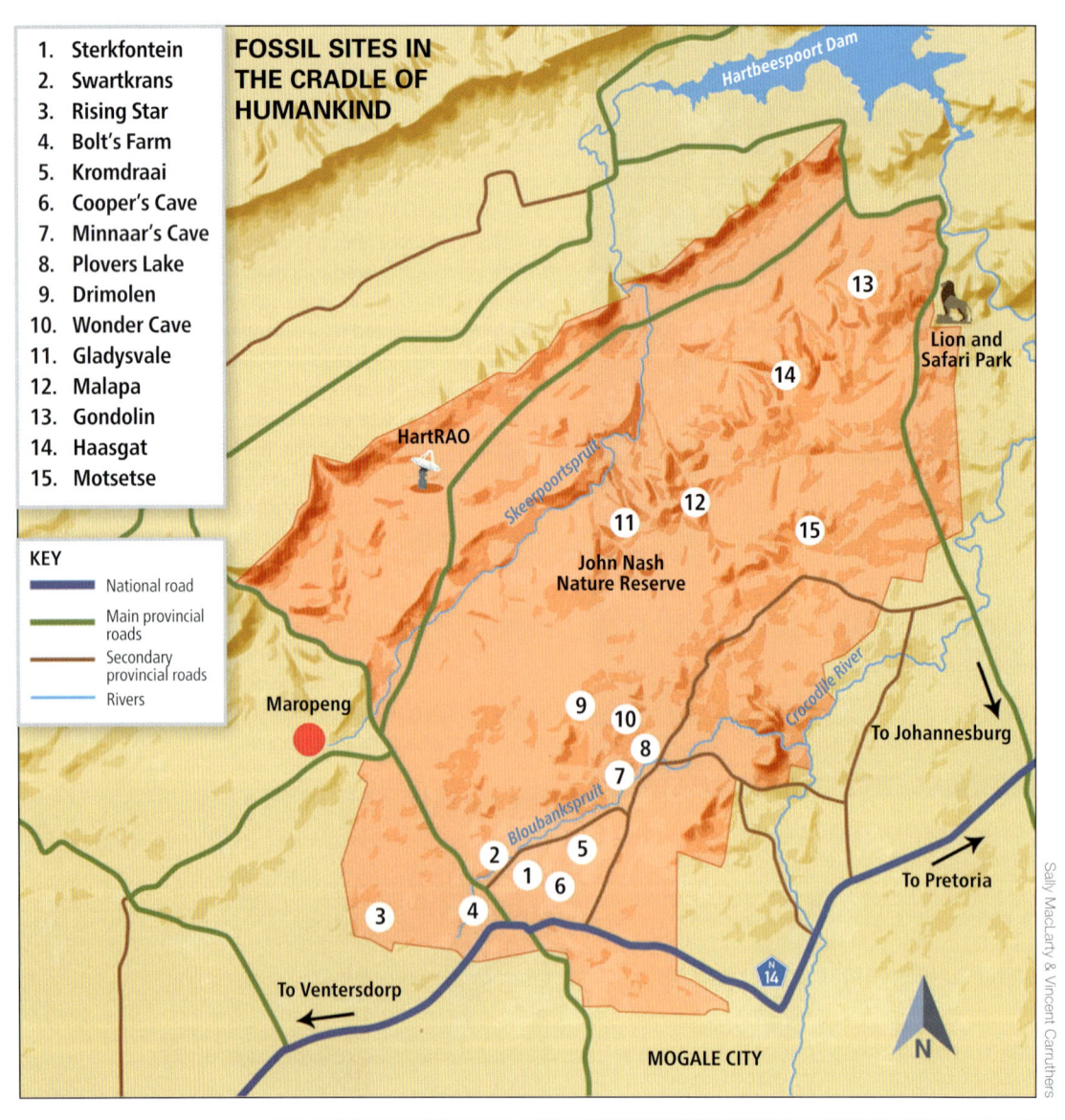

1. Sterkfontein
2. Swartkrans
3. Rising Star
4. Bolt's Farm
5. Kromdraai
6. Cooper's Cave
7. Minnaar's Cave
8. Plovers Lake
9. Drimolen
10. Wonder Cave
11. Gladysvale
12. Malapa
13. Gondolin
14. Haasgat
15. Motsetse

FOSSIL SITES IN THE CRADLE OF HUMANKIND

KEY

▬▬	National road
▬▬	Main provincial roads
▬▬	Secondary provincial roads
▬▬	Rivers

Sally MacLarty & Vincent Carruthers

1. Sterkfontein This extensive underground cave system has an open, de-roofed surface area where palaeoanthropologists have conducted research for more than a century. Renowned discoveries such as Mrs Ples and Little Foot, together with popular public tours, have made Sterkfontein one of the best-known fossil hominin sites in the world. This aerial view of Sterkfontein shows the excavated surface deposits where fossils were first found in 1895, and the visitor paths to the entrance and exit from the underground cave system that was discovered later that year. The museum and restaurant are in the background.

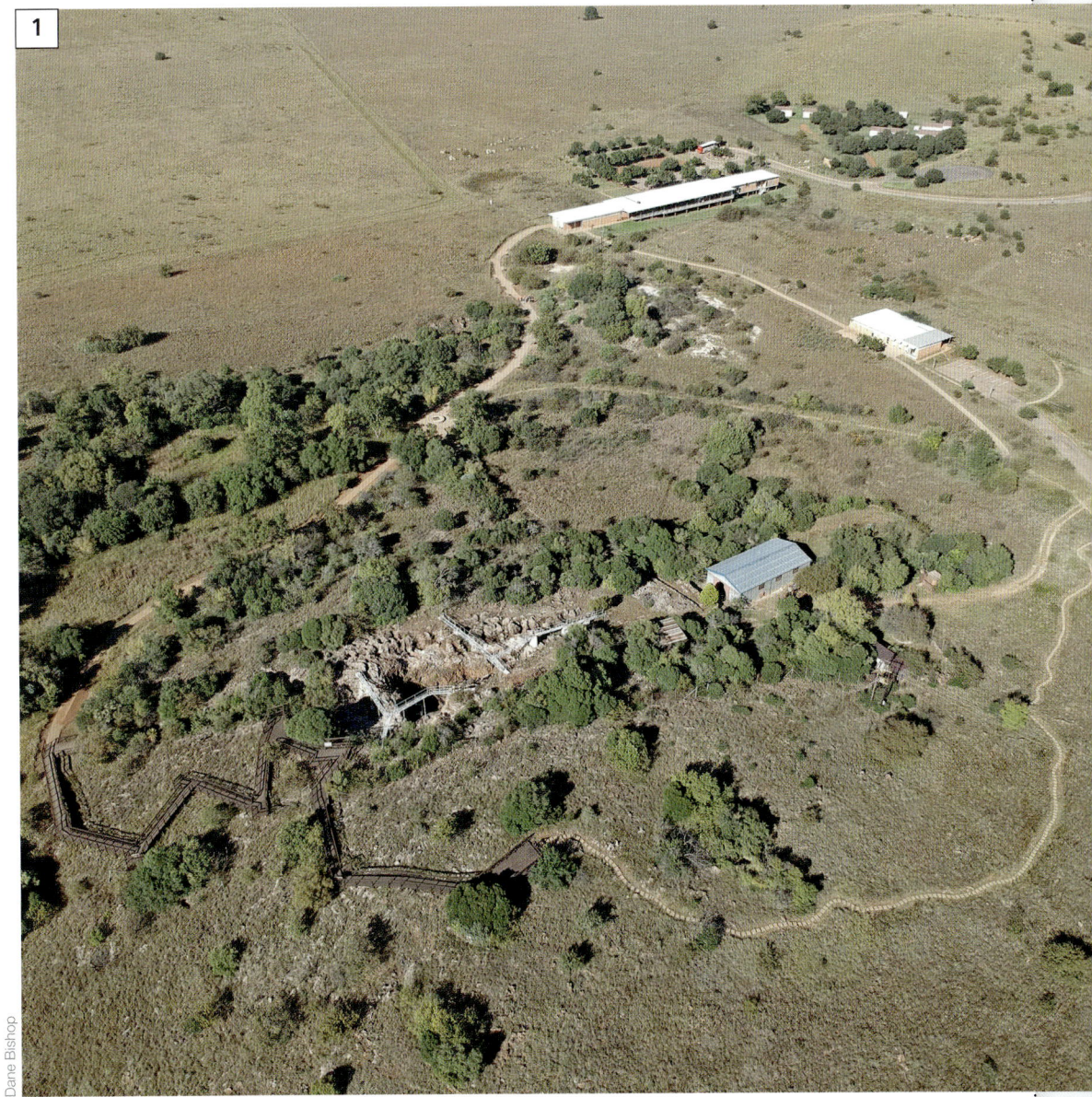

1

Dane Bishop

2. Swartkrans Situated near the crest of a small dolomite hill, Swartkrans has produced the largest of all assemblages of *Paranthropus robustus* fossils, including an almost complete skull found in 1948. Other important events have been Bob Brain's discovery of the early use of fire (discussed in Chapter 7) together with Early Stone Age artefacts.

Dane Bishop

3. Rising Star In this deep and largely inaccessible cave system (right) a new species, *Homo naledi*, has been found. This is the most recently discovered of the fossil sites and lies just to the west of the originally proclaimed area of the World Heritage Site. The site is unusual, because the fossils are preserved in sediments rather than breccia and there is an almost complete absence of other fauna in the chamber. The almost inaccessible Dinaledi Chamber is located deep in the Rising Star cave system and has yielded the largest assemblage ever found of fossils of a single hominin species.

Marina Elliott

4. Bolt's Farm This is a series of small fossil sites in and around an old lime quarry. Many of them have not yet been fully explored or excavated. No hominin fossils have been recovered, but fossils of other extinct fauna have been found, including primates, elephants, pigs, antelopes and the false sabre-toothed cat *Dinofelis*.

4

Dane Bishop

5. Kromdraai A de-roofed cave system, Kromdraai (right), is the site of Robert Broom's discovery in 1938 of *Paranthropus robustus*. In addition to that and other important palaeoanthropological discoveries, it contains a diverse faunal assemblage, including baboons, carnivores and ungulates. Fossil-bearing breccia has been removed by palaeoanthropologists over the years, leaving the dolomitic walls exposed. Kromdraai was one of the first sites in which hominin fossils were found in the 1930s and has been extensively excavated ever since.

5

Dane Bishop

6. Cooper's Cave An exposed cave floor, Cooper's Cave (left) is very close to Kromdraai. It was one of the early sites excavated in the area. A large number of fossils and numerous stone tools have been recovered from it, including remains of both *Australopithecus* and *Paranthropus*, as well as a wide variety of predators, ungulates and primates.

7. Minnaar's Cave This small cave system is located near Kromdraai and Cooper's Cave, and comprises four interconnected caverns and several excavation pits. Fossil-bearing breccia has been located, but no excavation has taken place, and little is known about the deposits here.

8. Plovers Lake This is a deep cave and a complex of exposed breccias. Fossils of several species of fauna have been identified, and artefacts from the Middle and Later Stone Ages have been found.

9. Drimolen Drimolen comprises two different deposits close to one another in the hills above the Rhino and Lion Nature Reserve. Main Quarry is dated at about two million years and Makondo Deposit, a few hundred metres away, at about 2.6 million years. Both are exposed caves from which numerous hominin fossils, including an almost-complete *Paranthropus robustus* skull, have been recovered, as well as other fauna such as sabre-toothed cats, an extinct elephant and colobus monkeys. Students are pictured below, excavating the fossil deposits in Drimolen Main Quarry.

10. Wonder Cave

Some of the beautiful stalactites to be seen in Wonder Cave (right), which lies close to Drimolen in the Rhino and Lion Nature Reserve. It is not a registered fossil site, but fine examples of speleothems can be seen in the cave as well as historical remnants of lime-mining activities.

Stuart McMichael

11. Gladysvale This is a large cave in the John Nash Nature Reserve. It was mined for bat guano and lime in the early twentieth century, and remnants of kilns and mining operations are still evident. A large number of fossils have been recovered, but the only hominin fossils are two *Australopithecus africanus* teeth. Below are the exposed deposits at the entrance to the cave being inspected by visitors.

11

12. Malapa Malapa is the site of the discovery of *Australopithecus sediba* in 2008. It is a re-exposed sinkhole into which hominins and other animals may have fallen to their death. It is now equipped with a state-of-the-art overhead viewing platform (see page 139), from which tourists are here viewing the excavations (right and far right).

12

Marna Elliott

13. Gondolin This partly destroyed dolomitic cave (above) is located in the Skurweberg on the northern side of the Cradle. An unusually large number of antelope and warthog fossils have been recovered here, as well as two hominin teeth. The large sample of mammals enabled Elisabeth Vrba to formulate the 'turnover pulse hypothesis', which she developed further at Yale University. In this picture the Gondolin cave is being set up for photogrammetry mapping.

14. Haasgat Situated in the remote northern area of the Cradle, Haasgat (left) is a deep tunnel that extends into the dolomite hillside. It was mined for lime in the early twentieth century, and these mining operations caused extensive damage to the natural cave. Palaeontological excavations only began in recent decades. They have thus far yielded numerous extinct primate fossils, but no hominins.

15. Motsetse This is an open cave floor located in the Cradle Nature Reserve. A diverse fossil assemblage of fauna, including bovids (antelopes and buffalo), carnivores and equids (horses and zebras) has been discovered here, but no hominin remains have yet been identified.

FOSSILISATION

Above: The fossilised tibia of a large mammal shows the quartz crystallisation of the inner bone.

The transformation of a deceased animal or plant into a fossil is exceptionally rare, and only takes place when a particular set of complex circumstances exists. These circumstances differ in different parts of the world but, in the case of the caves of the Cradle of Humankind, three factors make fossilisation possible.

The first of these is that the water and rocks in the caves are unusually rich in minerals, and over long periods of time these minerals impregnate the skeletal bones and change them chemically into a permanently durable substance while retaining their precise physical shape. The second is that the environment is well protected and climatically stable, so the slow process of fossilisation can take place without disturbance. The third factor that aids preservation is the high concentration of calcium carbonate (lime) in the water from the surrounding dolomitic rock. This combines with the detritus in the cave to form a concrete mix that encrusts the fossils and protects them for millions of years. The process can be summarised in the following series of events:

Stage 1: A dead organism is buried in a mound of debris in a cave, or in mud slurry that is washed into the cave. Bacterial decay removes all soft tissue, leaving skeletal and dental matter intact.

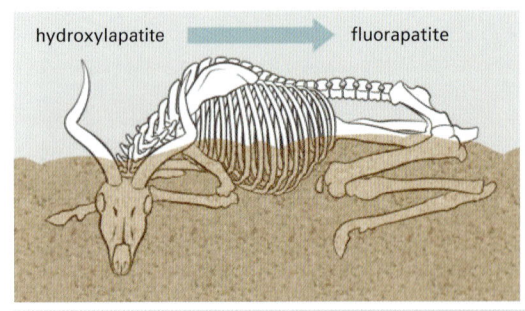

hydroxylapatite → fluorapatite

Stage 2: Bone from the dead organism absorbs minerals from the surrounding substrate and groundwater. A chemical reaction takes place, transforming hydroxylapatite, the main mineral component of bone, into other minerals, notably fluorapatite.

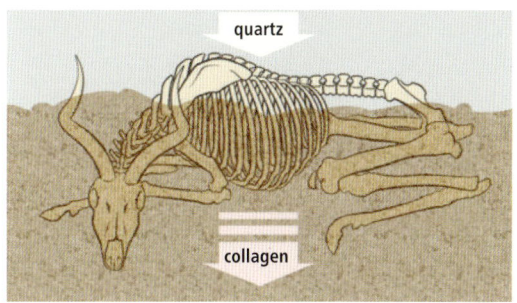

Stage 3: At the same time the organic components of the bone, such as fat, collagen and other proteins, break down, leaving pores in the bone structure that are filled by other minerals, notably silicon oxide (quartz), which frequently forms crystals in the fossil. Mineralisation of the bone preserves its morphological shape and improves its resilience to the hazards of burial, climate and compression by layers of rock and sediment. The replacement of the organic matter in the bone with minerals means that all traces of DNA are lost, and molecular analysis of the fossils and their phylogeny is not possible.

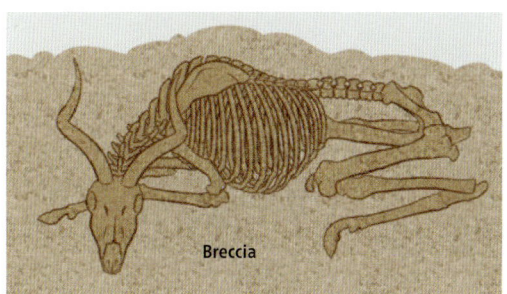

Stage 4: During the mineralisation processes, lime-rich water cements the bones together with pebbles and other bones into a concrete-like breccia.

Most of the fossils found in the Cradle are embedded in breccia, which has ensured their preservation for millions of years. However, it also makes them difficult to extract. Early palaeoanthropologists used methods ranging from dynamite to cold chisels to expose the fossils, often damaging them and compromising their scientific usefulness. Today, perfect fossils are recovered by highly skilled preparators using precision air scribes. Even more recent techniques include the use of computed tomography scanning (CT scans) to identify fossils in the breccia matrix, and then print perfect 3D copies without removing the fossil at all.

The fossils of *Homo naledi* are exceptional in that they have not been subjected to the above processes. Collagen and fats have been leached out of the bones but, probably because of their recent age, these organic components have not been replaced by other minerals like quartz. In addition, the hydroxylapatite has not been replaced by quartz, so the fossils have remained soft and fragile.

Bones, soil, pebbles and other debris are cemented into concrete-like breccia.

6 | THE CRADLE HOMININS

Our knowledge of early human ancestry comes almost exclusively from fossilised remains, and the rich fossil record in the dolomitic caves in the Cradle of Humankind is one of the world's most important sources of such information. Dolomitic caves are unstable structures. Their roofs frequently collapse, and their floors drop down into other cavities below them. This can make the dating of the different strata in a cave very difficult, but caves offer significant advantages to palaeoanthropologists conducting research. Fossils found in the caves of the Cradle are particularly informative because, unlike open fossil beds such as those in East Africa, the cave environment keeps the specimens *in situ* (i.e. in their original location), and restricts damage to them by the elements or by scavengers. Some fossils have been in their original place since the creatures entered the cave system millions of years ago. Caves also keep the fossils together with other fossils of plants and animals that lived at the same time, offering insights into the climatic and ecological conditions in which the creatures lived, the circumstances under which they died, and remnant clues about their way of life.

The collapse of the cave roof at Gladysvale in 2009 sealed one of the entrances and cut off the elevated walkway used by researchers for many years.

ost fossils are fragments of skeletal matter. Envisaging the complete morphology of an organism calls for skilled comparative anatomy, intuition and, often, a degree of guesswork from scientists. The discovery of a complete skeleton is exceptionally rare, and when it occurs it is important because it provides information about a species such as how its limbs were articulated, how it moved about in the landscape, its behaviour, and how it interacted with its environment. Complete skeletons give a far clearer picture of the role of the fossil in the evolutionary process than isolated fragments. In recent years, the complete or nearly complete skeletons of three different hominin species have been discovered in the Cradle. These have added immeasurably to our knowledge of human evolution and stimulated much scientific and public interest.

Between 3 and 1.5 million years ago climatic conditions continued to become cooler and drier on average, but within that trend Africa experienced a series of cycles of wet and dry periods, largely influenced by fluctuations in the Earth's orbit and the consequent Milankovitch cycles. Cold, dry periods peaked about 2.8, 1.7 and 1.0 million years ago, reducing the size of formerly widespread forests each time. Warmer conditions that existed between these periods of cold allowed for the partial revival of woodland, but with each cycle the expansion of the savannah and grassland biomes (which had begun 20 million years earlier) increased, at the expense of the forest.

During that time, the rate of evolutionary events, especially the emergence of new species, appears to have accelerated in response to climatic changes and habitat modification. Several species of hominin emerged and have been found in South Africa in the Cradle, Taung and Makopane's caves, and in East Africa.

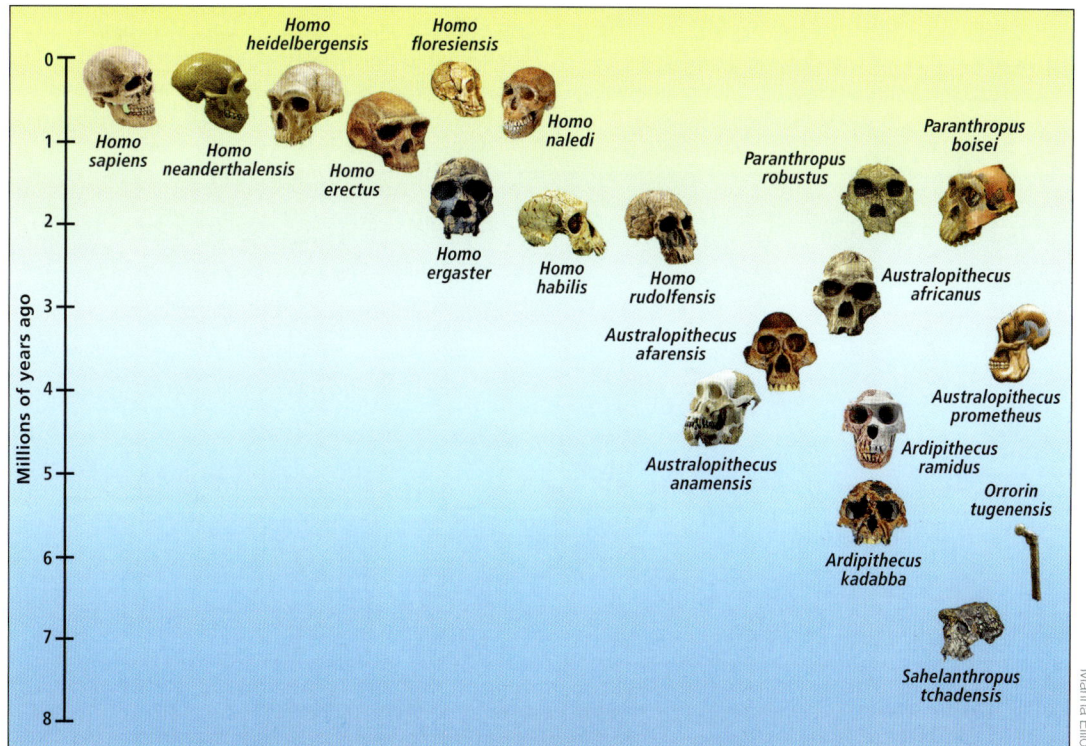

Marina Elliott

A composite chart of the hominin species. Changes in climate and habitat have led to the rapid evolution of new species and the probable extinction of others over the past five million years.

Age and evolutionary significance

Australopithecus prometheus is dated to 3.67 million years ago, which means it was contemporary with *Australopithecus afarensis* from East Africa and approaching the age of the oldest known member of the genus, *Australopithecus anamensis*. *Australopithecus prometheus* was first named and described in 1948 by Raymond Dart based on his find of the fossilised back of a brain case and an adolescent mandible from Makopane's Cave. The best-known and most important representative of the species, however, is the almost complete skeleton nicknamed Little Foot, discovered at Sterkfontein by Wits University palaeoanthropologist Ron Clarke. Some of its anatomical features, such as the large canine teeth and slightly splayed big toe, are primitive and similar to *Australopithecus anamensis*. It is therefore possible that *Australopithecus prometheus* could be an ancestor of *Paranthropus robustus.*

Discovery and naming of Little Foot

For many years *Australopithecus africanus* was the only species of that genus known to have occurred at Sterkfontein. Phillip Tobias, the head of the Anatomy Department at Wits University, and Alun Hughes, the director of Sterkfontein, had collected a large number fossil fragments from the caves over the years and in the 1980s Ron Clarke reconstructed a cranium from these fragments. Initially he did not attribute a specific name to the reconstructed cranium but, because of its distinct shape and larger teeth, he believed that it must be a different species of *Australopithecus.*

After the discovery of Little Foot in 1997, he recognised that the fragments of his earlier reconstruction and the Little Foot skeleton belonged to the same species which he named *Australopithecus prometheus*, the name originally given by Raymond Dart to a fossil from Makopane's

Kathleen Kuman

Ron Clarke, Stephen Motsumi and Nkwane Molefe looking at the Little Foot fossil soon after its discovery. It was found on a debris slope where it had died 3.7 million years before.

Cave some 50 years earlier. Clarke realised that his specimens from Sterkfontein and Dart's from Makopane were all the same species.

Prometheus was a Greek mythological Titan who angered the gods by giving fire to mortals; for this offence he was punished by being chained to a rock for all eternity. Dart chose this name for the species because of its association with fire, as some of the Makopane's Cave fossils appeared to have been charred (it was later shown that the black colour on them was caused by manganese staining). However, given the difficulties that Clarke experienced in extracting Little Foot from the rock, Prometheus's punishment makes the name even more appropriate.

The story of how Little Foot was discovered is a legend of serendipity and perseverance. In 1994, Tobias and Hughes suggested to Clarke that he should search for very old fossils in the Silberberg Grotto because of the great age of that section of the caves. In a box of faunal fossils that had been blasted from the cave by lime miners many years before, Clarke discovered the mis-sorted

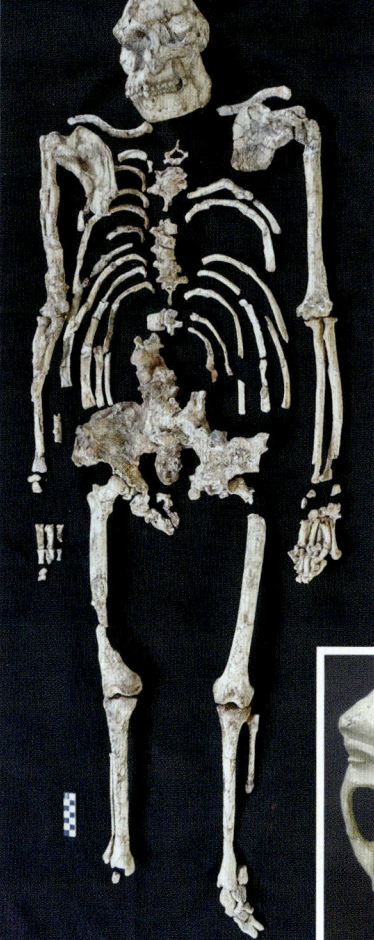

Ron Clarke

Right: The 3.7 million-year-old skeleton of *Australopithecus prometheus* shows anatomical differences when compared with other hominins, including relatively short arms.

Far right: The teeth of *Australopithecus prometheus* (left) are larger than those of *Australopithecus africanus* (right).

bones of a small *Australopithecus* left foot. Three years later, in 1997, he found more of the foot bones, as well the end of a shin bone and a foot bone from the right limb erroneously boxed with monkey and other animal fossils. The existence of portions of both legs and feet suggested that the rest of the skeleton might possibly still be in place, and he asked his two assistants, Stephen Motsumi and Nkwane Molefe, to try to find the rest of the shin bone which might still be embedded in the cave deposit. In a matter of two days, they found a perfect contact with the broken-through shaft of a right shin bone exposed in the breccia. Next to it was the broken-through shaft of the left shin bone. The hardness of the breccia and the soft condition of the bones made excavation of the fossil particularly difficult, especially as many of the bones were fragmented and scattered throughout the solid talus slope at different levels. It took Clarke and his team 20 years of slow and cautious work to locate, expose, clean and then reconstruct the fossils.

Anatomy

Little Foot is one of the most complete australopithecine skeletons yet discovered. This was probably a female who stood about 1.3m tall. The cranium is rounded at the

Marina Elliott

An aven opening into Sterkfontein Cave, similar to the one through which Little Foot might have fallen.

back, with a small sagittal crest and prominent cheekbones that anchored powerful chewing muscles. The teeth are comparatively large, with bulbous cusps and sharp, fairly well-developed canines. The low forehead and lack of a heavy brow ridge are also distinctive. Strong cheek muscles and large teeth suggest that this species survived on a diet of tough corms and other vegetable matter.

The hands and fingers of *Australopithecus prometheus* are shorter than those of apes, with a flat palm and opposing thumb that are suitable for grasping objects and the branches of trees. The legs are substantially longer than the arms, demonstrating permanent bipedal locomotion, and even though it retained tree-climbing capability, it would not have knuckle-walked as apes do, and as other very early hominins might have done.

The foot that gave it its nickname has a somewhat splayed big toe, useful for tree-climbing, but the heel is adapted for a well-developed stride.

The Australopithecus prometheus fossil when it was still deeply embedded in breccia and flowstone. It took two decades to extract it.

Most of the former were woodland species with a habit of climbing, and they probably fell while foraging around steep shafts or when using these as sleeping places. Bovids (antelopes and other grazing species that do not climb) are noticeably rare in the fossil assemblage in the Silberberg Grotto, but the takin-like *Makapania* is present. This may be an indication that the mosaic of habitats in this region included extensive forested areas around Sterkfontein at the time. None of the bones of Little Foot is gnawed, so it seems that the cave was never used as a den by carnivorous animals and was probably not accessible except through the avens. It seems likely that every animal preserved in the ancient grotto, including Little Foot, fell or was trapped there.

Little Foot died with one arm above its head on a debris slope, where the skeleton was cemented into breccia by calcareous sedimentation. Flowstone subsequently engulfed the body, and at a later stage erosion caused a collapse of the substrate and fractured the skeleton. In spite of this dismemberment, almost every bone has now been recovered.

Taphonomy

The avens that first brought daylight into the caves were death traps, and Little Foot was almost certainly a victim. Animals that fell into these shafts were in free fall from the roof of the cave to the floor, where they either died on impact or were trapped without an accessible exit. Little Foot died on a steep debris slope in the Silberberg Grotto, one of the oldest deposits in Sterkfontein. No other hominins have been found in this part of the cave, and most other fossils there have been those of extinct species of baboon and monkey and various members of the large cat and hyena families.

Dating Little Foot

The primary significance of *Australopithecus prometheus* is its completeness and extreme age, but establishing this with confidence has not been easy. The Silberberg Grotto has been known to be a particularly old part of Sterkfontein since the discovery of an ancient hyena fossil (*Chasmaporthetes*) there in 1946, but initial attempts to find an accurate date for Little Foot were based on the flowstones. This complicated the dating because these flowstones had developed long after fossilisation had taken place, and had intruded into cavities in the original breccia around the skeleton. A final date of 3.67 million years was determined using the cosmogenic isochronic burial dating technique (see 'Interlude 1: Measuring deep time' on pages 24–25).

Age and evolutionary significance

The juvenile *Australopithecus africanus* fossil from the limeworks at Taung, described by Raymond Dart in 1924, was to become one of the most important discoveries in the history of palaeoanthropology. Not only did it shift the focus of human origins to Africa, it completely revised our understanding of how human anatomy evolved. In particular it showed that the enlargement of the brain was not an early development in human evolution.

Many more fossils of *Australopithecus africanus* have since been recovered from the Cradle. They represent different age groups and both sexes over a long palaeontological record of 800,000 years. A great deal of information about the species has emerged since the 1920s and it has become the flagship species with which other fossil finds are inevitably compared.

Discovery and naming of *Australopithecus africanus*

Australopithecus africanus was the first hominin fossil to be discovered in South Africa. In 1924 a box of primate fossils from the Buxton lime quarry at Taung was brought to Raymond Dart, the recently appointed Professor of Anatomy at the University of the Witwatersrand that had been founded just two years earlier. Among the fossils in the box was a small cranium that differed from the others. Using improvised kitchen implements, Dart extracted it from the breccia matrix, exposing the skull of a four-year-old child with facial and jaw bones intact, and a perfectly preserved endocast of the brain. He published a description of it in the scientific journal *Nature* a few months later, and named it *Australopithecus africanus*, declaring that it was probably an ancestor of *Homo sapiens.* It was an extravagant claim from a little-known

Marina Elliott

The discovery of the Taung Child, *Australopithecus africanus*, in 1924 changed our understanding of human evolution.

Marina Elliott

'Mrs Ples', as she is commonly known, is one of the most celebrated fossils from Sterkfontein. Unlike most fossils, the skull is relatively undamaged by rock pressure.

anatomist at a new and obscure university, and it was almost unanimously dismissed by the established scientific community.

There were two main reasons for the rejection. First, the skull was that of a juvenile and most evolutionists at the time thought that it might merely be a young extinct ape. Dart needed an adult specimen to prove his claim. Second, and more importantly, the small brain directly contradicted the accepted view that human development had begun with the growth of the brain, as evidenced by Piltdown Man (see pages 94–96).

Robert Broom, the Curator of Palaeontology at the Transvaal Museum, discovered the first specimen of *Australopithecus africanus* (then named *Plesianthropus transvaalensis*) at Sterkfontein in 1936 and realised that it was the adult specimen required to confirm Dart's theory. A better specimen discovered later was nicknamed Mrs Ples. However, it was not until the Piltdown Man fraud was revealed in 1953 that the importance of *Australopithecus africanus* was internationally acknowledged.

Anatomy

Australopithecus africanus is a small-bodied species weighing 30kg to 45kg and standing 1.2m to 1.4m tall. The brain size is between 400cc and 500cc – slightly larger than in chimpanzees, but smaller than in most other hominins. The rounded forehead rises from a slightly projecting face which, when comparing the Taung Child with adult skulls, appears to become more prominent with age. The teeth, including the canines, are small, and set in a lightly built mandible which, together with the delicate cheek bones, is often described as 'gracile'. The smaller teeth may indicate that *Australopithecus africanus* had a more varied and nutritious diet than the largely vegetarian *Australopethicus prometheus*.

The pelvis is broad, similar to that of humans, and the lower limbs indicate that it was bipedal. The arms are relatively long in proportion to the legs, so it still retained the ability to climb trees. The hands appear to have had considerable dexterity, with relatively long opposing thumbs. The metacarpals show that it had a flat palm and strong insertion points for thumb muscles, while

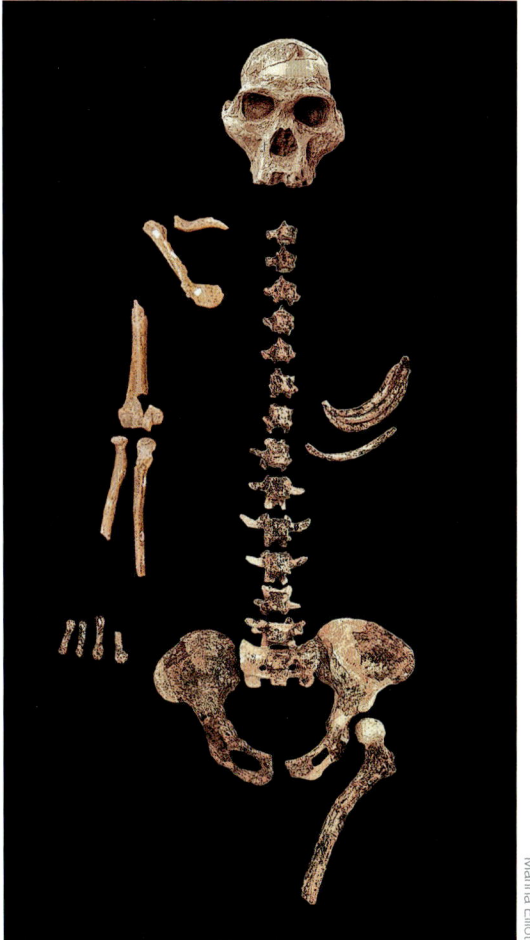

Marina Elliott

The pelvis and lower limbs of *Australopithecus africanus* show human-like adaptations while arboreal features such as long arms and a small brain are still evident.

broad fingertips gave it the ability to grip objects firmly and precisely. The end of the radius bone that connects with the wrist is flattened, as it is in humans. No tools have been associated with any of the *Australopithecus africanus* fossils, so it is probable that hands were used for manipulating general objects rather than for tool-making.

Males of the *Australopithecus africanus* species were only slightly larger than females and this, together with their small canine teeth, suggests that males were less competitive than male apes, which have relatively large canines. Molecular analysis of differences in strontium isotope levels of tooth enamel indicates that females dispersed from their immediate family gene pool to mate with outsiders, while males remained in their natal groups and were more closely related to one another.

Habitat

During the time of the existence of *Australopithecus africanus*, the climate of Africa became warmer and wetter after the glacial period of 2.8 million years ago. Patches of woodland that had been pushed back during the colder era began to revive as gallery forest interspersed with wooded savannah. In the strata of the Sterkfontein Cave where most of the *Australopithecus africanus* fossils have been found, palaeobotanist Marion Bamford, the current director of the Evolutionary Studies Institute at Wits University, has identified petrified wood from a liana named *Dichapetalum mombuttense* which today occurs in the tropical forests of the Congo. She has also found remains of *Anastrabe integerrima*, a shrub that grows on the margins of forests. It seems therefore that *Australopithecus africanus*, like many emergent hominin species, lived in the mixed woodland ecotone between forest and open woodland, in a habitat that was probably similar to the semi-tropical regions of KwaZulu-Natal today.

Fossil lianas similar to these have been recovered from Sterkfontein and show that the habitat of *Australopithecus africanus* included gallery forest.

Taphonomy and other species

In the fossil assemblages in which *Australopithecus africanus* has been found, almost all the bones are fragmented. Raymond Dart originally attributed this to the bloodthirsty nature of our ancestors, who broke bones to make weapons, not only for hunting but also for slaughtering each other. He called it the osteodontokeratic[13] culture and it was popularised by the writer Robert Ardrey in his books *The Territorial Imperative*, *African*

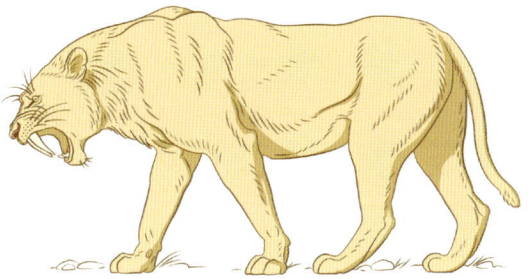

One of the species of sabre-toothed cats that may have preyed on *Australopithecus africanus*. The long upper canines were thrust down forcefully into the skull of its prey.

Colobine monkeys shared the Cradle forest with *Australopithecus africanus*. Today, their descendants occur only in central African forests. The ancestors of existing southern African monkey species did not occur in the Cradle area at that time.

Genesis and others. Research by Bob Brain at Swartkrans in the 1960s completely reversed Dart's theory. His analysis of many thousands of bones revealed that *Australopithecus africanus* was neither a weapon-maker nor a hunter. The protein in its omnivorous diet probably came from eating insects and other small creatures. The analysis also demonstrated that, together with antelope, three-toed horses, warthogs and monkeys in the fossil bed, the little hominin was the prey of some of the most powerful predators at the time. The caves in which they were found were evidently the feeding dens of extinct hunting hyenas, leopards and sabre-toothed cats.

Two species of sabre-toothed cats of the genera *Megantereon* and *Homotherium* are represented in the Cradle cave deposits. Unlike felines such as leopards, sabre-toothed cats killed by driving their long, serrated canines downwards into their victims. Powerful muscles connected from the neck to the top of their head gave enormous strength to the downward thrust, while the lower jaw opened wide to keep it out of the way. Tooth punctures in the skulls of several *Australopithecus africanus* show that they met their fate in this way.

Among the prey species found in the predators' dens was a large bovid the size of a water buffalo, *Makapania broomi*, which demonstrates the physical power that the predators must have had to bring it down.

Marina Elliott

The extinct wide-horned buffalo *Makapania broomi* is among the faunal fossils found in Sterkfontein Cave.

13 *Osteo* = bone; *donto* = teeth; *keratic* = claw

Age and evolutionary significance

The discovery of *Paranthropus robustus* at Kromdraai by Robert Broom in 1938 revealed for the first time that more than one species of hominin had existed at the same time and in the same place. Thus, human evolution had not been a single, linear progression, as scientists had previously thought. A large number of fossils of this species have now been recovered from numerous sites in the Cradle, especially from Drimolen where palaeoanthropologist André Keyser of Wits University found particularly good examples of crania and mandibles during the 1990s. The dates of these fossils overlap with those of late *Australopithecus* and early *Homo* species.

The robust dentition and skull suggest that this species may have descended from *Australopithecus prometheus* after a divergence from the *Australopithecus* line of evolution.

Discovery and naming

In 1938 Gert Terblanche, a local schoolboy, showed George Barlow, the quarry manager of Sterkfontein lime mine, a hominin palate with one molar in place. Terblanche gave guided tours to visitors, and had found the fossil on the neighbouring farm, Kromdraai. Barlow showed the fossil to Robert Broom, who recognised that it was distinctly different from the *Australopithecus africanus* fossils already discovered, and that it was embedded in a matrix different from that at Sterkfontein. Terblanche led Broom to the Kromdraai site 3km away, where the rest of the fragmented skull and more teeth were recovered. Broom named it

The Kromdraai fossil site where Robert Broom discovered *Paranthropus robustus*.

Marina Elliott

Paranthropus robustus has a distinct sagittal crest on top of the skull to which strong chewing muscles were attached.

Paranthropus robustus based on its distinctively large dentition and chewing muscles rather than a particularly robust body. Fossils of the body below the cranium are scarce, but those that are known show that it was not much larger or more robust than other gracile (slight-framed) hominins.

Despite this early success, subsequent excavations at the site yielded only a few more fossils. But in 1950 a more complete skull of a young *Paranthropus robustus* was found at Swartkrans, and many others have since been discovered at other sites, confirming the unusual morphology and Broom's designation of a new hominin species.

Anatomy

Paranthropus robustus was about the same weight and height as *Australopithecus* (about 40kg and 1.2m tall) but it had a slightly larger brain (about 500cc). Its defining characteristics were its massive premolar and molar teeth, a sagittal crest on the male skull to which powerful jaw muscles would have been attached, and the widely flared cheekbones (zygomatic arches) that also supported strong chewing muscles. The species was evidently specialised for a diet that required heavy mastication of tough, fibrous fruit, nuts and roots which might have become more abundant with the spread of mixed savannah. Some recent research shows that these types of foods may not have been the only components of its diet, but they would have enabled it to occupy specialised feeding niches that did not conflict with other species, and therefore to have co-existed with other competitive hominins at the time.

Ron Clarke & J.L. Heaton

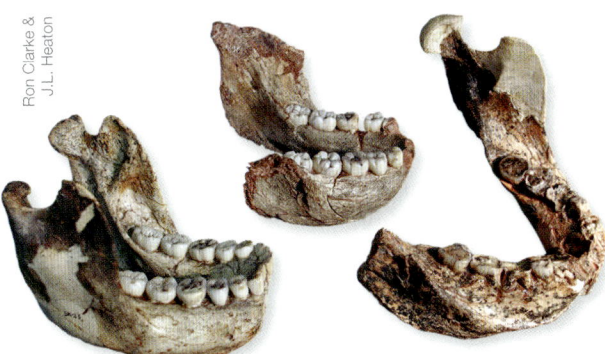

The massive jaw and robust dentition of *Paranthropus robustus* are evident in these three fossils from the Cradle.

This species appears to have been less bipedal (and therefore more arboreal) than other hominins. The limbs show pelvic and lower limb morphology indicative of a 'rolling' gait not well developed to move long distances on open ground. Only a few fossil fragments of upper limbs and hand bones have been found, but they too show that it had a strong grip and climbing ability suitable for an arboreal existence in the woodland-savannah habitat of the Cradle at that time.

Taphonomy and ecology

Paranthropus robustus existed during a period when the lush woodland and warm weather that *Australopithecus africanus* had experienced were declining, and the climate was generally becoming cool and dry. The arboreal adaptations that the species retained, however, would have allowed it to move about in the copses of trees and marginal forest that remained around the Cradle-Magaliesberg area. Slightly warmer conditions returned before the species became extinct but may have had little impact on its evolutionary adaptation.

Paranthropus robustus has been found in the same fossil strata as *Homo ergaster*, along with the stone tools and controlled fire associated with that species. However, the size of its brain, its lack of specialised articulated hands, and a partly arboreal lifestyle all suggest that it probably did not make or use tools, even in the later stages of its existence.

➤ 1.9 million years ago: Closer to human – *Australopithecus sediba*

Age and evolutionary significance

Australopithecus sediba has been found at a single site, Malapa, in the John Nash Nature Reserve. It is particularly informative because not only were multiple skeletons recovered together, two of them are more than 50 per cent complete and they represent different age cohorts, possibly within one family or a single small tribal group.

They have been dated at 1.98 million years ago, using two uranium-to-lead isotopes. This unusually accurate palaeomagnetic dating was possible because one of the rare inversions of the magnetic field (when the north and south magnetic poles are reversed) occurred during the deposition of flowstone around the fossil. The species is the most recent member of the *Australopithecus* genus. Although we cannot make assumptions about direct lineage between species, it is likely that *Australopithecus sediba* evolved from *Australopithecus africanus* and it may possibly be ancestral to the genus *Homo*.

Discovery and naming

The first fossil fragments of *Australopithecus sediba* were found by Lee Berger's young son, Matthew, while they were exploring a sinkhole and lime mine in the John Nash Nature Reserve. On revisiting the site two weeks later with a team of students, Berger discovered parts of what promised to be a complete skeleton of a juvenile hominin in soft, decomposing breccia in the pit. Later, a second and third skeleton were discovered, making this one of the most complete discoveries of a hominin species.

The site also contained numerous fossils of other animals that may have fallen to their death in the sinkhole. Berger named the species *sediba*, the Setswana word for a fountain or well, because of the likelihood that the site had been filled with water. However, when deciding on the genus, his team chose *Australopithecus* rather than *Homo* after the balance of features of both genera had been fully considered.

Jane Carruthers

Lee Berger and his son Matthew at the Malapa site shortly after the discovery of *Australopithecus sediba* in 2008.

Anatomy

The juvenile male and adult female specimens recovered from Malapa are both about 1.3m tall. The cranial capacity is small (420cc–450cc), but CT scans show that the brain may have had an unusual configuration. The impressions of the frontal lobes were similar to the frontal lobes of earlier fossils, while the position of the olfactory bulbs was more like that of humans. This suggests that some cognitive developments may have taken place before the evolution of a larger brain. Part of the breccia attached to one of the fossils has been retained to allow further research. The reduced jaw, small teeth and facial structure are also similar to later *Homo* species. The wide pelvis, robust, vertically oriented hips and thin pubic symphysis (the lower joint of the pelvis) all show that it was comfortably bipedal, and the weight of each stride seems to have been taken on the outer edge of the foot as is the case with humans.

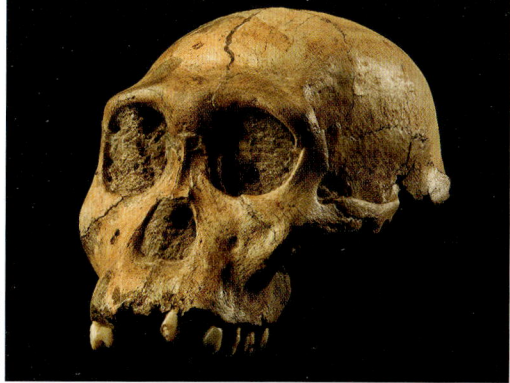

Marina Elliott

The low brow of the *Australopithecus sediba* cranium is indicative of the small brain capacity.

The hand also has some human-like aspects but the curved fingers, wrist features and relatively long arms indicate that *Australopithecus sediba* retained some climbing ability. The leg bones (femur and tibia) and heel are akin to those of *Australopithecus africanus*, but the foot is arched, and may have had an Achilles tendon. Therefore, although *Australopithecus sediba* may not have walked in exactly the same way as modern humans, it was clearly comfortably bipedal. Overall,

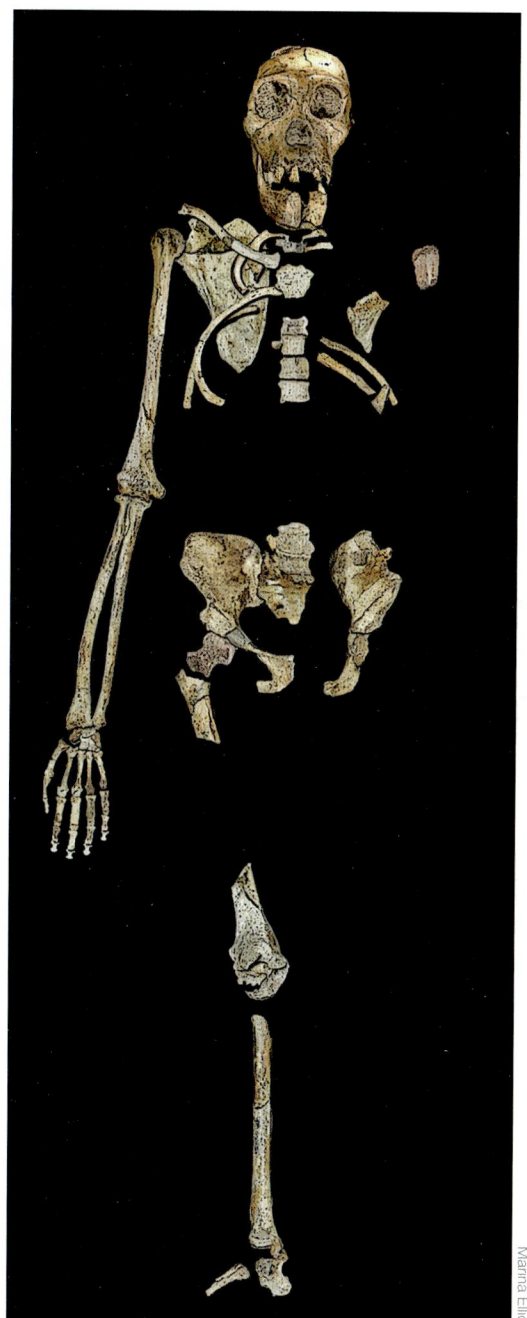

Marina Elliott

The almost complete skeleton of *Australopithecus sediba* is similar in many respects to *Australopithecus africanus* but shows several human-like features.

The landscape around the Malapa site has probably changed very little since the time of *Australopithecus sediba* two million years ago.

the skeleton has a body more like that of other australopithecines than of later hominins. It also shows that changes in the pelvis and dentition occurred before changes in limb proportions or cranial capacity, and this suggests that there was no single package of traits that led to subsequent evolutionary developments.

Ecology

A wide variety of fossils of other animals has been recovered from Malapa, including carnivores, herbivores and primates, and these, together with the group of hominins, suggest that the Malapa site may have been the scene of some unknown catastrophe that caused significant numbers of deaths.

Australopithecus sediba was also contemporary with *Paranthropus robustus* for some of its existence, at a time when the region was experiencing a cool, dry climate transitional between the lush, forested warmth of the *Australopithecus africanus* habitat and the cold grasslands in which the genus *Homo* evolved. The environment would have been characterised by savannah interspersed with patches of forest, not unlike conditions there today.

THE VIEWING PLATFORM AT MALAPA

Malapa, the site of the discovery of *Australopithecus sediba*, can be viewed from one of the most remarkable architectural structures in the Cradle. Designed by architect Krynauw Nel, the elliptical platform is suspended above the fossil site on eight insect-like steel legs that are bolted into selected outcrops of dolomite rock. These bolts constitute the total footprint of disturbance of the site, and add up to less than the size of an A5 sheet of paper. The legs are articulated, and the structure can be 'walked' to different viewing positions as excavations proceed. Up to 48 visitors can observe the excavation from the deck without obstructing the work or touching the sensitive substrate where the fossils are being found. A crane and gantry are slung below the viewing platform to lift large blocks of fossil-bearing rock.

To minimise disturbance to the fragile landscape, the structure was assembled and tested on a rugby field before being erected in pieces over the Malapa site. Hidden among the trees and camouflaged by its form, materials and colour, it is almost invisible to anyone approaching the site along the raised walkway. Once on the platform, the viewer looks down into the depths of the exposed cave that is illuminated by daylight from a round opening in the roof. The white ceiling reflects and amplifies the illumination, but nowhere is this visible from the surrounding landscape.

This amazing combination of aesthetics, engineering and environmental sensitivity has received many accolades and awards, and it is loaded with symbolism. Nel explains that the oval shape and entry way depict a hand mirror, reflecting the past from the cave below, while the shoulders of the articulated legs represent the clavicle bone which was the first fossil fragment found on the site by Matthew Berger.

The award-winning viewing platform overlooking the Malapa fossil site.

7 | THE HUMAN GENUS

This chapter describes the fossil discoveries in the Cradle that have been assigned to *Homo*, the genus that includes human beings and those extinct species that appear to have been closely related to us. Humans are the sole surviving member of this genus. The taxonomic hierarchy of the genus is shown below.

Taxonomic classification of *Homo*

KINGDOM	Animal
PHYLUM	Vertebrate (possesses a spinal column)
CLASS	Mammal (has hair; suckles young)
ORDER	Primate (hands that can grasp; bifocal vision; flat finger nails)
FAMILY	Hominids (includes orangutans, gorillas, chimpanzees, humans)
TRIBE	Hominins (humans and their fossil ancestors)
GENUS	*Homo* (as opposed to *Australopithecus, Paranthropus* and other hominin genera)
CRADLE SPECIES	*Homo habilis* *Homo ergaster* *Homo naledi* *Homo sapiens* (human beings)

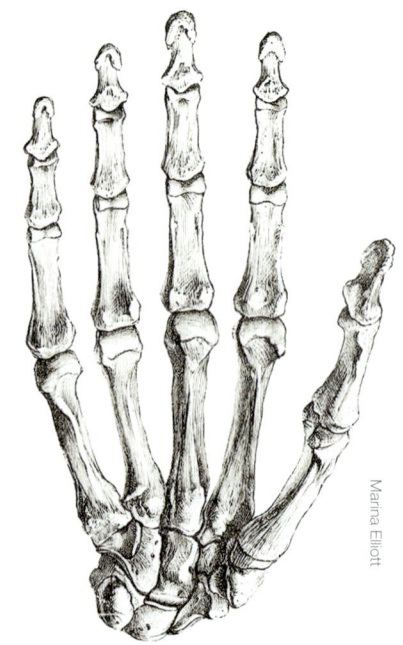

The difficulty in applying zoological taxonomy to fossil species is discussed on pages 104–105 in the text box on Fossil taxonomy, and those problems extend to the allocation of species to genera. In zoology, a genus is defined as a group of species descended from a common ancestor. In live animals this can generally be determined by DNA sequencing, and the group of species with a common ancestor can be placed in one genus. With fossils, however, a common ancestor can seldom be established scientifically. Palaeoanthropologists therefore define each genus in terms of a collection of physical attributes that suggest that several species have significant characteristics in common.

Until recently the most definitive feature of the genus *Homo* was the ability to use and make tools – skills associated with hand articulation and brain size.

Marina Elliott

Early palaeoanthropologists defined the genus *Homo* in terms of attributes such as a relatively large brain (larger than 700cc), small dentition without prominent canines, a hand anatomy consistent with making tools, arms shorter than legs, and a fully erect bipedal stance suitable for existence in grassland savannah. However, with the discovery of more fossil evidence, these attributes are no longer regarded as belonging only to *Homo*. For example, the defining characteristic of tool-making, which was once ascribed to *Homo* alone, cannot always be attributed to a fossil with certainty: some of the most primitive hominins had hands that were anatomically capable of making tools, even if they did not necessarily use them for that purpose.

Currently, palaeoanthropologists include species in the genus *Homo* based on an informed assessment of observed human-like features in the fossil. They often disagree with each other on these taxonomic assessments, and so the allocation of a species to one genus or another is seldom definitive or even useful. The four species described in this chapter have all been accepted for the present as members of the genus *Homo*, although this may change with time.

➤ 2.3–1.8 million years ago: The Earlier Stone Age – *Homo habilis*

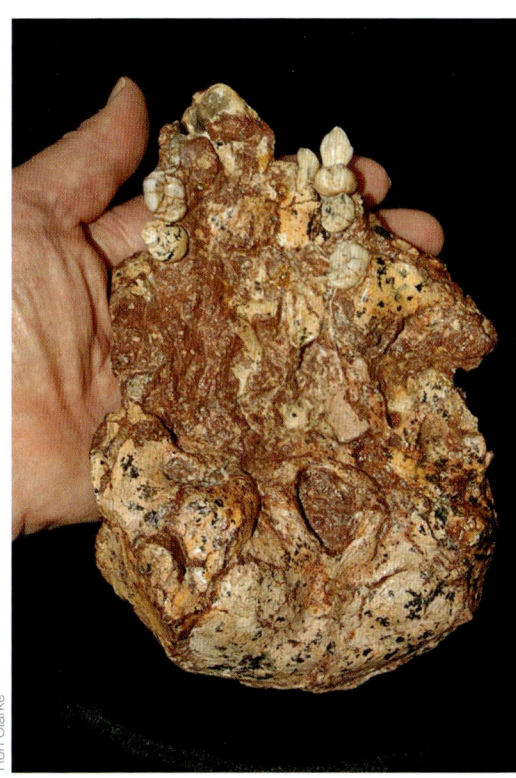

Ron Clarke

The distinctive underside of the partial cranium of *Homo habilis* from Swartkrans, reconstructed by Ron Clarke.

Age and evolutionary significance

For many decades *Homo habilis*[14] was regarded as the earliest hominin to have made and used stone tools. Many of the fossils assigned to this species come from East Africa, but only two fossil fragments have been recovered from the Cradle and assigned to *Homo habilis*. One is an infant from Sterkfontein, and the other a juvenile discovered by Robert Broom at Swartkrans. However, primitive Oldowan tools from Sterkfontein have been dated at 2.18 million years ago, which indicates that *Homo habilis* or some other tool-making hominin was evidently active for much longer than the fossil record of *Homo habilis* shows.

Fossils that have been attributed to *Homo habilis* are distributed in South and East Africa, and the variety of dates for them indicates that this species existed for half a million years. Across that timespan and geographic range, there is wide morphological variation, and palaeoanthropologists differ in their opinions about whether some of these fossils should be classified as *Homo* or *Australopithecus*. For many years Phillip Tobias held the view that *Australopithecus africanus* developed into *Homo habilis*, which then developed into *Homo ergaster* (which he called early *Homo erectus*). However, based on more recent discoveries and

14 *Homo* = man; *habilis* = handy

better dating, Ron Clarke and other palaeontologists disagree with this view because the evidence suggests that *Australopithecus africanus* may have been contemporary with early *Homo*.

Recent discoveries of very early specimens in Asia suggest that *Homo habilis* rather than *Homo ergaster* may have been the first hominin to venture out of Africa.

Discovery and naming

Homo habilis was first named in 1964 to refer to fossils from Beds I and II in Olduvai Gorge, Tanzania. It was described by three luminaries in the palaeoanthropological world: Louis Leakey, Phillip Tobias and John Napier. The first of these fossils, found in 1960, was from a sedimentary deposit rich in Oldowan stone tools and broken-up bones that date to about 1.8 million years ago. Raymond Dart suggested the name *habilis*, meaning 'handy', because the fossil was presumed to represent the maker of the tools.

A partial skull discovered in the Cradle in 1976 by Alun Hughes, director of Sterkfontein, was classified as *Homo habilis* because it was thought (incorrectly) to be associated with Oldowan tools that were found in the same strata. American palaeoanthropologist Donald Johanson also

attributed it to *Homo habilis*; but Ron Clarke has reconstructed the cranium from component parts and believes that it is a late specimen of *Australopithecus africanus*. Despite this taxonomic uncertainty and the fact that the number of fossils is meagre and fragmentary, the two Cradle specimens currently attributed to *Homo habilis* by Ron Clarke are the only South African representatives of the species until further evidence becomes available.

Anatomy

The brain capacity of the *Homo habilis* fossils found in the Cradle is not known, but Broom noted that the brain of the juvenile from Swartkrans was larger than that of *Paranthropus*. The face was less protruding than that of *Australopithecus*, with teeth slightly larger than in *Homo ergaster*, and the arms were proportionately shorter than in the australopithecines.

The Oldowan tool industry

The ability to make tools is the attribute most often emphasised in *Homo habilis*, and it was once regarded as the fundamental distinction between the genus *Homo* and earlier hominin genera.

Oldowan tools (named after the Olduvai Gorge in Tanzania where they were first found) are very

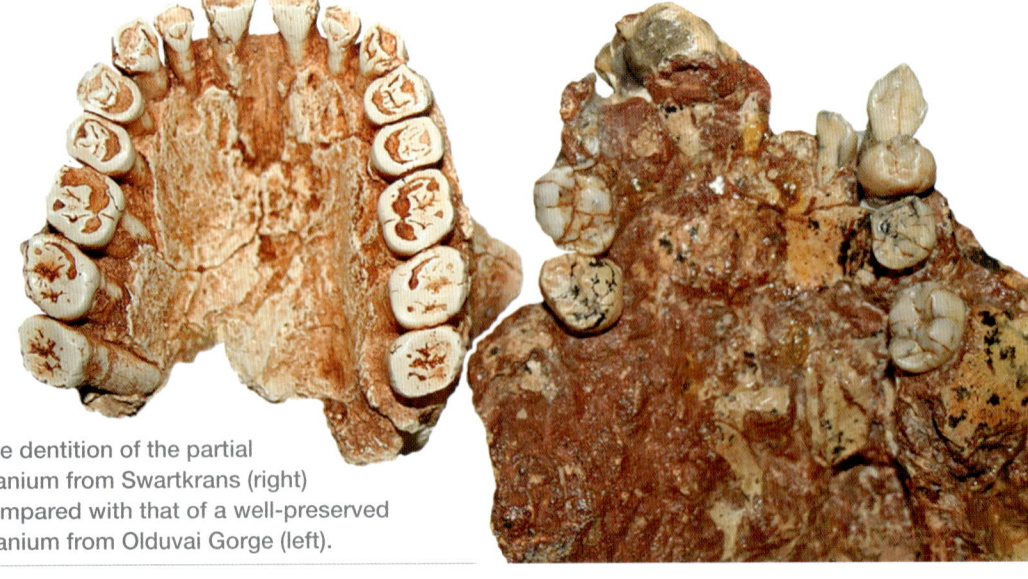

The dentition of the partial cranium from Swartkrans (right) compared with that of a well-preserved cranium from Olduvai Gorge (left).

Ron Clarke

Kathleen Kuman

Kathleen Kuman

Oldowan flakes (above) and a core stone (above right) from which flakes have been struck have been recovered from strata associated with *Homo habilis* at Sterkfontein. These early tools are about two million years old.

early stone tools made by chipping one or two flakes from a stone to give it a sharp edge for chopping or scraping. They are found at Earlier Stone Age sites in East Africa and they are present at Sterkfontein and Swartkrans, where they have been washed into the

caves from surface accumulations at cave entrances where they were manufactured. The Oldowan tools of Sterkfontein have been dated at about 2.18 million years and were possibly used by a hominin species even before the complete evolution of *Homo habilis*. The materials used were carefully selected. Quartz was favoured because it produced durable, sharp-edged flakes; chert was also used, especially at Swartkrans, and quartzite was collected at both sites from nearby river gravels.

From about 1.7 million years ago, the more sophisticated Acheulean tools appear in Africa. These were typically worked by knapping off a number of flakes to form pear-shaped or wedge-shaped scrapers. They were made and used by *Homo ergaster* at Sterkfontein. The name is derived from St Acheul, a village near Amiens in northern France where tools of this type were discovered.

➤ 1.9–1 million years ago: Fire and emigration – *Homo ergaster*

Age and evolutionary significance

Homo ergaster[15] was the first hominin to show fully modern body proportions and is widely regarded as being a direct ancestor of *Homo sapiens*. Its brain was less than 1,000cc, smaller than that of a modern human, which is about 1,400cc, but substantially larger than that of *Australopithecus* species, which are under 500cc.

During the long period of its existence, between almost two million and a million years ago, two significant evolutionary developments took place: hominins learned to control and use fire, and they developed more advanced tool-making technology. For a long time scientists believed that *Homo ergaster* was the first species to migrate from Africa to other continents, but there is now evidence that an earlier species of *Homo* may have entered Asia more than two million years ago.

15 *Homo* = man; *ergaster* = working

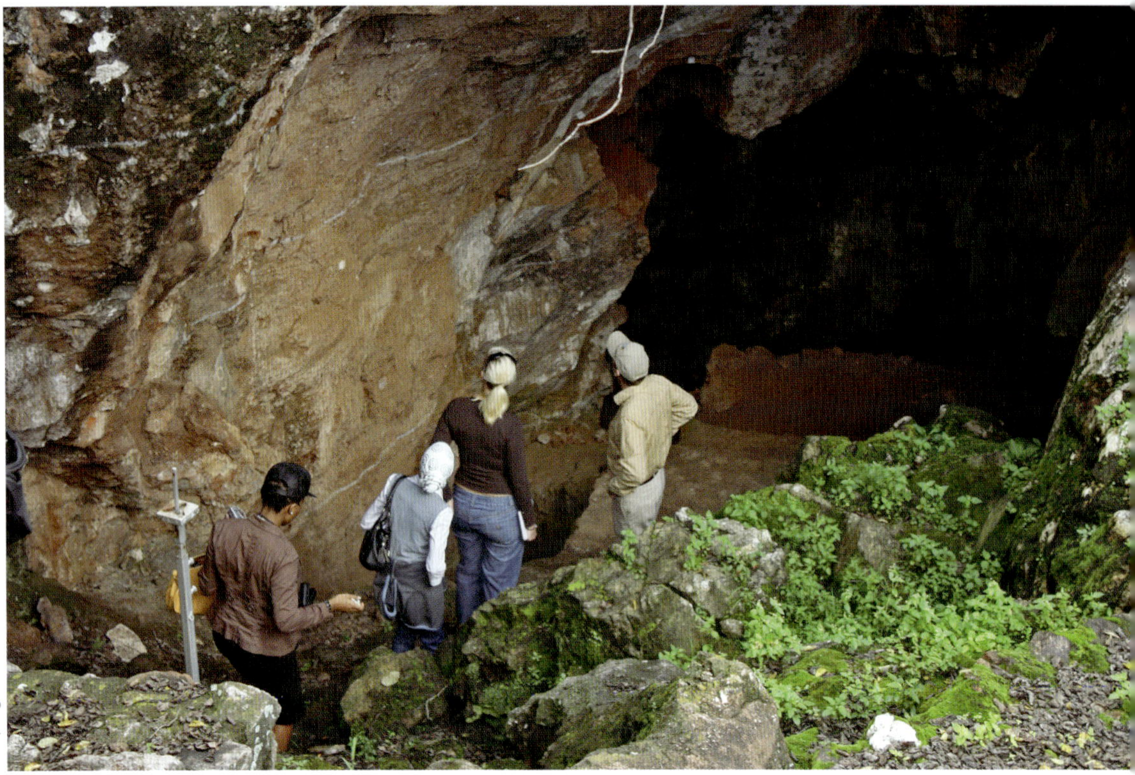

The Swartkrans site where Bob Brain found evidence of *Homo ergaster* and fire.

Discovery and naming

In 1949, a mandible, a mandible fragment and a partial upper jaw were recovered from Swartkrans and named *Telanthropus capensis* by Robert Broom and his colleague John Robinson. Twenty years later, Ron Clarke joined the upper jaw to a larger part of a cranium that had previously been classed as *Paranthropus*; Clarke identified it as belonging to the genus *Homo*, and subsequent scientists have considered it to be *Homo ergaster*.

The first specimen named as *Homo ergaster* was an isolated mandible recovered from Lake Turkana in 1971 by a member of Richard Leakey's field team. It was originally considered to be *'Homo, species*

The distinctive facial structure of a partial cranium of *Homo ergaster*, reconstructed from fragments (right) recovered from Swartkrans in the 1950s, is compared here with a cranium (left) from Lake Turkana, Kenya.

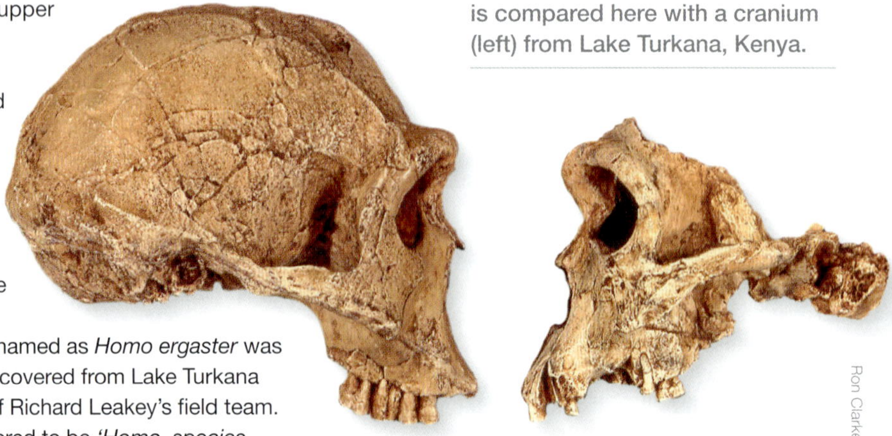

indeterminate', and in 1975 it was designated the type specimen of a new species, *Homo ergaster*, by Colin Groves and Vratislav Mazák.

A very similar species, *Homo erectus*,[16] is known from Asia, and dated to at least 1.5 million years ago. Many scientists consider *Homo ergaster* to be an early ancestral form of the species *Homo erectus* and thus they regard both of them as *Homo erectus*. Others regard *Homo ergaster* as a separate species ancestral to *Homo sapiens*. *Homo ergaster* is generally considered to be the more primitive form, and is the only one that is known from the Cradle or, indeed, from Africa. It existed for almost a million years with only very slight variations in anatomy during that long period. Its probable ancestral status is therefore accepted here.

Anatomy

No full skeletons of *Homo ergaster* have been found in the Cradle, but a skeleton from Nariokotome in Kenya shows that it had a general appearance that was decidedly human: a tall, erect posture with long legs and no special arboreal adaptations. Its brain capacity was about 850cc – about half or two-thirds of that of modern humans. The face was short, with a pronounced brow ridge over the eyes. The jaws were lightly built, and the nasal bones projected forward, unlike *Australopithecus* which had flat nasal bones. The sides of the brain case were less expanded than in modern humans, and there was a slight keel along the top of the skull.

Right: *Homo ergaster* exhibited a stature and physique very similar to *Homo sapiens* but with a somewhat smaller brain and a pronounced brow ridge over the eyes. This species is widely regarded as being a direct ancestor of *Homo sapiens*.

Technology

At Swartkrans, Bob Brain of the Transvaal Museum discovered evidence of the controlled use of fire by *Homo ergaster*: burnt bone fragments that had been subjected to prolonged heat, as occurs in a campfire, as opposed to superficial veld-fire damage. The bones are thought to have been heated in campfires at the surface and washed into the cave, where they have accumulated in a 1 million-year-old deposit. It seems, therefore, that fire management was mastered by hominins between 1.4 million and 1 million years ago. Initially, they probably collected burning embers from natural fires, and carefully kept them smouldering in the cave for later use. It was very much later, possibly only after the evolution of *Homo sapiens,* that the ability to ignite fire deliberately was learned.

The use of fire was a considerable advantage in the development of humanity. It gave warmth and protection from predators; it extended the productive hours of the day; and, most importantly, it provided the ability to cook meat and digest it more readily. Access to a more diverse and protein-rich diet improved hominins' physical and mental capabilities. It also resulted in the stomach region being smaller in *Homo ergaster* than it had been in the vegetarian or fruit-eating hominins.

Above: The controlled use of fire, evidence of which was discovered at Swartkrans, would have had a significant effect on the evolution and development of *Homo ergaster*.

The use of fire probably happened at the same time as the development of Acheulean stone-cutting tools, which are characterised by distinctive heavy-duty hand axes and cleavers that are typically associated with *Homo ergaster* in Africa. Unlike earlier, more primitive, Oldowan cores and flake tools, the Acheulean tools were skilfully faceted for specific purposes. Sharp-edged cleavers and pointed hand axes enabled users to butcher meat and perform other functions, such as digging for roots or working wood. They may even have enabled their users to hunt for meat rather than to depend merely on scavenging. These simple instruments represented a major technological leap forward, and were the dominant toolkit of humanity from 1.76 million years ago until they began to be phased out about 300,000 years ago. This is a time span four times longer than the entire period that *Homo sapiens* has existed.

Kathleen Kuman

For more than a million years Acheulean tools like this hand axe and cleaver were the prinicipal instruments of hominin survival.

Distribution and mobility

Tools are essentially a means of accessing food, and the *Homo ergaster* toolkit and use of fire might have enabled it to survive in more varied habitats and climates. Armed with these capabilities, the species was able to spread beyond the African continent into central Europe and Asia about 1.5 million years ago.

Homo ergaster was generally believed by scientists to have been the first hominin to migrate out of Africa, but recent discoveries in Asia suggest that it may have been preceded by an earlier species such as *Homo habilis* about 2 million years ago.

➤ 335,000–236,000 years ago: The enigma – *Homo naledi*

Age and evolutionary significance

Homo naledi [17] differs significantly from any other hominin yet described, and many aspects of the species present an evolutionary enigma. Its scientific significance lies not only in its unusual anatomy, age and taphonomy, but also in the novel way in which it was discovered and retrieved from the depths.

Dated between 335,000 and 236,000 years ago, it is the most recently deposited fossil in the Cradle other than *Homo sapiens*. It is characterised by a unique combination of human and pre-human morphology, and the relatively recent age means that *Homo naledi* and *Homo sapiens* may have been contemporary and perhaps lived in the same area. This means it could not have been an ancestor of *Homo sapiens*, and the two species probably split from a common ancestor in the distant past.

The Rising Star cave site has yielded an exceptional volume of skeletal material. To date 2,000 fossils representing 18 individuals have been recovered from the two subterranean chambers – the single largest discovery of a hominin species in Africa, and one of the largest assemblages of such material in the world. This collection of fossils provides a great deal of information, but it also poses many puzzling questions.

17 *Homo* = man; *naledi* = star, after the Rising Star cave system where the fossils were found

The discovery of *Homo naledi* provided science with a new perspective on hominin evolution.

Marina Elliott

Discovery and extraction

In 2013 the fossils were discovered by three speleologists, Rick Hunter, Steven Tucker and Pedro Boshoff, in the depths of the Rising Star cave system. That part of the cave, later named the Dinaledi Chamber, was accessible only through an extremely narrow and dangerous passage. Lee Berger put together an international team of scientists who were qualified palaeoanthropologists, athletic cavers, and physically small enough to fit through the passage. The first scientists to enter the cave and begin to excavate the fossil assemblage were Marina Elliott and Becca Peixotto.

E. Feuregel

Palaeoanthropologist Becca Peixotto working in the cramped and dangerous conditions of the Dinaledi Chamber.

The fossils of *Homo naledi* were scattered over the floor of the cave in soft sedimentary deposits. The chamber contains no other species.

The volume of material demanded a particularly large team and the number of scientists working on the fossils once they had been extracted eventually numbered more than 50; among them were geologists, palaeobotanists, climatologists, biochemists and anatomists, as well as scientists from other disciplines.

Anatomy

With almost every bone in *Homo naledi*'s body represented multiple times in the fossils found, scientists have been able to reconstruct what it looked like with more accuracy than for almost any other hominin. The brain is similar in size to that of *Australopithecus* (465cc–610cc), but it shares with other species of *Homo* a relatively high, thin cranial vault and a flexed occipital region – meaning that the neck could be flexed like a human neck and not held rigid like that of an ape. The size of the cranium is no larger than that of much earlier fossil species but the shape of the internal surface suggests that the frontal lobe may have given this species greater intellectual ability.

The teeth are remarkably uniform, relatively smooth, and thickly enamelled. Primitive multi-rooted upper molars become larger towards the back of the jaw. The canines are unique, showing a leaf-shaped morphology unlike that of any other known hominin.

Adults were slightly smaller than modern humans, about 1.3m to 1.5m tall and weighing 40kg to 50kg. The shoulders are ape-like, and the fingers are curved to facilitate climbing, but they are combined with a human-like wrist and a long, robust thumb that is indicative of strong manipulative

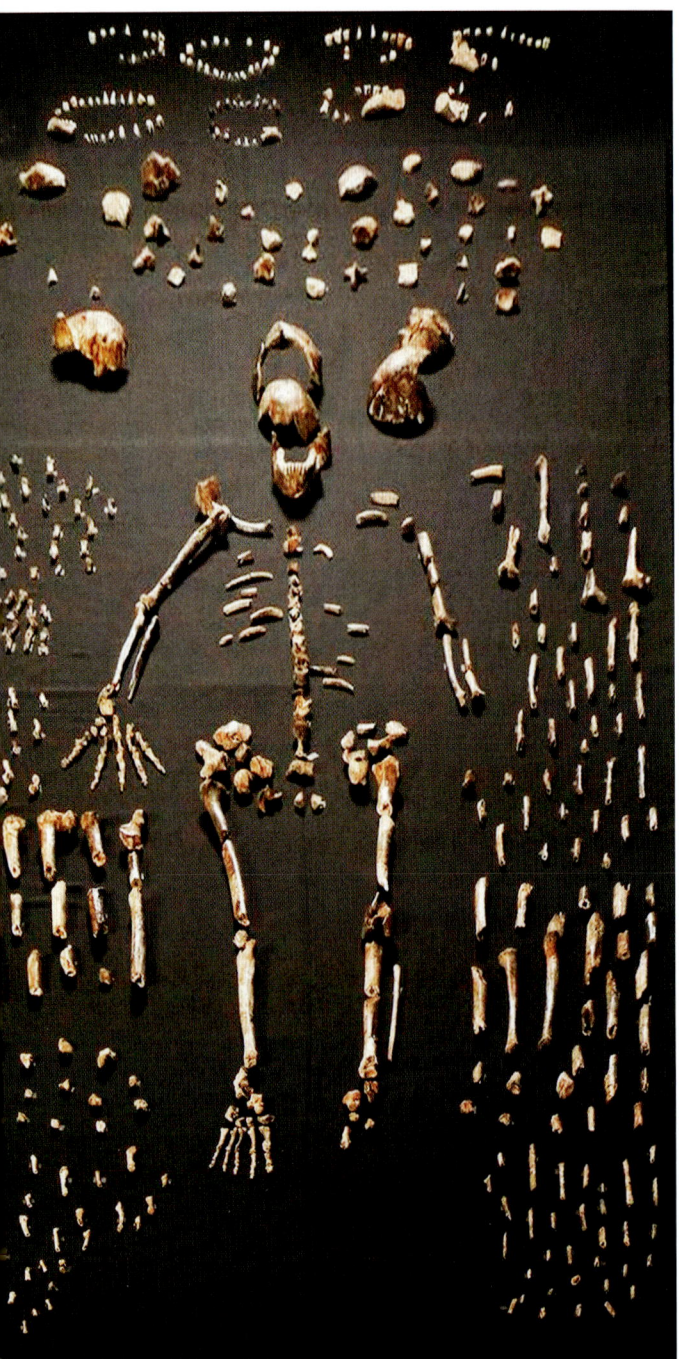

The *Homo naledi* fossils from the Rising Star cave is one of the most comprehensive assemblages of one species of hominin ever found.

Marina Elliott

abilities. The hips and lower body are primitive, but the lower legs and feet are similar to those of humans and well adapted to walking in the open woodland savannah that prevailed at that time.

Taphonomy

Perhaps the most enigmatic aspect of *Homo naledi* is its taphonomy. A large number of skeletons were deposited on the floor of two of the deepest and most inaccessible chambers of the extensive Rising Star cave system. The fossils are in an excellent state of preservation, and the entire assemblage comprises just one species; virtually no other plant or animal fossils are present in the deposit, and no stone tools or other artefacts have been found in the chambers. The structure of the sediments shows that the fossils were not washed in by floods, and the geology suggests that an alternative entrance has never existed. There is no sign of predation, and the state of preservation indicates that the hominins entered the cave before there was any significant decomposition of soft tissue. Access to the chamber is extremely difficult and has evidently prevented casual entry by other animals for hundreds of thousands of years.

One explanation that Lee Berger's team has suggested for this curious situation is that the bodies were deliberately deposited in the cave after death. That a small-brained, semi-arboreal creature consciously disposed of its dead a quarter of a million years ago seems highly improbable, and there is no other evidence of such behaviour by hominins as early as this. Many other palaeoanthropologists have challenged the idea and suggested alternative possibilities, but continuing work on the taphonomy of the skeletons seems to strengthen the possibility that this was purposeful posthumous disposal.

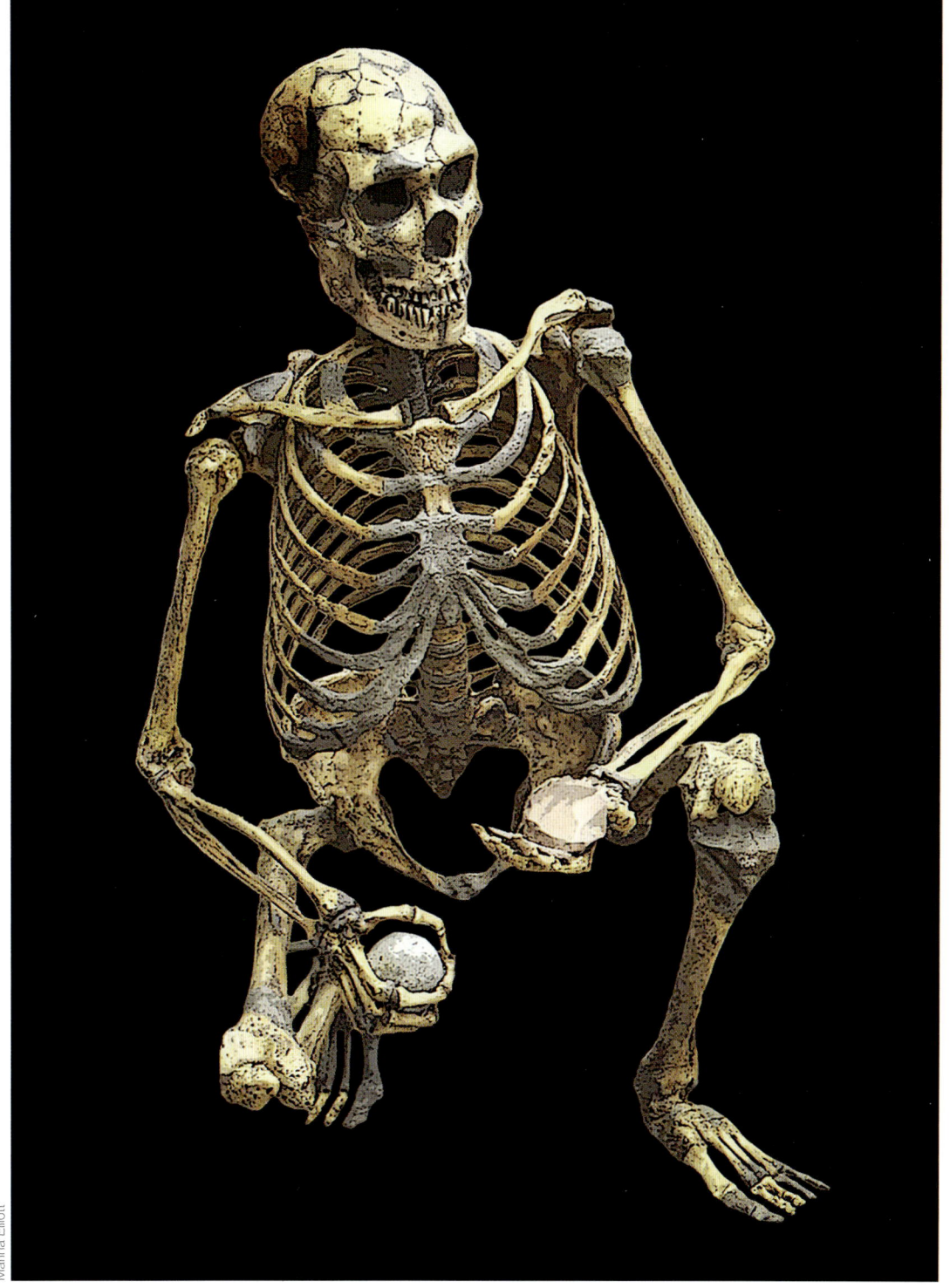

Skeletal features that typify our species are a large, high-domed brain case, short arms, considerable dexterity and bipedal mobility.

Age and evolutionary significance

Homo sapiens[18] is the only surviving hominin on the planet. Compared with other fossils found in the Cradle of Humankind, relatively few human remains have been unearthed in the region. However, the presence of Middle Stone Age stone tools demonstrates that humans have lived in the Cradle-Magaliesberg region since at least 200,000 years ago and may have been there continuously since the evolution of their modern anatomical form.

Anatomy

The human species is characterised by a large brain (1,400cc) housed in a high, domed cranium situated on the spinal column, with the unique ability to tilt back and forth called bicranial flexation. The arrangement of the brain within the cranium is also unique in maximising the space for the frontal lobes that are responsible for rational thought and speech.

The brow ridges are smaller than in other hominins and separated over each eye. The face is comparatively flat, with a prominent chin. The dentition comprises spatula-shaped incisors, single-rooted canines, multi-cuspid molars and thick dental enamel.

Below the head, the body has the familiar proportions of relatively short arms and long legs. The rib-cage is relatively narrow at the base, unlike in other hominins, and the lower pelvic girdle is shorter and narrower than that of ancestral species.

Our most distinctive morphological characteristic is the size of our brain. This gave us the intellectual aptitude to develop innovative survival techniques in a wide variety of habitats and climates. Walking upright on two legs allowed our ancestors to move comfortably across almost any terrain as they migrated across the planet, and their manual dexterity allowed them to perform a range of functions with their hands that are impossible for most other animals, including the manufacture and use of continuously improving tools.

However, there are many disadvantages to a large head, particularly the difficulty it brings in childbirth – a pelvis capable of efficient upright walking is not ideal for delivering large-headed offspring. Evolutionary selection has resulted in a compromise that allows the pre-natal brain to remain relatively small, with further growth after birth combined with a long period of parental dependence.

Technology

Large brains are more energy-consuming than small ones, and higher-calorie diets are needed to sustain them. As the climate changed, many animals evolved adaptations that were suited to the expanding grassland. Herds of grazers were followed onto the plains by hunting predators, and humans developed the Middle Stone Age culture to be described in Chapter 8. Their hunting weapons and scavenging tools improved, their verbal communication developed into language, and they obtained better nourishment from cooked food. Their improved diet accelerated their mental and physical development and thus the advance of technology.

Image by meisjedevos from Pixabay

The dexterity of the human hand was a significant evolutionary advantage, providing us with the ability to make and manipulate articles.

18 *Homo* = man; *sapiens* = wise

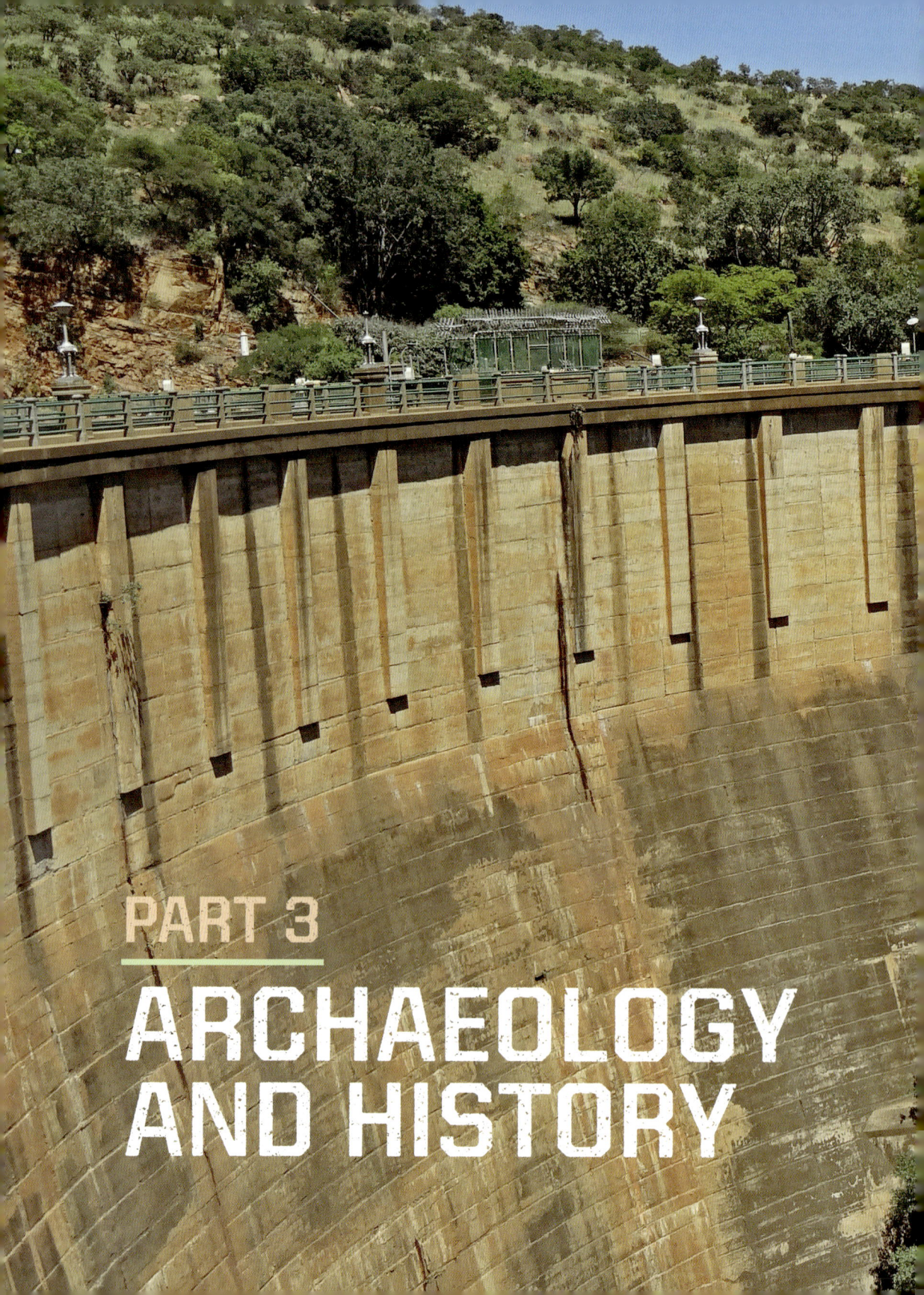

PART 3
ARCHAEOLOGY
AND HISTORY

Socio-political dispensation		Date	Events in the Cradle-Magaliesberg region
Early Stone Age		1–2 million years ago	Early dispersal of hominins (*Homo habilis* or *Homo ergaster*) out of Africa.
Middle Stone Age hunter-gatherers		200,000 years ago	First anatomically modern human.
		125,000 years ago	First migrations out of Africa.
		60,000 years ago	Stone Age people populate the world.
Later Stone Age hunter-gatherers		10,000 years ago	Later Stone Age people introduce microliths, bows and snares into the region. Stone etchings and ornaments appear.
Early Iron Age settlement		1,600 years ago	The first herder-farmer settlement is established at Broederstroom. Animal husbandry, iron smelting and pottery are introduced.
Tswana chieftainships	Cameron Watson/ Shutterstock.com	500 years ago	Early Tswana migrate from Botswana.
		300 years ago	Stone-walled structures introduced.
		300 years ago	People agglomerate to form ever larger settlements.
		1780–1820	Cradle-Magaliesberg occupied by BaPô, BaKwena and others.
		1823	BaPedi raid Cradle-Magaliesberg.
Ndebele kingdom under Mzilikazi 1827–1838		1821	Mzilikazi flees Shaka's Zulu kingdom.
		1827	Mzilikazi invades Cradle-Magaliesberg.
		1829	Robert Moffat visits Mzilikazi in the Magaliesberg.
		1836	Andrew Smith expedition into Cradle-Magaliesberg.
		1838	Boer-Tswana forces drive Mzilikazi from region.
Potchefstroom (Mooi River) Boer administration 1840–1852		1840–1850	Boers establish farms and consolidate the frontier society.
		1850–1890	Naturalists and explorers visit the Cradle-Magaliesberg region.
		1849	Kgosi Mogale flees to the Sotho king for protection against Boer reprisals.

Socio-political dispensation		Date	Events in the Cradle-Magaliesberg region
Zuid-Afrikaansche Republiek 1852–1877		1852	Transvaal granted independence.
		1853	Gold discovered by Pieter J. Marais in the Jukskei River in the Cradle.
		1862	The Pô acquire the farm Boschfontein north of the Cradle, including their ancestral home.
		1867	Kgosi Mogale returns to his people in the Magaliesberg.
British annexation 1877–1881		1877	British annexation of the Transvaal.
		1880–1881	Transvaal War.
Zuid-Afrikaansche Republiek 1881–1899		1881	First gold mined in the Cradle.
		1886	Gold discovered on the Witwatersrand.
		1890	MacArthur-Forrest gold extraction process creates demand for lime from the Cradle.
		1895	Sterkfontein Cave discovered by Guglielmo Martinaglia.
South African War and aftermath 1899–1910		1899–1902	South African War.
		1905	Economic recovery planned in the Cradle-Magaliesberg region. Hartbeespoort irrigation and poverty relief scheme initiated.
Union of South Africa 1910–1961		1914	Rebellion against participation in World War I.
		1924	Hartbeespoort Dam wall completed.
		1924	Taung Child discovered. Palaeoscience starts in SA.
		1936	First adult *Australopithecus* discovered in Cradle.
		1938	*Paranthropus robustus* discovered at Kromdraai.
		1947	Mrs Ples fossil discovered.
Republic of South Africa 1961–1994		1961	Hartebeesthoek tracking station established.
		1965	Pelindaba nuclear facility established.
		1977	Magaliesberg declared a Protected Area.
Republic of South Africa 1994–present		1997	Little Foot fossil discovered.
		1999	Cradle of Humankind listed as World Heritage Site.
		2011	Evolutionary Studies Institute founded.
		2013	*Homo naledi* fossils discovered.
		2015	Magaliesberg Biosphere Reserve proclaimed.

Wits Archaeology

Revil Mason addressing a meeting of the Archaeological Society at Broederstroom in 1980. Stone and Iron Age sites in the Cradle-Magaliesberg provide important insights into the societies that once lived there.

To follow the history of the Cradle-Magaliesberg region for the 200,000 years of human existence we need to make use of historical sources in the widest sense. The following chapters will draw on written, oral and archaeological material from a number of different disciplines and researchers and integrate them to construct an overarching historical narrative of the region.

ARCHAEOLOGY

The archaeological record is the principal source of information for the greater part of this long time span, and the many archaeological sites in the Cradle-Magaliesberg have been extensively researched for decades. Early discoveries of the archaeological wealth of the region were made by Revil Mason in the 1950s. As a young commerce student, he explored the caves in the Hennops River valley and his finding of ancient copper smelting in Uitkomst Cave, in what is now the Cradle of Humankind, persuaded him to change his career and qualify as an archaeologist. He went on to become Professor of Archaeology at Wits University. He excavated most of the major Stone Age and Iron Age sites in the Magaliesberg and his discoveries motivated him to develop an educational programme through which he hoped to have pre-colonial history taught in schools.

Mason's work in the Magaliesberg was followed by that of Tom Huffman and others who specialised in the Iron Age, and by Lyn Wadley who worked on the Middle and Later Stone Ages. Other well-known archaeologists who have worked in the Magaliesberg are Amanda Esterhuysen, Jan Boeyens and Julius Pistorius. Huffman used the distribution of pottery patterns, and linguistic connections between African languages across the continent, to trace the migration patterns of Iron Age cultures into the area, and he combined this with ethnological information to unravel the social complexity of farming communities in the region over more than a thousand years. Wadley demonstrated the use of ceremonial ornaments and natural resources, such as seeds, fruits and ochre, by hunter-gatherer communities, and she investigated their possible relationship with immigrant cattle owners. From all this research has come a growing understanding of the lives and cultures of the early people in the region.

ORAL HISTORY

An important aid to interpreting archaeological sites and artefacts is the oral tradition that was deeply embedded in African culture, but this valuable resource has all but disappeared in recent decades as the traditional art of storytelling has declined. The oral histories of the Tswana people living in the Cradle-Magaliesberg were, however, meticulously documented by government ethnographer Paul-Lambert Breutz, who contributed a number of volumes to the ethnological publications of the Department of Native Affairs in the 1950s and 1960s. In the course of hundreds of interviews, Breutz collected and transcribed the lineage, customs and oral history of each Tswana chiefdom in the area. He accurately estimated that the first migrations of the Tswana into the Magaliesberg region had been in the fifteenth century, yet he persistently denied that the stone-walled settlements in the Cradle-Magaliesberg had been built by the ancestors of the very people he was interviewing. He also held decidedly pro-Nazi sympathies during and after World War II.

The work of the Ethnological Section of the Department of Native Affairs was intended to facilitate the apartheid policy of segregating the histories of all ethnic groups from one another. Despite the sinister intentions of the government, and Breutz's own prejudices, his work was a major contribution to our knowledge of pre-colonial society. His publications were supervised and rigorously edited by the more enlightened director of the Ethnological Section, Nicolaas van Warmelo, and his ideological bias was eliminated from the published material, which survives as a valuable historical resource.

More recent reinterpretations of oral and other contemporary sources have since been published by historians Phil Bonner, Fred Morton and Bernard Mbenga who have provided interesting insights and a better understanding of early Tswana history.

UNION OF SOUTH AFRICA

DEPARTMENT OF NATIVE AFFAIRS

Ethnological Publications No. 28

THE TRIBES
OF
RUSTENBURG
AND
PILANSBERG DISTRICTS
by
P.-L. Breutz

THE GOVERNMENT PRINTER, PRETORIA.
1953
G.P.-S.10924—1952-3—1,000.

Research by P.-L. Breutz in the 1950s captured a permanent record before the oral history traditions were lost.

GENETICS

The value of genetics in the study of history is not always appreciated. Using cladistics, human evolutionary development can be traced from living individuals back to common ancestors, thereby providing insights into lineage, migrations and evolution. Work by Trefor Jenkins and Himla Soodyall, both based at Wits University, has confirmed that the lineage of all living humans converges on a common ancestral gene pool deeply rooted in Africa, probably in southern Africa.

Their work shows in particular that the Cradle-Magaliesberg region was inhabited by hunter-gatherer communities for tens of thousands of years before the arrival of Bantu-speaking cattle-herders and farmers one or two thousand years ago, and that some of the oldest mitochondrial DNA (mtDNA) lineages in the world are retained in Khoisan populations whose ancestors might once have lived in this area.

In summary, genetic analysis of human populations shows that the ancestors of all humans who have ever existed came from Africa. African populations have accumulated the greatest number of mtDNA mutations and have hence been in existence for longer than any other group.[19]

Captain William Cornwallis Harris whose paintings and publications drew the attention of European scientists to the Cradle-Magaliesberg region.

WRITTEN HISTORY

The first written account of the people of the Cradle-Magaliesberg region was provided by Robert Moffat, who visited the powerful Ndebele king, Mzilikazi, in 1829 and gave detailed descriptions of life under his reign following his conquest of the Tswana people. More information came from the journals of the explorer Andrew Smith and the hunter William Cornwallis Harris a decade later. Subsequent travellers have also recorded their impressions of early Boer settlers in the area, and from the mid-nineteenth century a considerable body of written history exists, including diaries, illustrations, press reports, and formal published histories by a large number of authors. The digitisation of archival records is now commonplace and has greatly increased the scope of information available and facilitated its accessibility.

History is never a simple list of dates and facts. South African historiography is strongly influenced by the views and cultural perspectives of those who write it, as well as the social norms and standards at the time it is written. This does not necessarily mean that the information is wrong or inaccurate, but when considering any account of the past we must be aware of the subjective nature of the sources and, indeed, of our own prejudices and partiality.

The South African War of 1899–1902 and the century that followed it divided white South Africans, including historians, into different political camps. Initially, these divisions were aligned either with Boer or British sympathies. Little attention was given to the history of black South Africans, although some ethnologists and anthropologists began to publish important works on early African traditions.

The emergence of the apartheid state in 1948 exploited pre-colonial history to justify the creation

19 Based on Mark Stoneking, 'Genetic evidence for our recent African Ancestry', in Soodyall (2006)

of homeland territories, which further polarised academic historians. By the 1970s, there were three forces retarding pre-colonial historical studies. First, academics felt that any study of pre-colonial times would lend legitimacy to the homeland policy, and many of them therefore remained resolutely disengaged. Second, Afrikaner nationalist historians, following the lead of Gustav Preller, focused on the trials and fortitude of Afrikaners and defended their historical right to a separate identity. Third, the influence of French-inspired Marxist history in English-speaking universities led some historians to view class divisions in African societies as more significant than tribal or ethnic structures, and they focused on industrialisation and the socio-economic origins of the growing resistance to apartheid and what today is termed 'struggle history'.

At the start of the twenty-first century politically polarised historiography began to diminish, and there has been a substantial resurgence of broader studies that once again embrace the early history of the people of the Cradle-Magaliesberg region. Parastatal bodies, private history societies, tourist associations and museums flourish. Battlefield tours to the South African War and Anglo-Zulu War sites have become popular, while world heritage sites such as the Cradle of Humankind and Mapungubwe have been registered, calling for wide-ranging historical research.

The Cradle-Magaliesberg has been the beneficiary of this resurgence. Wits University historian Philip Bonner, archaeologist Amanda Esterhuysen and geneticist Trefor Jenkins brought together a multidisciplinary team to produce a volume of historical studies of the region, *The Search for Origins: Science, History and South Africa's Cradle of Humankind* (Witwatersrand University Press, 2007). Visitor centres such as Maropeng, the erection of information plaques at historical sites and many private heritage enterprises now play significant roles in preserving the history of the region.

In line with the worldwide practice of erecting Blue Plaques at historical sites, this plaque introduces visitors to the rich heritage of the Cradle-Magaliesberg.

Military cemeteries, fortifications and archaeological sites provide a wealth of historical evidence in the region.

8 | THE FIRST PEOPLE

People have lived and thrived in the Cradle-Magaliesberg for as long as the *Homo sapiens* species has existed. During those 200,000 years, they improved their methods of subsistence and found new ways of manipulating the environmental balance in their favour. Spears replaced clubs, arrows replaced spears, and hunting was supplemented by animal husbandry. From time to time, some of the inhabitants dispersed through Africa, and a few left the continent altogether – their offspring going on to populate the world. This chapter is about those who remained.

André Wedepohl

The dry-stone walls built by the herders and farmers who inhabited the Cradle-Magaliesberg are reminders of the rich heritage of the past.

The direct ancestors of many South Africans alive today farmed and herded cattle in the Cradle-Magaliesberg region. They had displaced earlier societies that had used rudimentary stone tools and stealth to hunt and gather food from the veld.

Over the centuries people manufactured and used different sets of tools and implements, some of which have survived and provide the archaeological evidence of life in the Cradle-Magaliesberg in the past. Archaeologists call the different time periods the Stone Age and Iron Age, based on the durable materials that people used – stone and iron. These 'ages' are often referred to as cultures or industries, and the transition between them was seldom abrupt or clear-cut. In some places, Stone Age hunter-gatherers appear to have lived together with Iron Age cattle herders for extended periods, so that the archaeological evidence of one culture overlaps with that of the other. In other places, people's lives and the implements they used simply changed gradually over time, as each generation introduced technical innovations and improved lifestyles.

The transition from a way of life based on Iron Age pastoralism to life under the rule of colonial powers encompassed five completely different and often repressive regimes of government in the space of 100 years. The South African War was the final and most disruptive event of the nineteenth century before the start of an erratic process of post-war restoration of the economy and society.

➤ 200,000–60,000 years ago: Peopling the world

From their evolutionary places of origin humans have tended to disperse and occupy new territory wherever their technical and intellectual competence enabled them to survive. The earliest migrations out of Africa may have begun as many as a million years ago, when Early Stone Age hominins – perhaps *Homo ergaster* or *Homo habilis* – spread into Europe and Asia. Their descendants possibly evolved into *Homo erectus* in Java and China, and Neanderthals and Denisovans in Western Europe and Russia, all of which are now extinct.

There are two views on how anatomically modern humans, *Homo sapiens*, came to populate the world following those earlier hominin dispersals. Until the latter part of the twentieth century the most commonly accepted theory was that the early hominin species that were widely dispersed in the northern hemisphere evolved simultaneously into *Homo sapiens* with different regional characteristics. This view, originally called the Multiregional model, has been modified to embrace the concepts of hybridisation and fluid movement among populations that enabled a single human species to emerge from the earlier diversity.

In 1987, however, three geneticists from the University of California, Berkeley – Rebecca Cann,

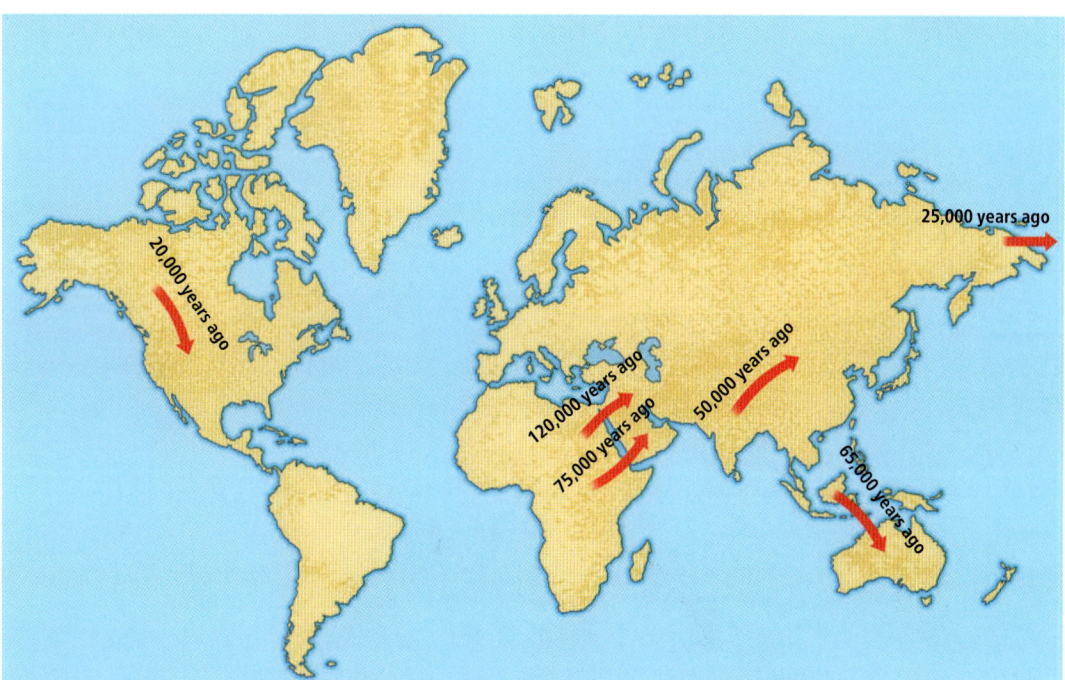

Human migrations from Africa may have started 120,000 years ago, and were only successful as little as 75,000 years ago. They gave rise to all humanity throughout the world.

Multiregional model

The hypothesis that early migrations from Africa gave rise to regional populations and that interbreeding allowed a single species of *Homo sapiens* to persist is now largely discredited or severely modified.

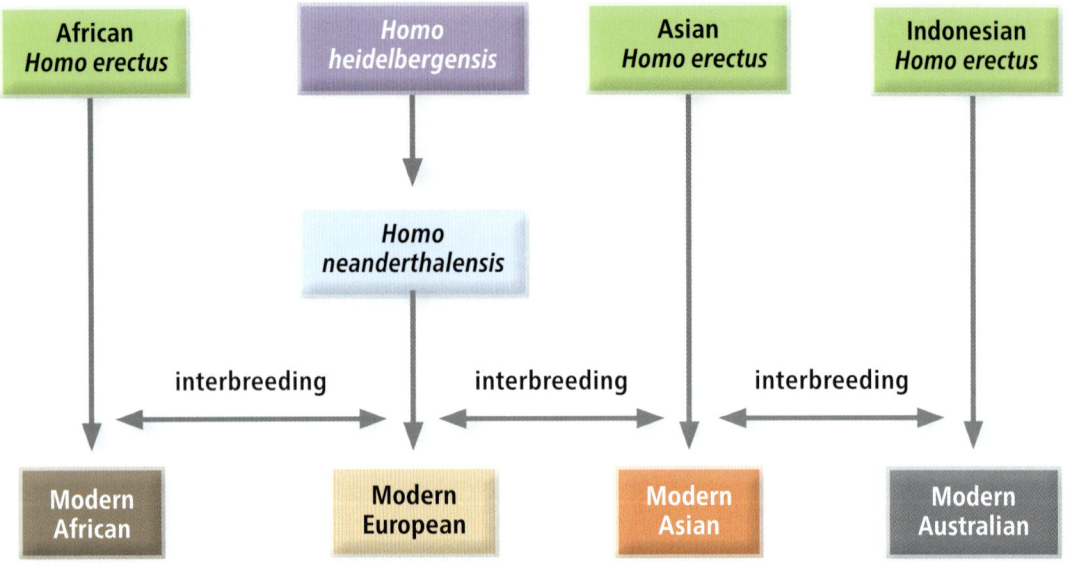

Out of Africa model

It is now thought that the first migrations of *Homo ergaster* from Africa started to take place 1.8 million years ago and gave rise to subsequent species of *Homo* that are now extinct.

Later migrations of *Homo sapiens* began from about 80,000 years ago and subsequently gave rise to all existing regional populations.

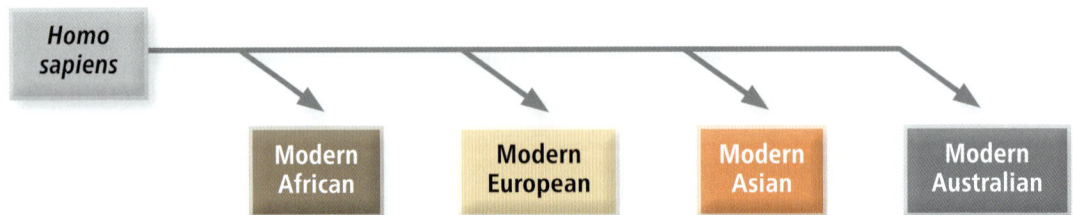

Maropeng Visitor Centre

The entrance to the Maropeng exhibition hall emphasises the Out of Africa model. MtDNA analysis has shown that all modern humans are descended from one common African ancestral gene pool and that genetic characteristics developed subsequently.

Allan Wilson and Mark Stoneking – analysed the mitochondrial DNA (mtDNA) from a wide sample of women in Asia, New Guinea, Australia, Europe and Africa. MtDNA is inherited exclusively through the female line and can indicate the time elapsed since a common ancestor was shared by two or more people. The locality of that ancestor can also be determined.

The work of Cann and her colleagues produced the startling evidence that every living human today is descended from one ancestral gene pool in Africa about 200,000 years ago. Diversity and regional genetic distinctions all occurred *after* the evolution of anatomically modern humans, not before, as suggested by the Multiregional model. Earlier

ancestral species and the Eurasian descendants of *Homo erectus* were either replaced by, or absorbed into, this more recent African exodus, which is accordingly called the Out of Africa model.

Subsequent studies by genetic scientists using the all-male Y chromosome confirmed the Out of Africa model, and refined it further to show that at least two, and probably many more, migrations occurred. New research also demonstrated that occasional interbreeding may have taken place between humans and Neanderthals and other earlier hominin groups, and that tool styles and manufacturing skills were probably exchanged among the groups.

The influence of climate change

In the early period of their existence, the first humans in the Cradle-Magaliesberg were part of a metapopulation of *Homo sapiens* (all of the geographically dispersed groups that made up the entire species) that roamed over much of sub-Saharan Africa. Until about 145,000 years ago, the global climate was mainly cold and dry. The Sahara Desert was a harsh and impenetrable barrier, and North Africa straddled the width of the continent like the lid on an African pot. Humans were confined to the mosaic of woodland and grassland savannah in the southern part of the continent where they were an endemic sub-Saharan species.

From time to time, however, variations in the Earth's orbit and the tilt of its polar axis produced periods of warm humidity. Although they were fairly

Pixabay.com

For short periods the Sahara Desert was more extensively vegetated, similar to the modern Kalahari, and humans and other animals were able to move beyond the confines of sub-Saharan Africa.

brief in geological time, these interludes caused lakes and grassland to develop across the Sahara and allowed savannah wildlife as well as humans to spread northwards.

One of these warm cycles occurred about 120,000 years ago, and human hunter-gatherers followed the game northwards, crossing the Sinai land bridge into the Middle East. Burial sites of these early migrants have been excavated in Israel and dated to about 100,000 years ago. However, that initial foray out of Africa appears to have failed to prosper, and probably terminated about 90,000 years ago when the warm cycle ended and cold, arid conditions returned.

A second, larger, dispersal took place 80,000 to 75,000 years ago, probably in a series of sporadic migrations of small populations. The climatic window of opportunity on this occasion was only a few thousand years, but it allowed a small group of people to cross the southern end of the Red Sea and give rise to a dynasty that ultimately populated the world. Using a route through southern Sinai and Southeast Asia, the human population expanded gradually, driven simply by their own population growth. From Asia, they crossed the frozen Bering land bridge about 20,000 years ago, and settled in North and, eventually, South America. Others moved south-east and reached Australia about 65,000 years ago. Evidence also shows that groups of humans returned to Africa after at least one of the migrations outwards, and that in general, populations moved into and out of the continent from time to time.

The migrations coincided with the beginnings of an upsurge in technological development and marked the gradual transition from Middle Stone Age to Later Stone Age culture. New hunting methods and tools such as throwing-spears emerged, bone awls were used to stitch clothing made of animal skins, and spiritual symbolism and decorative materials, such as ochre body paint, began to be used. Clothing and weapons were probably some of the innovations that helped the emigrants to succeed in occupying the diversity of habitats and climates they encountered in different places.

➤ 200,000–20,000 years ago: Middle Stone Age hunter-gatherers

As humans evolved anatomically into our present form about 200,000 years ago, more sophisticated tools started making an appearance in what archaeologists call the Middle Stone Age. This was an important period because it signified the beginning of more advanced technical development, following almost two million years during which the tools used by our ancestors had been limited to Oldowan flakes and Acheulean hand axes.

Marina Elliott

Middle Stone Age tools on display in the Origins Centre show the advances in knapping technique and fit-for-purpose developments over the Earlier Stone Age axes.

A core from which flakes have been knapped to make Middle Stone Age tools.

Middle Stone Age tools were made from specially selected core stones from which hunter-gatherers knapped flakes to make the tools. The cores were specially selected for their suitability, and they were often carried by the nomadic hunter-gatherers for some distance to tool-making sites. Some tools were blades about 100mm long, with sharp, skilfully chipped cutting edges. Others were spearheads, shaped at the base to allow them to be bound to a shaft to make spears; these spears were sufficiently effective to bring down small antelope, and stone spearheads have been found buried in animal fossils from this period. Middle Stone Age artefacts from this era have been found at several sites in the Cradle-Magaliesberg, including Sterkfontein, Plovers Lake and Swartkrans, and examples of tools from the region can be seen in the Origins Centre at Wits University in Johannesburg.

Spearheads were bound to a shaft with leather thongs and glued with mastic made from acacia resin and red ochre.

The emergence of *Homo sapiens*

Equipped with their Middle Stone Age tools, hunter-gatherer communities roamed across sub-Saharan Africa including the Cradle-Magaliesberg region. Lyn Wadley, one of South Africa's foremost archaeologists, has given us some insights into the lifestyle of these early inhabitants of the region. They were a nomadic people, following the seasonal movement of game and camping temporarily at selected sites. Ash residue in the hearths at the campsites indicates that they cooked their food, and were able to ignite fires rather than being dependent on gathering smouldering coals from natural bush fires as their Early Stone Age predecessors had been. Occasionally they camped on the banks of streams, but more frequently they sheltered in caves and rock overhangs, where multiple layers of ash and debris indicate that the sites were revisited regularly over many years. Their propensity to roam some distance away from streams suggests that they could carry water with them, possibly stored in leather bags or ostrich shells.

Most of the Middle Stone Age fell within a warmer interglacial climatic period in southern Africa, similar to the climate that we experience today. Hunters would have been able to find a variety of small and medium-sized game animals, which they ambushed in the woodland thickets or pursued with their rudimentary spears. Edible herbs and roots would have been abundant, and those who ate these plants were evidently knowledgeable about them.

However, from about 75,000 years ago, during the latter part of the Middle Stone Age, glacial conditions returned and very much lower temperatures were experienced in southern Africa. Under these cold conditions grassland expanded at the expense of woodland, bringing large herds of ungulates such as eland, wildebeest and zebra onto the plains of the Cradle. Middle Stone Age hunters would have had to become adept at stalking big game in open country, probably cooperating in hunting parties, and using fire to drive animals towards armed and concealed hunters. But the task was difficult, and the success rate unpredictable.

Corms of the African potato *Hypoxis hemerocallidea* are among the debris found at Middle Stone Age campsites.

Kevin Gill

Animal protein meals may have become less frequent than they had been in earlier times – the bones of prey animals at campsites were crushed for their interior marrow, suggesting that every scrap of nourishment was precious. The remains of seeds and the corms of the African potato *Hypoxis hemerocallidea* at the sites reveal how hunting for meat was augmented by plant-gathering.

Climate and environmental change over tens of thousands of years stimulated new developments in tool technology and lifestyles, and led to the emergence of what is called the Later Stone Age. And it was at about this time that groups of Middle Stone Age people began to leave the African continent and populate the rest of the world.

The transition between the Middle and Later Stone Ages took place over a long period of time and across wide geographic areas, with artefacts from both cultures often occurring together at the same site. This suggests that changes were either introduced by immigrant groups and gradually adopted by the local communities, or that they were innovative developments among existing communities themselves. They were unlikely to have been the result of a sudden replacement of one population by another. The new lifestyles may possibly have been responses to climate change.

Marina Elliott

Later Stone Age tools were smaller and more finely wrought than those of the Middle Stone Age, but the transition between the two was slow and overlapped in different regions.

The tools that characterise the Later Stone Age are particularly abundant in the Magaliesberg and can often be found exposed on river banks, or on the floors of rock overhangs and shelters. They are smaller than those of the Middle Stone Age, usually less than 50mm in length, and they were purpose-built for specific uses. Bi-faceted arrow-heads, flat-shaped scrapers and flat-backed blades were part of a complex toolkit, and they are often remarkably sharp, even thousands of years after their manufacture.

Hunting and gathering

Later Stone Age artefacts from other parts of South Africa date back 40,000 years or more, but those that have been recovered from the Cradle-Magaliesberg are 10,000 years old or younger. By that time, the cold climate that had prevailed for the previous 75,000 years had dissipated and the Cradle was enjoying much warmer days.

Grassland vied with woodland as climates changed, and the Cradle-Magaliesberg became the frontier across which the two vegetation types

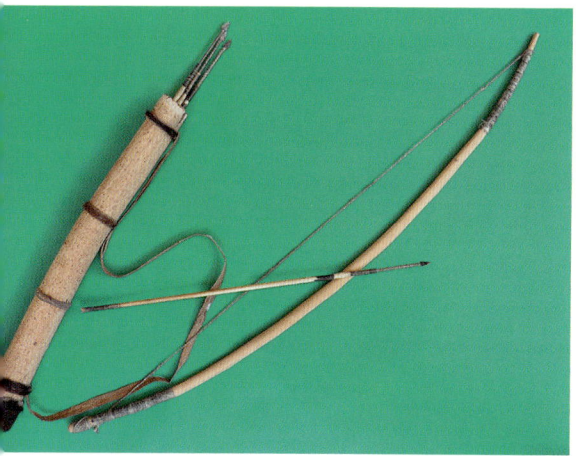

Bows and arrows, the latter often with detachable poison tips, were probably in use in the Cradle-Magaliesberg 5,000 years ago.

A bored stone was wedged onto a stick to give it greater thrust for digging.

battled for dominance – a confrontation that continues today. The warmer moist conditions of the Later Stone Age meant that there might have been slightly more woodland than there is today, but open savannah would still have been interspersed among the trees. Small browsing animals were common, and their remains are frequently excavated from shelters in which the Later Stone Age hunter-gatherers once camped. The two primary methods used to hunt small creatures were the bow and arrow, and trapping. Lengths of twine were plaited from the sinewy leaf fibres of *Sansevieria aethiopica*, a type of hemp, and used to string bows and to make snares to catch ground-dwelling birds and small game. Arrow-heads were made of bone or wood and tipped with poison. They were often notched, so that they snapped on impact and remained buried in the victim while the poison took effect. Small bows could be used in a wooded environment, but snares were more energy-efficient.

Gathering roots and underground plants was made easier by the invention of a weighted digging stick, and these remarkable implements can occasionally be found in the Cradle-Magaliesberg. A hole was bored through the centre of an elliptical stone, a bit bigger than a doughnut, and threaded onto a sharpened stick until it was wedged fast in place. The weight of the stone added momentum to the digging action.

Ornaments and celebrations

Personal ornamentation was another aspect of Later Stone Age life. Simple leather loincloths were worn by men and aprons by women. Hide cloaks provided warmth. Bedding was made of grasses and herbs such as *Artemisia afra*, which is a repellent against lice and other vermin, and it is probable that these nomadic hunter-gatherers were well acquainted with the medicinal uses of many of the plants that occur in the area.

Ostrich eggshells were used as water containers and were often decorated, and shards of eggshell – perhaps recycled after accidental breakage – were filed down into beads and strung into necklaces and other adornments. Some may have had ritual, as well as decorative, purposes.

Although people were nomadic and small family groups spent most of their time hunting independently of each other, research by Lyn Wadley at Jubilee Shelter in the Magaliesberg found that they had congregated together periodically at specially selected sites, where groups would exchange information and gifts and hold ceremonies and celebrations. Jubilee Shelter was used repeatedly for these assemblies over many hundreds of years, beginning more than 5,000 years ago. Large numbers of ornamental artefacts, beads and shells have been recovered from such shelters, indicating that the gatherings had considerable social and, possibly, also spiritual significance. These well-used shelters with a rich variety of artefacts and implements are very different from other Later Stone Age sites where small hunting parties stopped temporarily, and where the artefacts to be found are limited to tools that were functional for survival.

The places where they gathered for celebrations also inform us about gender roles at that time. Eggshell beads and bead-making debris were concentrated in areas to the left of the hearth,

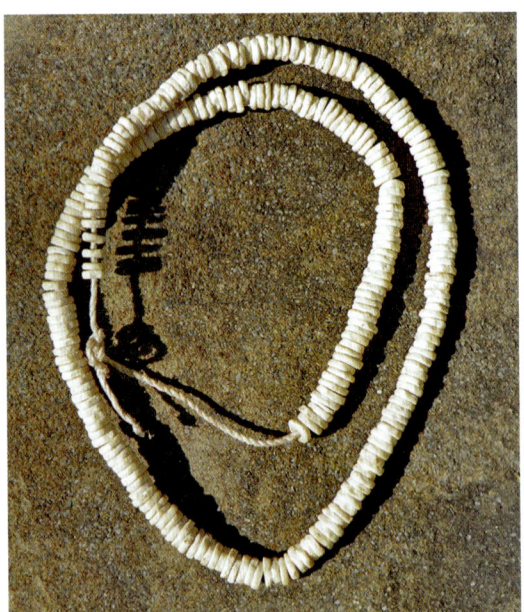

Ostrich eggshell beads were a common ornament and probably served as exchange items at ceremonial gathering sites.

suggesting that women gathered in that part of the cave, while bone and stone tools were crafted, presumably by men, to the right of the hearth.

The Stone Age culture did not end abruptly, but it gradually changed with the arrival of immigrants who led an entirely different way of life, the people of the Early Iron Age. Jubilee Shelter is not far from the Broederstroom Early Iron Age site, and Wadley's work has shown that celebratory gatherings declined noticeably after the establishment of the new settlement there. Stone tools have been found in the middens at Broederstroom, and it appears that interaction may have taken place between the two different cultures. This probably took the form of servitude or collaboration, and the timing coincides with the steady decline of the Stone Age in the Cradle-Magaliesberg.

Rock etchings in the Magaliesberg may have had ceremonial or spiritual significance.

Rock etchings

Some of the most fascinating remnants of Later Stone Age life are the stone engravings (petroglyphs) that can be found in several places on the southern slopes of the Magaliesberg near the Cradle. Rock engravings occur elsewhere in South Africa, but those in the Magaliesberg are unique in that they are line drawings etched into the rock, rather than produced by pecking which is the more common method. Almost all the images depict animals (there are virtually no human forms) and they are so exquisitely crafted that each species is immediately recognisable.

The Magaliesberg etchings have been subjected to relatively little scholarly anthropological study. Many of them show hammer marks and scratching, suggesting perhaps that the images were part of a

spiritual ritual. Rock art in the Drakensberg has been shown to be ritualistic, and induced by shamans in a state of trance.[20] This may give some insights into what the Magaliesberg etchings meant to the people of the time. Eland are the most commonly depicted animals in both the Magaliesberg and Drakensberg rock art, and we know that these massive antelope had great practical and spiritual significance in hunter-gatherer societies. Rhinoceros also feature in both types of art and are symbolic of rain animals. Some of the Magaliesberg rhinoceros etchings have been cut across, as though they were part of a rain-making ceremony. But the rock engravings of the region remain largely unexplained, a reminder of how much there is still to be learned about the fascinating society that lived here thousands of years ago.

➤ 1,600 years ago: Early mixed farming at Broederstroom

Near the village of Broederstroom on the southern bank of Hartbeespoort Dam lies the archaeological site of one of the oldest farming and herding settlements in South Africa. It comprised several small interlinked homesteads and was first excavated by the pioneering Wits University archaeologist Revil Mason in the 1970s.

The inhabitants of this settlement were the first Iron Age people in the area, and another leading archaeologist at Wits University, Tom Huffman, used styles and patterns on potsherds from the site to trace their origins via the KwaZulu-Natal east coast through East Africa and back to the birthplace of Bantu languages east of Nigeria. The

20 See, for example, Lewis-Williams (1983); Lewis-Williams & Dowson (2000)

The Broederstroom archaeological site at the time it was being excavated in 1972.

site reveals that people were practising agriculture, farming livestock, making pottery and smelting iron in South Africa 1,600 years ago. They brought with them the linguistic roots of the Bantu languages now spoken by 80 per cent of South Africans, and introduced methods of farming and animal husbandry that gave them considerable advantages over the Stone Age nomadic hunter-gatherer way of life that had existed in the region until then.

Farming and animal husbandry

The people who lived in this area tilled the land, and stored their produce in sealed underground pits lined with cattle dung. Methane gas from the dung lining of the pit controlled insect infestations, and grain stored in this way could last for several seasons. For daily use, grain was also kept in thick-floored wicker storage bins raised on stones to keep out the damp.

Later Stone Age artefacts were found at the Broederstroom site, and it is probable that as Stone Age culture declined in the face of Iron Age competition, those people were absorbed into, or

The remains of a stone platform on which a tightly woven wicker grain bin was placed to keep it off the damp ground.

subjugated by, the new settlers. The types of stone tools recovered are similar to those found at Jubilee Cave and were used for scraping and preparing hides, and the Stone Age people probably worked as servants performing that type of task.

The arrangement of dwellings and cattle kraals shows that the male-dominated central cattle pattern was introduced into South Africa at this early stage, together with the concept of bride-wealth, *lobola,* which characterises social structures, kinship and power in many South African societies to this day. Cattle were central to their economy, and a number of social norms were implicit in the central cattle pattern. Society was ranked according to kinship, with hereditary male leadership. Women were associated with agriculture and crops, and grain bins were situated in the female areas of the settlement. People lived in small circular *rondavel* huts clustered around the central cattle kraal. Each hut was about 3m to 4m in diameter, and was made of interwoven saplings plastered with clay under a conical thatched roof. Ritual burial of the dead was also practised, and the bodies of important male personages were buried in the cattle kraal in keeping with the significance of cattle in the society.

Cowrie shells found at the Broederstroom site indicate that some form of trade or exchange through middlemen was evidently taking place with people along the Indian Ocean coast who used cowries as currency.

Iron smelting

Mixed farming and food storage allowed these communities to settle in one place and to lead lives that were not constrained by the need to hunt and gather every day. While this was important, a more significant aspect of the Broederstroom site was the iron production that gives this period its archaeological name, the Early Iron Age.

Iron was produced in three stages, mining, smelting and forging, and Early Iron Age settlements were usually located close to accessible ore deposits. At Broederstroom the ore was mined from surface deposits next to the settlement, and other banded iron formation deposits were worked, possibly at a later date, on what is now the farm Welgevond, a few kilometres away.

The miners took the ore to a smelting furnace where charcoal was brought to temperatures between 1,200°C and 1,500°C. The high temperatures may have been achieved by drawing air into the furnace through surrounding lateral pipes. Small amounts of iron were produced in the furnace, leaving quantities of slag behind. Although we do not know the

Wits Archaeology

Important personages were buried in a sitting position in a grave in the central cattle kraal.

Above: Ferruginous deposits at Broederstroom from where iron ore was extracted.

Right: An iron ingot recovered from Broederstroom is about 1,600 years old. It is about 120mm long and had been cast as part of the refining process.

details of this process, the inclusion of clay charms in furnaces at Broederstroom suggests that iron smelting had ritual significance; and smelting furnaces were located close to the chief's quarters which indicates that metal workers and their craft held an elevated standing in the community.

The metal bloom from the smelters was cooled and the metal workers broke it up to separate the iron from unwanted slag and carbon. Metallurgical tests on an ingot block from Broederstroom showed that it had been cast by wrapping the pieces of impure iron in a fire-clay mould, and heating them in the furnace to weld them together and separate the remaining slag and charcoal contaminants. The mould would then have been removed from the fire and broken away to reveal the refined ingot, which was taken to the forging furnaces for conversion into hoes, spears and other implements. This method is similar to that used by fourth-century iron smelters in Taruga,

Nigeria, and supports Tom Huffman's findings that the Broederstroom community originated from that region of West Africa, passing their iron-smelting skills from one generation to another as they migrated southwards.

Five iron slag heaps have been unearthed at Broederstroom, suggesting that it was probably a fairly large production site. Smelting furnaces, as opposed to forges, have not been discovered, and may have been situated some distance away from the village. Few iron artefacts have been recovered; iron products could have been removed from the site by the people using them, and cast aside to corrode away over thousands of years.

The Broederstroom settlement lasted for only a few centuries, after which there is a gap of 1,000 years in the archaeological record in the Magaliesberg. However, the site was to be reoccupied centuries later by the ancestors of the modern Tswana.

➤ 500–200 years ago: The Tswana cattle economy

When viewed from the air, numerous clusters of circular dry-stone walls can be seen on the slopes of the Magaliesberg. They are remnants of a once vigorous Tswana cattle farming community that thrived in the Cradle-Magaliesberg region for more than 500 years.

Settlements and chieftainships

The first inhabitants of these settlements began to migrate into the Cradle-Magaliesberg area in about 1500. Tswana oral tradition places their origins at the sacred water-hole of Lowe at Matsieng, not far from Mochudi in Botswana – a site rich in petroglyphs that have spiritual significance. From there, people spread gradually south-east across the Marico River as their population increased and they sought new grazing for their growing cattle herds. Other people from an Nguni background arrived in the

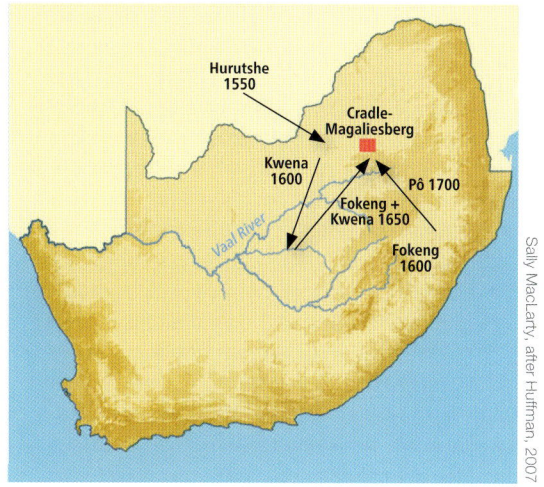

Migrations of Tswana groups in and around the Cradle-Magaliesberg region, where a number of chieftainships were later established.

Molokwane was one of the towns governed by Kgosi Kgaswane in 1800. Large towns replaced scattered homesteads in the Cradle-Magaliesberg towards the end of the eighteenth century.

Cradle-Magaliesberg some time later, and trace their ancestral roots to the hill of Ntsuanatsatsi south of the Vaal River.

Tswana society was characterised by repeated homestead break-ups as contending factions within a community split away from one another. In this way, a number of chieftainships developed in the region. The people all spoke Setswana, but they had no written language. They were grouped into clans each headed by a hereditary *Kgosi*, or chief, whose power was determined by his cattle wealth and his ability to support or defend his people. His authority, however, was limited by elders who held council over the affairs of the clan at meetings of the *lekgotla* (the tribunal where community matters were decided). Unlike some of the later Nguni chieftainships, Tswana chiefs seldom achieved dominance over one another, and they did not develop a hierarchy under what might be called a 'paramount chief'. Chieftainships were defined by the people who owed allegiance to the *Kgosi*, rather than by any territorial region; but their settlements and grazing grounds effectively established localities with which they were associated. This system of rule was effectively maintained for many centuries. The chiefs managed large-scale agricultural systems, dispensed justice to their people, and manoeuvred against competing chiefs for trade and the acquisition of cattle.

The Hurutshe were probably the first Tswana group to move east from what is now Botswana, in about 1550. During the following decades the migrations continued, and the Kwena broke away from the Hurutshe. One Kwena group spread further east into the Magaliesberg region, while another moved south of the Vaal River onto the southern Highveld. Here they encountered the Fokeng, an Nguni group who had come from the eastern coastal region and settled in what is now the Free State. The two groups, Kwena and Fokeng, integrated, retaining the name Fokeng (or *Bafokeng* in Setswana) but adopting the Tswana language and customs and retaining the Kwena crocodile totem.

In the treeless grasslands of the Highveld the Fokeng had developed the craft of dry-stone walling, but they retained their Nguni homestead pattern of placing an outer circle of dwelling huts around the central cattle kraal. By about 1650 the united Kwena-Fokeng group had moved north again, bringing their stone masonry skills into the Cradle-Magaliesberg. They settled at Phokeng, north of modern Rustenburg, and their building expertise passed from one chieftainship to the next. By about 1700 stone-walled enclosures and villages had spread throughout the region, and by 1800 extensive stone-walled towns such as Olifantspoort and Molokwane (both near Rustenburg) had become established, often with newer buildings resting on the foundations of older ones. The simple circular pattern of huts around a

Hut floors were compacted with mud and cow dung. This floor at Olifantspoort has survived in the open air for almost two centuries.

Doorways were closed by a wooden or stone slab sliding on a stone runner across the threshold.

cattle kraal had become more complex, with the outer perimeter walls scalloped to accommodate small stock pens, granaries and dwellings, and the chief's apartments set prominently on high ground.

Early explorers frequently commented on the skill with which the walls were crafted. Houses were separated within enclosures, and each house was built of stone usually plastered with clay, with a thatched roof supported independently on poles. A low, semi-circular doorway was the only opening, and inside the smoke from a central cooking hearth escaped through the thatch.

During the eighteenth century one group, the Kwena ba Modimosana ba Mmatau, constructed settlements and cattle outposts along the southern slopes of the Magaliesberg from Magatasnek (modern Rustenburg) as far as the Cradle area. Their chief in 1800 was Kgosi Kgaswane, one of the most respected leaders in the region. Griqua and Korana traders and raiders who traversed his country called the mountain range after the chief, and the name 'Cashan', a corruption of Kgaswane, persisted and appeared in all the early references to the Magaliesberg area until about 1840.

Cattle

Cattle were central to the Tswana economy and social structure. The cattle were husbanded exclusively by men, and were a source of wealth and a means of acquiring wives. Cattle were precious, and were only slaughtered for meat on special occasions. People generally obtained venison and leather by hunting wild game. Women tended the children and cultivated the land, using hoes with iron blades mounted in the knob of a long *kierie* (wooden stick). They grew sorghum and millet in communal fields; maize was introduced after about 1650, first for medicinal use and later as a food. They ground the grain on concave grindstones with handheld rounded stones, and stored it in large clay pots or tightly woven baskets raised on upright stones similar to those that had been used at Broederstroom 1,000 years earlier. All households possessed several types of basketware, pottery, wooden spoons, and iron tools and weapons.

Metal work

Besides farming, the principal industry was metal-working, and the process had changed very little from the Early Iron Age. Smelting was still undertaken exclusively by men, and many settlements had smelting and forging furnaces. The symbolic comparison between iron production and childbirth was often emphasised, and furnaces were occasionally shaped to resemble female bodies, with womb-like, oval-shaped clay ovens; these were filled with charcoal and clay-pipe bellows inserted at either end. Smelted iron was

André Wedepohl

Crops were an important food source and grindstones were common household ware.

Museum Africa

Iron-smelting furnaces reached temperatures of up to 1,500°C.

collected on the floor of the furnace and taken to a forging furnace, where it was congealed and beaten into spearheads, hoes and other necessary articles in the centuries-old manner.

Underground mines were dug in several places in the region, but the mines were kept secret and, even after all the ore had been removed, they were often refilled with earth to make them inconspicuous. Iron ore was not all used for smelting; red ochre obtained from the ore was crushed and used as a paste for decorating pottery and, probably, as body paint, wall decoration and for medicinal purposes.

Furnaces consumed considerable amounts of charcoal, and smelters were set up close to woodland as it was easier for the metal workers

to bring ore to the furnace than to carry large amounts of wood to a distant site. This, together with the mild, frost-free climate, may have been a contributing reason for the expansion of settlements in the Bushveld regions of the Cradle-Magaliesberg. People traded ironware from the area for livestock and other goods from grassland regions where there were no trees.

Uitkomst Cave, in a remote part of the John Nash Nature Reserve, where copper-smelting furnaces have been found.

Among the artefacts found at Broederstroom was a chain made of short lengths of copper wire bent into links. It may have been manufactured at Uitkomst.

Copper and trade

One of the most interesting metal-working sites in the Cradle is Uitkomst Cave in the John Nash Nature Reserve, which was discovered by a youthful Revil Mason in 1951 and led to his taking up archaeology as a career. The cave contained a copper-smelting furnace with numerous potsherds and other Iron Age artefacts. The copper ore came from the nearby Hennops River and yielded a fairly high grade of metal. Copper was a valued commodity and was extensively used for ornamental wear such as amulets and earrings. It was also an important trade commodity. Below the Later Iron Age artefacts found at Uitkomst Cave were signs of much earlier Later Stone Age occupancy dated at about 9,000 years ago.

Copper ornaments, decorated potsherds, plaited matting, wooden bowls and spoons, as well as iron hoes and spears have been found at archaeological sites in the Cradle-Magaliesberg area and give us an idea of domestic life two centuries ago.

Copper earrings were commonly worn by the ancestral Tswana, and they have been found at several archaeological sites in the Cradle-Magaliesberg and as far afield as the Free State. The English naturalist and explorer William Burchell commented on these earrings during his journey among the Tswana in 1824: '… they are fond of wearing some ornament in their ears. That which is in most general use is the *manjena* or eardrop, a small pendant made of copper wire … very neatly wound about another of larger

dimensions and terminated by a small knob formed by a piece of copper hammered round the end; the upper part being bent into a ring by which it is fastened to the ear'.[21]

Uitkomst never supported an Iron Age community other than the metal workers themselves, and there are no dwellings or other signs of settlement around the cave. However, archaeologists have found signs of a nine-thousand-year-old Stone Age community on the cave floor below the copper works. We can imagine that the copper smelters were a specialist group plying their craft away from the main population. In modern archaeological terms the cave is important, and its name, Uitkomst, is used to refer to the distinctive pottery of an entire Iron Age community living in the Cradle-Magaliesberg region between Rustenburg and northern Johannesburg.

Until the end of the eighteenth century, the southern Magaliesberg, including the Cradle, was occupied mainly by the Kwena ba Modimosana ba Mmatau. But new Nguni groups had also begun to migrate into the region from the south and east. Among them were the Pô, who established a settlement at Tlhogokgolo below Wolhuterskop, an isolated hill near modern Hartbeespoort Dam. Although of Nguni origin, the Pô eventually adopted Tswana customs and language and were assimilated into their society. These two groups, the Kwena and Pô, were the principal inhabitants of the Cradle until 1827.

Travellers recorded the presence of elephants in the Magaliesberg well into the nineteenth century; ivory was an important item of trade for the people of the region. A lone bull, probably the last one in the region, was shot on the site of the Hartbeespoort Dam shortly before the start of the South African War in 1899. Initially, the ivory trade routes linked the region with the coast of East Africa, crossing the Lowveld to Sofala and other Indian Ocean ports. Later, the Korana and Griqua frontier clans north of the Orange River operated as middlemen for the trade, and opened commercial links between the Magaliesberg and white colonists at the Cape. By 1800 the trade in ivory, leather, gold and copper from the area was well established.

21 See Burchell (1967: 566–567)

The decline of the Late Iron Age

In the latter part of the eighteenth century, disorder began to disrupt the lives of people in the Cradle-Magaliesberg. The size of the cattle enclosures, formerly very similar in all chieftainships, became much larger, signifying greater wealth for some chiefs and centralisation of power, and possibly also the need to provide more security for the herds. The number of dwellings in each settlement also increased, as tensions grew between rival chiefs. This accords with the oral traditions collected by Paul-Lambert Breutz (see Interlude 6 on pages 156–159), which speak of cattle-raiding, succession disputes and growing rivalry between chiefs. Large towns, such as those at Olifantspoort and Molokwane, and the Pô settlement in the Cradle-Magaliesberg near Hartbeespoort Dam, replaced the more vulnerable scattered homesteads of former years, and the change is evidence of the increasingly troubled times that weakened the power of the Tswana chiefs.

At the same time, widespread disturbances and migrations, collectively referred to as the Difaqane, were disrupting communities in what is now the Free State, and strong regional military leaders were emerging. The declining power of chiefs in the Cradle-Magaliesberg attracted the unwanted attention of these warlords from the south. The Northern Sotho chief Sebetwane threatened the region as he moved from his base in the Free State en route to founding the powerful Kololo kingdom in Barotseland, south-western Zambia. In 1823, Maleleku, son of the Pedi chief Sekwati, led a successful raid into the Magaliesberg, capturing cattle and women, and further weakening the resilience of the local Tswana chiefs. The final destruction of the Tswana chiefdoms and traditional way of life in the Cradle-Magaliesberg came when Mzilikazi, one of the most powerful military leaders on the continent, invaded the region in 1827.

Museum Africa

Cornwallis Harris painted and hunted herds of elephants in the Cradle-Magaliesberg during his visit in 1836.

9 | THE NINETEENTH CENTURY

By 1820 internal strife and inter-regional raids had weakened pre-colonial Tswana society, and the region was ill-equipped for the tumultuous century that lay ahead. This chapter takes us into those difficult years when the Cradle-Magaliesberg experienced a series of invasions, settlements and subjugation. By the end of the nineteenth century traditional ways of life had been violently disrupted and the people of the region had been cast into a role of subservience that lasted for another hundred years.

Perhaps surprisingly, that time of intense political and military confrontation was also a period of discovery and enlightenment. Explorers, hunters and naturalists ventured into the region from the south and documented its natural wonders, its people and its potential mineral wealth. Many of the naturalists who visited then are now immortalised in the scientific nomenclature of the plants and animals named after them, and the prospectors have left a legacy of the richest mines in the world. All of them helped to expose the wonders of this landscape, and they contribute to the romance of its extraordinary story.

The life-size statue of Mzilikazi Khumalo on exhibition at Maropeng. He dominated the Cradle-Magaliesberg region from 1827 to 1838.

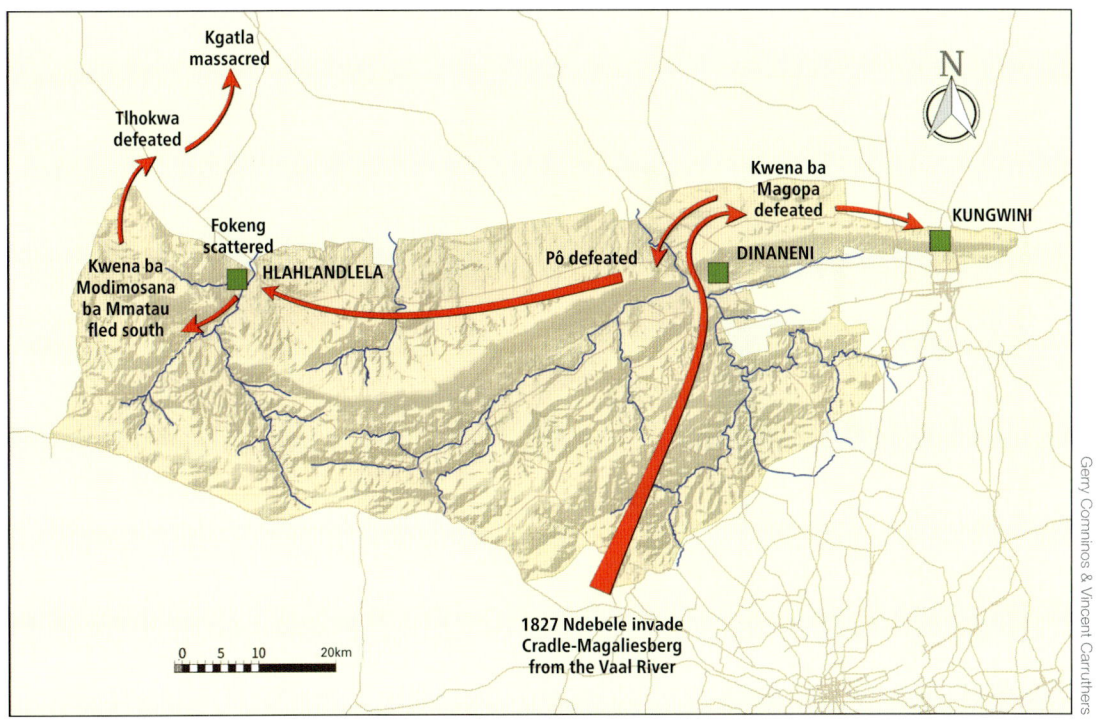

The Ndebele conquest of the Cradle-Magaliesberg region: in 1827 Mzilikazi led his people from the Vaal River through the Cradle and across Mohane Pass (now Kommando Nek). He defeated the Kwena ba Magopa in the north of the Magaliesberg, and established military camps at Kungwini (near Tshwane/Pretoria) and Dinaneni in the Magaliesberg (now Silkaatsnek). He then moved west, crushing each Tswana chieftainship in turn – the Pô, the Fokeng, the Kwena ba Modimosana ba Mmatau, the Tlhokwa and the Kgatla – and establishing a third military camp at Hlahlandlela (Rustenburg). Arrows on the map show the route of the Ndebele conquest through the Cradle-Magaliesberg.

The army that Mzilikazi led into the Cradle-Magaliesberg region in 1827 was one of the most formidable military organisations on the subcontinent. Mzilikazi had been chief of a minor branch of the Khumalo people, who fell within the orbit of Shaka's expanding Zulu empire. In 1821, he flouted the authority of the Zulu king and fled with a few hundred followers, beginning his rapid rise to power. For two years he pillaged the farming communities in what is now Mpumalanga. With each victory, he enlarged his cattle herds and coerced more recruits into his army. They were called the Ndebele and in time they numbered more than 10,000, at which stage they moved west and settled for several years on the banks of the Vaal River. Here, however, they were constantly attacked by bands of Griqua and Korana, who were opportunistic raiders from the northern Cape frontier. Although these invaders came with horses and firearms, the military superiority of the Ndebele always drove them off. But to escape the incessant raids Mzilikazi eventually led his followers north into the Magaliesberg.

No 127 - Machaka (umm: Woming) Conducting a train of tributary Bacquains with supplies fu Matgelikatzi — 1835

Tswana subjects carrying tribute to Mzilikazi, as recorded by Charles Bell while travelling with Andrew Smith's expedition in 1835.

The invasion of the Magaliesberg

Unlike the earlier raiders who had simply stolen cattle and returned to their homelands, Mzilikazi's objective was conquest and subjugation of the people of the region. His route north from the Vaal River followed the Oori (Crocodile) River through the Cradle countryside, crossing the Magaliesberg at Mohane (now Kommando Nek). He established two great military kraals, one at Kungwini north of modern Tshwane/Pretoria, and the other at Dinaneni (now Silkaatsnek – the name is a corruption of Mzilikazi's Nek). From these strongly held bases, he attacked the local Tswana chieftains.

Mzilikazi's men were disciplined along Zulu lines and equipped with short stabbing assegais and body-length shields. These were more effective than the weapons of their opponents, whose fighting gear comprised a pair of throwing javelins with an axe for close combat, and a small H-shaped shield to deflect the spears of enemies. Unable to resist the military strength of a Zulu-style army under its extremely skilled commander, each of the Tswana clans was defeated. The first to be overpowered were the Kwena ba Magopa. Thereafter, the Pô, Fokeng, Kwena ba Modimosana ba Mmatau, Tlhokwa and Kgatla were vanquished in a succession of swift, brutal attacks. Young men from the conquered tribes were recruited into the Ndebele army and a third military kraal, Hlahlandlela, was established near modern Rustenburg to accommodate the expanded militia. Subjugated chiefs were obliged to pay tribute to the Ndebele armies, leaving their own people destitute. Many fled and took refuge with kindred Sotho-Tswana tribes in the south.

Mzilikazi expanded his influence from the Vaal to the Limpopo River. Within a decade of his leaving Zululand, he had created a kingdom

Museum Africa

Cornwallis Harris's portrait of Kalipi, Mzilikazi's senior general, in fighting regalia. The Ndebele were better armed and more disciplined than the Tswana.

threat came from Zululand to the east, from where Shaka's successor, Dingane kaSenzangakhona, sent a large army against Mzilikazi in 1833. A furious battle took place north of the Magaliesberg, and although neither side was the absolute victor, Mzilikazi was forced to abandon his military kraal at Kungwini and move further west.

Mzilikazi's methods of warfare and subjugation were ruthless and, until recently, he has universally been labelled a tyrant by historians. However, to those of his people who were loyal, he ultimately brought prosperity and security. His skill as a leader and as a general is undeniable, and he managed to weld his disparate conquered peoples into the great Matabele nation that settled in what is now western Zimbabwe.

equal to that of his former overlord, Shaka. Nonetheless, while he aggressively expanded his power base and area of conquest, he was constantly under attack from outside enemies and from treachery within. Later in his life Mzilikazi justified the brutality of his governance by citing the need for constant vigilance against sedition, because the great majority of his followers had once been his enemies.

The Griqua chief, Barend Barends, and his Korana rival, Jan Blom, both sent well-armed cattle-raiding parties into Ndebele country. Although both were soundly defeated, Mzilikazi developed a deep suspicion of anyone who approached his kingdom through what he termed 'the forbidden route' that led from the Vaal River through the grasslands of the Cradle. It was this concern that led to his later confrontation with the Voortrekkers. Another

Carruthers (2014)

Robert Moffat, a missionary at Kuruman, whose long friendship with Mzilikazi suggests that the powerful king was more than a mere despot.

Charles Bell's illustration 'The Kashan Mountains from the banks of the Oorie River – 1895' was painted on the Andrew Smith expedition. The valley is now flooded by the Hartbeespoort Dam.

Nº 116. The Kashan Mountains from the banks

Oorie Rivir — 1835 — ... from the Banks of the tirie

C: Bell.

Robert Moffat

One indication that Mzilikazi was more than a mere despot was his extraordinary relationship with Robert Moffat, a politically astute missionary based at Kuruman. Mzilikazi had heard about Moffat from two hunter-traders, Robert Scoon and William McLuckie, and he sent an emissary to Kuruman in 1829 to persuade the missionary to visit his kingdom. The rapport between the two very different men was immediate, and they established a friendship that lasted until the king's death 40 years later. Moffat was fully aware of the tyranny of Mzilikazi's regime. He spoke Setswana – which most of the Ndebele did not – and was able to obtain first-hand details of the brutal subjugation of the Tswana from those who had experienced it. Moffat's reports to his superiors described the massacres in the villages and the frequent executions of innocents by Mzilikazi's warriors, and he persistently railed against Mzilikazi to stop the ritual killings and mass murder. Yet he believed he could be more influential if he retained the admiration and trust of the king, and this he did.

An important consequence of the trust between Moffat and Mzilikazi was that it opened up what was known as 'the missionary road' via the Kuruman mission station. Unlike the 'forbidden route' across the Cradle, this route allowed access to visitors, explorers and traders who approached the Ndebele kingdom with Moffat's approval, and they were welcomed by Mzilikazi without suspicion. It was this accessibility that made possible the visits of Andrew Smith and William Cornwallis Harris to Mzilikazi in 1835 and 1836.

The Voortrekkers

In 1836 an advance party of Boer emigrants from the Cape, later to be known as the Voortrekkers, entered the region along the 'forbidden route' across the Vaal River. Led by Stephanus Erasmus, they camped on the bank of the Crocodile River upstream from where the Hartbeespoort Dam is today. Suspicious of this unannounced visit, the Ndebele surprised and attacked the camp. Several of the Boers were killed, but Erasmus escaped to warn the main Voortrekker party under Hendrik Potgieter who were camped south of the Vaal

The monument at Vegkop where the Voortrekkers withstood a strong Ndebele attack but lost all their cattle.

River. The Ndebele launched a full-scale attack at what is now called Vegkop, several days later. The Boers were overwhelmingly outnumbered, but they successfully withstood the onslaught by forming a defensive circular wagon laager. Hundreds of Ndebele were killed with the loss of only two Boers. However, the Voortrekkers lost all their cattle which were outside the laager, and they had to borrow draft oxen from the friendly Barolong people in the area to pull their wagons back to Thaba Nchu, where they regrouped and prepared for war against Mzilikazi.

In June 1837, Dingane sent another Zulu army into the region, which pushed Mzilikazi and the Ndebele settlements further west, and captured most of the cattle taken from the Boers at Vegkop. In the same year, the Voortrekkers retaliated and, with the help of Tswana refugees from Mzilikazi, they destroyed the last of the Ndebele military camps. By October 1837 the Boers were in full control of the Cradle-Magaliesberg. Early white explorers had called the region 'Cashan', a corruption of the name of the chief of the Kwena ba Modimosana ba Mmatau, Kgaswane, who was killed by Mzilikazi. The Boers now gave it the name Magaliesberg after Mogale, the chief of the Pô, an ally who had fought with them against Mzilikazi. The power of the Ndebele had been broken, and Mzilikazi retreated further north where he re-established his kingdom at Bulawayo.

Andrew Smith and William Cornwallis Harris

The 'missionary road' through Moffat's mission station at Kuruman enabled a 40-man exploratory expedition from the Cape to visit the Ndebele kingdom in 1835. It was led by Andrew Smith, a military doctor, scientist and government emissary from Cape Town (where he had, incidentally, started the South African Museum). His detailed journal was fully illustrated by the expedition's three artists, George Ford and Henry Lowe, who specialised in biological subjects, and the renowned Scottish artist Charles Bell, who painted exquisite landscapes and sketches

A portrait of Andrew Smith whose expedition provided detailed information about the natural history and people of the Cradle-Magaliesberg region.

of the people of the region. The expedition travelled along the south of the Magaliesberg as far east as the Crocodile River and documented in detail the natural wonders of the area. They marvelled at the size and sophistication of the Tswana settlements, and the politics and power of the Ndebele king who had destroyed them.

Smith's visit was followed a year later by the hunter-naturalist William Cornwallis Harris, an officer in Britain's Indian Army who had taken his 'home leave' to visit Africa. The Indian Army was a separate service from the British Army and comprised mainly British officers and Indian non-commissioned ranks. Travelling with a fellow army officer, William Richardson, he hunted and painted

This gorge painted by Charles Bell on the Andrew Smith expedition in 1835 is now impounded by the Hartbeespoort Dam.

Harris [1840] (1986)

One of Cornwallis Harris's paintings of wildlife in the Magaliesberg. This sable antelope was the first to be recorded for science.

his quarry and later published beautifully illustrated accounts of his adventures. His return journey took him south across the region that is now the Cradle, where he encountered parties of Voortrekkers after the battle of Vegkop.

Prospectors and collectors

The published works by Smith and Harris were the first to reveal the wealth of biodiversity in the Cradle-Magaliesberg to the Western world. Their accounts elicited widespread interest and, even after Mzilikazi had been driven out of the area, botanists, geologists and naturalists from all over Europe began to visit the region and to discover a paradise of fauna and flora, many of which bear scientific names based on the names of their discoverers.

Joseph Burke was one such person. He was employed by Lord Derby to bring samples of

plants and animals from around the world to add to Derby's natural history collection at Knowsley Hall, near Liverpool. On Burke's arrival in Cape Town in 1840 he teamed up with Carl Zeyher, a German professional collector and naturalist with some 18 years' experience of collecting in southern Africa. At that time, collecting and selling natural history specimens was a lucrative business. Together, the two men set out with three wagons and many local assistants, following the route of the Voortrekkers who had recently displaced Mzilikazi.

In May 1841 they reached the Cradle-Magaliesberg area and for several weeks they collected bird and animal skins in the region, which the locals were already calling the Magaliesberg after the chief of the Pô. They established a base camp at the confluence of the Magalies and Crocodile rivers, where Hartbeespoort Dam is today, and for the next six months they made short

The spreading crown of the wild syringa *Burkea africana*, named after Joseph Burke, who was employed by Lord Derby to collect samples of plants and animals for his collection in England.

excursions along the mountain range and into the Cradle area. They were the first Europeans to record the marked differences in fauna and flora between the northern and southern sides of the mountains, differences that we now ascribe to the division between the grassland biome in the Cradle and the savannah biome of the Bushveld.

Numerous plants have been named in honour of Burke and Zeyher, and many of them were collected in this area. They include the wild syringa *Burkea africana*, an African cucumber *Cucumis zeyheri*, the large-fruited bushwillow *Combretum zeyheri*, the wild apricot *Dovyalis zeyheri*, the red ivory *Berchemia zeyheri*, the milkwood (moepel) *Mimusops zeyheri* and the elephant-root *Elephantorrhiza burkei*.

While Burke and Zeyher were camped on the Crocodile River, they were visited by the Swedish naturalist Johann Wahlberg. He had arrived in the Magaliesberg from Natal, where he had used his skills as a man of learning to help the Voortrekker community lay out the town of Pietermaritzburg. He, too, collected specimens from the Magaliesberg valley. Wahlberg was a prolific and knowledgeable collector, and the diversity of his interests is evident from the fact that he is commemorated in the names of Wahlberg's eagle *Aquila wahlbergi*, Wahlberg's epauletted fruit bat *Epomophorus wahlbergi*, Wahlberg's snake-eyed skink *Panapsis wahlbergii* as well as in the names of other lizards and various plants.

Not all of the Victorian explorers were in pursuit of natural history. The geology of the region also fascinated many, and the potential mineral wealth of the Cradle-Magaliesberg attracted treasure hunters and prospectors, particularly after the badly kept secret of a gold strike by Pieter Jacob Marais. The discovery of viable mineral deposits in the area is usually attributed to the eccentric German explorer Karl Mauch. In his search for the lost biblical city of Ophir, he traversed south and central Africa for a decade from 1865 to 1875, travelling alone and on foot, identifying and mapping the mineral wealth of the subcontinent. Mauch studied the geological structure of the dolomites of the Cradle and the minerals of the Bushveld Complex, using his own intuitive methods to discover copper, silver and lead deposits near the Crocodile River. He also found the important chrome ore deposits north of the Magaliesberg that led eventually to the large-

Carruthers (2014)

Karl Mauch, who discovered several minerals in the Magaliesberg area before travelling north to find the ruins of Great Zimbabwe.

scale mining of today. Mauch may have known that pre-colonial miners had smelted copper ornaments in past centuries, and he rediscovered copper near the Crocodile River. He also found chrome deposits north of the Magaliesberg. Eventually his relentless search took him further north, where he discovered the ruins of Great Zimbabwe.

➤ 1836–1867: Mogale and the Boer republics

Adam Madebe's statue of Mogale-wa-Mogale outside the Mogale City municipal buildings.

A river, a mountain and a city in the Cradle-Magaliesberg region all bear the name of Kgosi Mogale-wa-Mogale, chief of the Pô, although for much of his life this leader lived in exile from his ancestral lands.

Mogale inherited the chieftainship when his father was killed during Mzilikazi's conquest of the Magaliesberg in 1827. The young heir managed to escape, and fled with his people to comparative safety south of the Vaal River. Ten years later he and the Pô fought alongside the Boers to drive the Ndebele from the area, and helped to win back their home territory at Tlhogokgolo (Wolhuterskop).

The eviction of Mzilikazi from the area in 1837 opened up the region for resettlement by the original Tswana inhabitants together with their Boer allies, but it did not bring peace. The alliance between white and black settlers soon soured, as the Boers tried to establish an independent national state under their control. Their pursuit of independence and their need to dominate the region were to be the causes of conflict throughout the nineteenth century.

In 1838 the Boer leader Hendrik Potgieter founded the Republic of Potchefstroom, which incorporated the Magaliesberg district. Gert

Kruger, an uncle of the more famous Paul, was appointed as magistrate of the district, and he established his farm Hekpoort along the banks of the Magalies River. Like many of the initial attempts by the Boers to establish independent polities, the Potchefstroom Republic did not last and was replaced, ultimately, by the Zuid-Afrikaansche Republiek in 1852.

The confluence of the Magalies and the Crocodile rivers was a particularly fertile valley and several prominent Voortrekker leaders took up farms there. General Hendrik Schoeman, who later played a prominent role in both the Transvaal War of 1880–1881 and the South African War of 1899–1902, took a farm that he called Hartebeestpoort, which is now the site of the dam of that name. Andries Pretorius, a rival of Potgieter, took Grootplaas, which today is also mostly under the waters of the Hartbeespoort

Dam, and his two brothers, Bart and Piet, named their neighbouring farm Broederstroom; part of this farm is included in the Cradle of Humankind. Other members of the Pretorius and Kruger families, including the future president Paul and his father, Casper, also took up farms in what is now the Magaliesberg Biosphere Reserve.

Boer labour demands

Boer supremacy in the interior was based on land ownership and demand for labour. In the 1860s land was surveyed into farms each about 3,000ha in size, and claimed by Boer settlers as theirs by right of conquest. To meet their insatiable need for farm workers, the Boers required local chieftains to recruit labourers from among their subjects and send them to work on the farms. Where the chiefs

Thomas Baines's painting of children being taken into slavery by Transvaal Boers in 1870. He hoped that the picture would help prevent further child slave raiding.

refused to cooperate, the Boers carried out punitive raids against them, capturing cattle and young children in retribution. The children were 'booked' into the custody of a Boer farmer by a magistrate, and they were indentured as *inboekelings* (child labourers) until they were adults. Having been dislocated from their childhood roots, and thus ignorant of their mother tongue throughout most of their lives, these indentured workers had little choice after their release but to remain as labourers on the farms where they had grown up; they 'belonged' to the farm, but had no rights of ownership. Although child slavery was prohibited by the Sand River Convention negotiated between Britain and the Boers in 1852, it persisted until the late nineteenth century. The artist Thomas Baines found a Boer slave train returning to the Transvaal from Botswana in 1870.

Mogale in exile

Mogale, like many of the other chiefs, resented the system of child slavery, and tensions and suspicions escalated between him and the Boers. In 1849 an informer hinted to Gert Kruger that Mogale was helping to arm Kgosi Mgombane Kekana, known as Makopane, who was a strong adversary of the Boer regime in the north-central Transvaal. Kruger summoned Mogale who, anticipating serious consequences, fled with a number of his followers to

the sanctuary of the Basotho king, Moshoeshoe, in the Caledon River valley, where he had found refuge from Mzilikazi many years before.

Angered by their chief's enforced exile, the Pô were a constant threat to the security of the Boer farmers in the Cradle-Magaliesberg, and Gert Kruger made several attempts to persuade Mogale to return and re-establish peace. On one occasion he sent Mogale's mother to visit her son with promises of reconciliation. On another, the chief did in fact meet with Kruger at Hekpoort but, as nothing was satisfactorily resolved, Mogale slipped away again at night in fear of possible reprisals.

The sacred rock pool in the old town of Tlhogokgolo, traditional home of Kgosi Mogale and the Pô.

As the nineteenth century progressed, the ethnic divide between white farm owners and landless Tswana labourers became increasingly entrenched. In response to land acquisition by white settlers, several chiefs in the Magaliesberg region sought to purchase farms for their people. Using missionaries as intermediaries and funds collected from migrant labourers, they bought back extensive tracts of their ancestral lands; a century later these properties would become the core areas for territorially based apartheid and the Bophuthatswana homeland. It was by this means that in 1864 the Pô managed to purchase the farm Boschfontein, which included their traditional homeland and the graves of their ancestors. In 1867, after 18 years in exile, Mogale returned to his home in the mountains that had been named after him. There he remained, and some of his descendants still live in the area. The settlement of Majakaneng has sprung up around the original town of Tlhogokgolo, but the sacred sites at the foot of Wolhuterskop remain in the seclusion of a large forest of *Euphorbia* trees.

A forest of *Euphorbia* trees shades the ruins of the ancient home of Mogale, chief of the Pô.

10 | BOERS AND BRITISH

This chapter describes the ebb and flow of enmity between the Boers and Britain as the tensions between them grew more intense throughout the nineteenth century. On two occasions these erupted into military conflict and the Cradle-Magaliesberg often found itself in the middle of this extended confrontation, with a good deal of the military activity taking place in the area.

The ruins of a British fort at Kommando Nek. The Cradle-Magaliesberg was a strongly contested region during the guerrilla phase of the South African War.

The Voortrekkers who had driven Mzilikazi out of the Magaliesberg in 1839 were themselves fugitives from the more egalitarian legislation being introduced by the Cape colonial government, whereby all people were equal before the law. In what became known as the Great Trek, many

Boer families migrated north and settled in the Magaliesberg. Technically they remained citizens of the Cape Colony, and they were wary of Britain reasserting its authority over them. The two Boer leaders, Hendrik Potgieter and Andries Pretorius, differed on how they should achieve their independence. Potgieter preferred to put as much distance as he could between the Trekkers and the Cape, while Pretorius favoured negotiation with the colonial authorities. In 1852, Pretorius successfully negotiated autonomy from Britain in terms of the Sand River Convention, but the discovery of minerals and other circumstances soon drew the two adversaries into conflict once more.

➤ 1877–1881: British annexation and the Transvaal War

The Sand River Convention gave the Transvaal its independence from Britain in 1852. It was formally named the Zuid-Afrikaansche Republiek (South African Republic), although the name Transvaal continued to be used informally. The independence of the Oranje Vrystaat (Orange Free State) followed two years later. Conflicts with local African chiefs and internecine squabbling among the Boers themselves weakened the fledgling republics and within 20 years the Transvaal government faced financial collapse. At the same time, German and French colonisation was fuelling the 'Scramble for Africa', and the benign British colonial policy of the 1850s was replaced by a more aggressive imperialism. The British High Commissioner for South Africa, Sir Bartle Frere, was a fervent imperialist determined to federate all of southern Africa under the British flag. He saw the Transvaal's difficulties as an opportunity to annex the territory and in 1877, in flagrant violation of the Sand River Convention, he sent prominent Natal politician Theophilus Shepstone to do so.

The monument at Paardekraal where the Boers proclaimed their independence in 1880. The original stone cairn was surmounted by the main monument in 1891.

Annexation was accomplished peacefully, more because of Boer apathy than agreement. A number of British settlers moved into Pretoria and the Magaliesberg, and many of their descendants remain in the area today. Annexation might even have succeeded were it not for the contemptuous arrogance of Shepstone and his successor Sir Owen Lanyon towards the Boers. Self-government, which had been promised to them by Shepstone, was persistently delayed, and over the next four years Boer frustration increased. In 1880 resentment turned to resistance, and on 16 December about 4,000 burghers (citizens of the Boer republics), led by a triumvirate of leaders – Paul Kruger, Marthinus Wessel Pretorius and Piet Joubert – proclaimed the independence of the Zuid-Afrikaansche Republiek at Paardekraal, north of Krugersdorp. The old republican Vierkleur flag was hoisted and the following day the proclamation was presented to Sir Owen Lanyon in Pretoria by Hendrik Schoeman of Hartebeestpoort in the Magaliesberg. Lanyon's response was uncompromising. He rejected any discussion and proclaimed martial law with immediate effect. Colonel William Bellairs, the overall commander of the British troops in the Transvaal, was instructed 'to restore the authority of Her Majesty's Government and put down the insurrection wherever it may exist'. It was a declaration of war, and the start of the Transvaal War of 1880–1881.

The British military contingent in the Transvaal consisted of 3,600 men, most of whom were based in Pretoria under the command of Colonel William Bellairs, with the remainder posted as small garrisons in seven outlying towns. While much of the fighting took place on the border with Natal, the garrisons in each town were besieged by the Republican forces in order to prevent them from taking an active part in the war. The sieges of Pretoria and Rustenburg affected the Cradle-Magaliesberg region directly.

Bellairs and his senior officer, Lieutenant Colonel Gildea, made repeated attempts to break out of Pretoria to join forces with the invading army in Natal. In one such attempt, they defeated the besieging force under Commandant D.J. Erasmus and took all the Boers prisoners. However, their ultimate objective was thwarted because, once they were beyond the town limits, the British lines of communication became too extended to be maintained. Erasmus was replaced by Hendrik Schoeman of Hartebeestpoort as commander of the siege of Pretoria, and he was somewhat more effective.

Gildea led three other attacks on the Boer camps around the town – two to the farm Rooihuiskraal on what is now the road to Johannesburg, and one westwards along the Daspoort Rand. All were driven back into Pretoria. The Boers, for their part, made no attempt to attack the town and were content to simply keep the British garrison bottled up.

One of the two guns built by Marthinus Ras.

The shed where the cannon was built still stands on what was Marthinus Ras's farm near Wolhuterskop.

In Rustenburg the situation was far more desperate than in Pretoria. Captain Daniel Auchinleck had only 62 men of the Royal Scots Fusiliers to defend the town against the Boers. On Christmas Day, the garrison and a few volunteers took up a position behind an earth-walled fort 22m square. Early in the siege Auchinleck was seriously wounded in the face and had to relinquish command for a few weeks.

Unable to defeat the British with rifle fire, the Boer commander, Commandant Pieter Riekert, enlisted the initiative of a local farmer, Marthinus Ras, who skilfully built a cannon from old wagon parts. Several rounds were fired, but they fell short of the fort and the cannon exploded. Ras began building a second larger cannon, but it was not completed before the war had ended.

In the meantime, Riekert had begun digging a trench towards the fort. One night, Auchinleck, partly recovered from his wounds, led a sortie to drive the Boers from this trench and damage the diggings. He was successful but was wounded once again in the engagement. Finally, the Boers attempted to divert the Dorpspruit River to flood the fort, but that too was unsuccessful.

In March, Auchinleck and his men learned that their gallant three-month defence of Rustenburg had been in vain. On 28 February the invading British army had been defeated at the battle of Majuba on the Natal border, and the commanding officer, General Sir George Pomeroy Colley, had been killed. The Boers had regained their independence.

➤ 1853–1925: Gold, lime and guano

Gold

The discovery of gold in the Transvaal Republic was one of the main factors that shaped events in the Cradle-Magaliesberg during the latter part of the nineteenth century. Rumours of gold in the interior of southern Africa had persisted for centuries, but nothing had been found before the first gold strike by Pieter Jacob Marais in what is now the Rhenospruit Conservancy.

Born in the Cape, Marais had joined the Californian and Australian gold rushes and, on his return to South Africa in 1853, he tried prospecting along the rivers of the Transvaal. Near the confluence of the Crocodile and Jukskei rivers, he found traces of alluvial gold. The Boer government was ambivalent in its reaction to his discovery. They had signed the Sand River Convention granting independence to the Transvaal only the

A monument on the banks of the Crocodile River commemorates Pieter Marais's discovery of alluvial gold on the borders of the Cradle in 1853.

The difficult working conditions in the early gold mines in the Cradle can be seen in the old Kromdraai mine museum near Sterkfontein.

previous year, and they feared that news of a gold strike might give Britain reason to renege on the agreement and try to take control of the territory once again. The government paid Marais a reward but swore him to secrecy, threatening him with severe penalties if he disclosed his find.

Marais kept to his word, but the secret could not be contained and prospecting continued with enthusiasm in the newly fledged Zuid-Afrikaansche Republiek. Panning for gold in the rivers never produced worthwhile quantities, but in 1874 Henry Lewis, an Australian digger, discovered payable gold in a narrow seam in the quartzite of the Black Reef on the farm Zuikerboschfontein, near the modern town of Magaliesburg, on the western boundary of the Cradle. The farm belonged to James Jennings, who had settled in the Transvaal in 1876, and he and Lewis set up the Nil Desperandum Co-operative Quartz Company to raise the necessary capital to mine the reef. Lewis and Jennings started the Blaauwbank United Gold Mines Company Limited the following year.

Other mining operations in the Cradle soon followed. Stephanus (Fanie) Minnaar discovered gold on the farm Kromdraai, not far from the Sterkfontein Caves, and started mining there in 1881. A third mine at Tweefontein was started by a German prospector with the appropriate name of Siegmund Hammerschlag. His water-driven hammer mill was erected on the Blaauwbank

stream and served both the Kromdraai and Tweefontein mines. These early finds in the Black Reef preceded the far greater gold strikes on the Witwatersrand, which was geographically fairly close but geologically completely different. The Witwatersrand operations soon overshadowed the mines in the Cradle, but the Cradle mines remained in production until well into the twentieth century. Not many of the old shafts are safe to enter today, but two of them – the Kromdraai mine near Sterkfontein Caves and the Blaauwbank mine outside the town of Magaliesburg – are open to visitors.

Lime

The discovery of the world's greatest goldfields on the Witwatersrand created an enormous demand for lime to be used in the gold extraction process, and brought a mixed blessing of short-term prosperity and permanent environmental damage to the Cradle.

Speleothems develop at an average rate of about 10mm per century, and hundreds of thousands of years of their growth was mined in just a few decades. The magnificent beauty of the dolomitic caves was destroyed, but some people argue that a beneficial by-product of the lime-mining industry was the discovery of fossils that were exposed as the breccia was dynamited. The story of these fossils is told in earlier chapters in this book, but for every fossil found, hundreds of tons of fossilised evidence of human and other evolution were turned into cement or slurry.

At first, lime was used to make cement to build the expanding mining towns of Krugersdorp and Johannesburg, but an unexpected and even greater demand came later from the mines themselves. The wealth of the Witwatersrand gold lay deep underground, and at these deep levels the chemical nature of the gold ore changes and conventional methods of refining it were unsuccessful. Less than five years after the discovery of the Witwatersrand, the mines were closing, markets slumped, and investors in the mines lost their fortunes because the gold could not be extracted from the ore. The solution to this problem was eventually provided by three Scottish chemists, John MacArthur and the brothers Robert and William Forrest, who

The kiln (above) and furnace (inset) at Gladysvale are typical of many lime extraction operations in the caves of the Cradle.

Entrance to the lime mine at Kalkheuwel.

developed a technique of using potassium cyanide to extract gold from the deep-level ore. Cyanide, however, is toxic, and an alkali such as lime has to be added to the ore slurry to prevent the lethal hydrogen cyanide gas which contaminates the ore from being released into the air.

The MacArthur-Forrest process called for many thousands of tons of lime, and from 1890 until well into the twentieth century every accessible dolomitic cave in the Cradle was stripped of its lime deposits to meet the insatiable demand. Flowstones, stalagmites and stalactites, and any other available form of limestone were blasted out of the caves and converted into lime. The process is relatively straightforward: calcium carbonate, of which speleothems are typically composed, is heated in kilns to form quicklime. The volatile quicklime is then doused in water to form slaked lime, which is strongly alkaline and can be added to the cyanide slurry.

In many places, miners dug tunnels into the dolomite hillsides to exploit the limestone, and

An old track and cocopan wheels in Wonder Cave in the Cradle are reminders of the lime-mining days.

A colony of Natal long-fingered bats roosting in a cave in the Rhenosterspruit Conservancy.

roads were constructed – often from fossil-bearing breccia – for the wagons to transport the lime away. Today, derelict kilns are to be found at many cave entrances in the Cradle, reminders of an age of large-scale lime mining in the area.

Guano

Several species of bat roost in the caves of the Cradle. One of these, the Natal long-fingered bat *Miniopterus natalensis*, migrates into the region during the winter months and roosts in tightly compressed colonies of up to several thousand animals, hanging from their hind feet from the roofs and walls of the caves or clinging to rocks with their feet and wing-claws. They mate when they arrive in autumn, and hibernate in the relative protection and constant temperature and humidity in the caves. Their droppings accumulate in large quantities on the cave floor; during the late nineteenth and early twentieth centuries this guano was extracted and sold to farmers as fertiliser. Robert Cooper, after whom

Cooper's Cave is named, was a businessman and past mayor of Krugersdorp who held mineral rights to Sterkfontein and other caves. According to Raymond Dart, Cooper had an advertisement in the window of his shop in Krugersdorp in 1935 which read: 'Buy your missing link'.[22]

In summer the bats disperse northwards to caves in present-day Limpopo and Mpumalanga provinces, where the young are born and mature during the seasonal abundance of insect life.

Lime mining and guano extraction a century ago disturbed many of the bat colonies in the Cradle area and depleted their numbers. At the time miners and others working in the caves seem to have paid little attention to histoplasmosis, the disease associated with bat droppings; there is a fungus in the droppings that can infect people who inhale it and sometimes proves fatal, and for this reason it is unwise to enter bat caves without a protective face mask. Today conservationists have taken steps to protect the bats from being disturbed by irresponsible caving and other damaging activities.

22 See Phillip Tobias in Bonner, *et al.* (2007: 228)

Battlefields and forts in the Cradle-Magaliesberg area

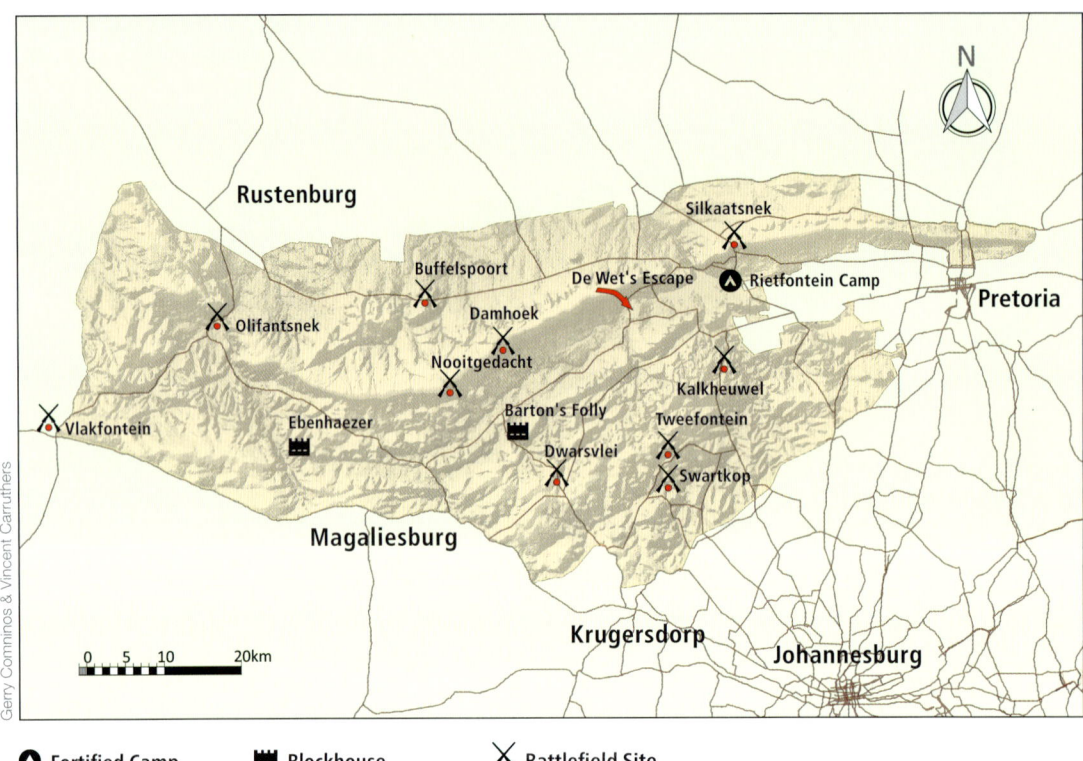

Gerry Comminos & Vincent Carruthers

Legend:

🅰 Fortified Camp   ⛫ Blockhouse   ✕ Battlefield Site

✕ **Kalkheuwel** June 1900. A column of British cavalry was ambushed in the Kalkheuwel Pass.

✕ **Dwarsvlei** July 1900. Krugersdorp Commando attacked the Gordon Highlanders and Royal Horse Artillery.

✕ **Silkaatsnek** July 1900. De la Rey defeated a column of Scots Greys at the battle of Silkaatsnek.

✕ **Olifantsnek** July 1900. Lord Methuen regained control of the town of Rustenburg from surrounding Boer commandos.

✕ **Swartkop** July–November 1900. Krugersdorp Commando held the koppie as a lookout and raiding base.

✕ **Tweefontein** and **Kromdraai** mines January 1901. Boers fought rearguard battles from the mines while retreating from the Cradle area.

✕ **Damhoek** 1900–1902 and 1914. First held by the Krugersdorp Commando (January 1901). Later fortified by British forces and used as part of the blockhouse enclosures (February 1901–May 1902). Used again as a base for General Beyers's rebel forces in the 1914 Rebellion (October 1914).

Rietfontein Camp 1900–1902. A major British fortified supply depot and hospital in what is now the suburb of Ifafi on the banks of Hartbeespoort Dam. The military cemetery remains.

Buffelspoort December 1900. Generals De la Rey and Smuts captured a British convoy of 140 wagons.

Nooitgedacht December 1900. A major Boer victory by the combined forces of Generals Beyers and De la Rey over General Clements's column.

Ebenhaezer 1900. The Boers raised a stone cairn to celebrate their victory at Nooitgedacht. It was later reconstructed as a commemorative monument.

Vlakfontein May 1901. In a vigorous battle, Jan Kemp first captured the British guns at Vlakfontein but was later driven off by the Derbyshire Regiment. The site is now the town of Derby.

Barton's Folly 1901. The last remaining intact masonry fort in the Magaliesberg, built by General Barton overlooking the Hekpoort road.

Lord Roberts leading the British victory parade after the occupation of Pretoria in June 1900.

A Boer position overlooking Kalkheuwel Pass. The car park of the Lion and Safari Park on the right is where the British column was trapped.

The South African War between Britain and the two Boer republics was the largest and most devastating military conflict ever fought on southern African soil. The Cradle-Magaliesberg area became one of the critical theatres of the war, and events took place in the region that affected both the outcome of the war and the future of South Africa.

In the late nineteenth century the British government held the view that the extension of its empire, including control of the mineral wealth of the Transvaal, would bring justice and prosperity to the region. At the same time the Boers in the Transvaal and Orange Free State republics were determined to retain their autonomy and racial dominance of the region. The clash between British imperialism and Boer desire for independence was politically irreconcilable.

When war broke out on 10 October 1899, the burghers of the Cradle-Magaliesberg area joined the Krugersdorp Commando under Commandant (later General) Sarel Oosthuizen and took part in the early Boer victories in Natal. By February 1900, however, the tide had turned. The Boers were in full flight before the advancing armies of Lord Roberts of Kandahar, who had been brought out of retirement to head the British forces in South Africa after the earlier reverses in Natal. Many of the burghers surrendered their arms, took an oath of neutrality, and returned despondently to their farms. Few of them suspected that the conflict would reach their own homes in this quiet rural district, but by June 1900 the British were closing in on the Transvaal capital, Pretoria, and the guns at the battle of Kalkheuwel would have been audible throughout the Cradle.

While Lord Roberts moved along the Johannesburg–Pretoria road, he despatched General John French with a column of about 4,500 cavalry and artillery from various regiments to encircle the capital from the west. The column was made up of regiments from all over the Empire including Canadians, Cape Colonists and men from the colonies of New South Wales and Western Australia, which had yet to be amalgamated into the modern federation of Australia. The route that French took is now the R512 highway past Lanseria Airport and through the Kalkheuwel Pass to Broederstroom. In 1900 it was a narrow, winding wagon track close to the stream.

In the late afternoon of 3 June the column of mounted British soldiers entered the lengthening shadows of the pass. On the hillsides on either side of the valley, close to the modern Lion and

Safari Park, a commando under Sarel du Toit lay in ambush. In the growing dusk, the Boers opened fire at almost point-blank range, killing the two leading British horsemen. Pandemonium broke out. Some of the soldiers retreated along the confined track while others tried to push forward into the attack. In the confusion, the artillery could not bring their guns to bear, and for a while the entire column seemed immobilised. Eventually, order was restored as troops climbed the hillsides to take commanding positions. Throughout the night both sides remained pinned down by each other's gunfire. The Boer losses were severe – 20 men killed – while the British losses were relatively light, in spite of the earlier chaos. At dawn the Boers fell back, leaving French to continue the advance towards Pretoria. But Du Toit had achieved his purpose: while he had held the British column at bay all night, a large convoy of supply wagons which he had been protecting had been able to escape, undetected, to the safety of the Bushveld.

Boer revival at Dwarsvlei and Silkaatsnek

Pretoria was occupied by the British on 6 June 1900 and, having taken the capitals of both Boer republics (Bloemfontein had been taken on 13 March), Lord Roberts believed the war was over. However, the Boers reorganised the remnants of their army into four discrete forces, with each under an independent general responsible for reviving Boer morale and re-recruiting burghers who had surrendered. The Magaliesberg region fell under General Jacobus (Koos) de la Rey and his two fighting generals, Hermanus Lemmer and Sarel Oosthuizen. Within a month, Lemmer had raised enough men to surround Rustenburg, and Oosthuizen had recruited a strong force in the Cradle area.

On 11 July the British despatched a column of infantry and artillery from Krugersdorp under General Horace Smith-Dorrien. The plan was to join a second column encamped at Rietfontein, where Hartbeespoort Dam is today, and the two columns were then to proceed together to relieve Rustenburg. However, General Oosthuizen, who owned the farm next to the present site of the

New South Wales horsemen caught in the ambush at Kalkheuwel in the northern part of the Cradle.

Wilson (1902)

Above: The view over the Dwarsvlei battlefield and the Krugersdorp–Rustenburg road from the ridge where Oosthuizen's men were concealed.

Left: The British artillery brought their guns too close to Boer rifle fire and suffered severe losses. Victoria Crosses were awarded to the men who tried to save the guns.

Wilson (1902)

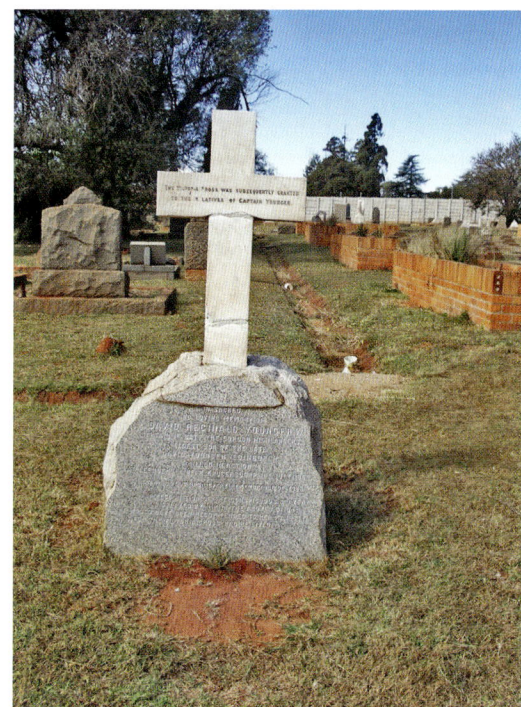

The graves of General Sarel Oosthuizen (left) and Captain David Younger VC (right) lie a few metres from each other in the Mogale City Sterkfontein Cemetery.

Maropeng Visitor Centre, placed his newly recruited Krugersdorp Commando on the ridges overlooking the Krugersdorp road as it approached his land. As Smith-Dorrien's column reached the intersection that now leads to Maropeng, the Boers opened fire.

In their haste to engage the enemy the British artillery brought their guns within range of the Boer rifles. It was a mistake they had made six months previously at the battle of Colenso, and it had similar consequences. Within minutes, most of the gunners and their horses had been killed or wounded. The Boers commanded the ridges but could not advance, and the British could not withdraw their guns from danger. Captain David Younger continued to fire his crippled gun until he was killed. He and Captain William Gordon were awarded the Victoria Cross for trying to save the guns. The battle lasted all day and both sides showed extraordinary courage. Just before sunset, Oosthuizen led a final charge against the guns. He was mortally wounded, and his men withdrew. He

died a month later and his body lies in the Mogale City Sterkfontein Cemetery, a few metres from the grave of Captain Younger.

On the same day, the column from Rietfontein that had been due to meet up with Smith-Dorrien had also suffered a serious defeat at the battle of Silkaatsnek and had been forced to retreat to Pretoria. These two battles in the Cradle-Magaliesberg marked the turning point in the war. They demonstrated to the British that the war was far from over, and they revived the Boer resolve to fight on with a determination that endured for the following two years.

The great escape of De Wet and Steyn

The change in Boer fortunes was confirmed a month later in another pivotal episode in the Cradle, and one of the most famous escapades in military history. In July 1900 the Orange

Free State army had suffered a serious defeat near the Lesotho border, but the Orange Free State president, Marthinus Steyn, and the Chief Commandant, Christiaan de Wet, had escaped with about 2,500 men. Steyn was intent on meeting President Kruger of the Transvaal, who had left Pretoria and was contemplating negotiating for peace. Steyn was determined to dissuade him from doing so.

With the remarkable evasive skill for which De Wet was to become legendary, the Orange Free State commando rode north, with a British force ten times its size in hot pursuit. Abandoning prisoners, wagons and guns so as to maintain their speed, they reached the foot of the Magaliesberg on 13 August 1900. General Ian Hamilton had been ordered to hold the pass at Olifantspoort but had failed to do so. De Wet's commando crossed into the safety of the Bushveld and, after a brief rest, moved east towards the British garrison at Kommando Nek.

Once there, De Wet sent a contingent to escort Steyn to meet Kruger, while he and a few men escaped once again via an unmarked route over the Magaliesberg. They then crossed the Cradle area to return to the Orange Free State.

This episode was far more than an exciting escape. On meeting Kruger, Steyn persuaded the Transvaalers not to capitulate to the British. That decision led to two years of bitter guerrilla war waged by the Boers, merciless retaliation by the British, great suffering, and inconsolable bitterness among some Boers that would permeate South African politics for the next century. No person in southern Africa was unaffected, and even those who were neither Boer nor British were all swept into the conflagration.

Scorched earth

Faced with the prospect of a sustained guerrilla campaign waged by the Boers, the British embarked on a scorched-earth strategy by

Wilson (1902)

Pursued by almost 30,000 British troops, De Wet and Steyn rode furiously towards the Magaliesberg.

Graves and memorials commemorate whites who died in the Krugersdorp Concentration Camp, but black graves are unmarked.

destroying all the farms from which the Boer commandos were receiving support, or whose owners remained on commando. Under orders from Lord Kitchener and Sir Alfred Milner, women, children and servants were sent to refugee camps that were run under appalling conditions of maladministration. Those from farms in the Cradle-Magaliesberg, mostly *bywoners* (landless Boers who lived on the properties of other farmers and contributed temporary labour and produce to their landlords) and African workers, were sent to two camps in Krugersdorp (one for whites, the other for blacks) where many of them, especially the children, died.

Initially, the burghers in the Cradle area avoided having their homes destroyed by remaining on their farms during the day, while secretly serving with their Veldkornet (an elected local official who had both civil and military responsibilities in Boer society) in the Krugersdorp

Commando at night. They occupied the summit of the saddle-shaped Swartkop Hill in the southern part of the Cradle, where the remnants of their fortifications are still visible. From this point they had a good view of the British military movements around Krugersdorp and Johannesburg, and could carry out swift raids against British patrols and target the properties of fellow Boers who were known to be British sympathisers.

Another of the activities of the local burghers was to regain what they regarded as 'proper control' of the African people living in the area. The British occupiers had introduced legal rights not previously enjoyed by black people in the Zuid-Afrikaansche Republiek. Most disturbing to the Boers was the right of black people to give evidence against white farmers. In the retreat in early 1900 many Boers had surrendered and taken the oath of neutrality, which allowed them to return to their farms provided they took no

By the end of the war practically every farm building in the Cradle-Magaliesberg had been destroyed.

further active part in the war. Most, however, secretly dishonoured their oath and went back to fight. They were greatly distressed when the evidence of local Africans was accepted in court – something which had never been allowed under republican rule – and exposed their breech of the oath. Many farms in the Cradle-Magaliesberg area were destroyed by the British as a result of this information. The men under the Swartkop

Veldkornet retaliated with random murders and atrocities against anyone they considered to be an informer.

Towards the end of 1900, Major-General Geoffrey Barton, the British commander of the Krugersdorp area, sent large columns of troops to clear the Boer counter-activity from the Cradle-Magaliesberg district. Running battles took place in the area between the Kromdraai and Tweefontein mines, and most of the burghers fled to Damhoek, an isolated part of the Magaliesberg range. As they left, however, their farms and crops were burnt by the pursuing British, and their cattle and other livestock killed. Women, children and servants were rounded up and sent to concentration camps. Today, there are barely any farm buildings in the Cradle-Magaliesberg that pre-date the purge of 1900.

The battle of Nooitgedacht

The final battle in the Cradle-Magaliesberg area took place at dawn on 13 December 1900. Having successfully raided a wagon convoy in the Magaliesberg a few days before, General De la Rey joined forces with General Christiaan Beyers (who would later be one of the leaders of the 1914

The Boers observed British army movements and conducted raids from trenches on the saddle-back summit of the Swartkop koppie in the Cradle.

Rebellion) to attack a British column camped at the base of the cliff. The column under Major-General Ralph Clements had been destroying farms along the Magalies valley, and had camped on the farm Nooitgedacht belonging to a pro-British farmer named George Hinds.

During the night, Beyers led four of his commandos up the northern face of the mountain, while a fifth commando under Commandant Christoffel Badenhorst attacked the camp at the base of the cliff. The battle began at first light. Badenhorst was repulsed, but the commandos on the summit overpowered the picket guard and fired directly onto the camp below while De la Rey attacked it from the south. Surprised by this onslaught, and outnumbered by about two-to-one, the British column managed to drag their artillery away from the mountain, and retreat with considerable loss of life and equipment. From a distance they shelled the Boers as they pillaged the captured campsite, but the day had been a resounding Boer success.

A hastily built rifleman's sanger on the Nooitgedacht battlefield.

Three days later the British returned with reinforcements and drove the Boers out of the Cradle-Magaliesberg region for the rest of the war.

The British continued to destroy farmland, and by the end of the war forts and blockhouses linked by barbed wire fences enclosed the entire region of burnt-out farms.

The site where a British column was defeated at the battle of Nooitgedacht.

With most of the draft animals killed, the guns were dragged to safety by men under heavy fire.

The ruins of a blockhouse on Breedtsnek. The blockhouse system ultimately defeated the Boers in the Cradle-Magaliesberg area.

Burning farms and building forts and fences was a slow and brutal strategy to restrict Boer supplies and mobility, but ultimately the Boer resources were exhausted and they were forced to capitulate. In May 1902, 60 Boer generals and officials gathered at Vereeniging to negotiate terms of peace. Some were reluctant to surrender, but the hopelessness of their situation led inevitably to a majority voting of 54 to six to accept the British conditions. On 31 May the peace was signed in Pretoria. Lord Kitchener (who had replaced Lord Roberts as supreme commander) and Lord Milner (the High Commissioner for South Africa)

Major-General Barton built this fort in the Hekpoort Pass. It was nicknamed 'Barton's Folly', referring to the decorative garden follies popular in Victorian times.

Peter Delmar

signed for the British, and ten Boer leaders, including the acting presidents of the two republics, Schalk Burger and Christiaan de Wet, signed for the Boers.

The Boer republics lost their independence and became British colonies. However, in the light of growing public opposition to the war, the British negotiators had conceded several important clauses in the treaty. Three of these were to have a significant impact in the Cradle-Magaliesberg in years to come. One was a large financial grant for economic reconstruction, and it provided for the building of Hartbeespoort Dam. The second was the provision for responsible government for the ex-republics, and within five years the Transvaal became a self-governed colony under the leadership of the Boer general Louis Botha. Most critically, the treaty met the Boer demand to withhold black political rights until after self-government. This was a violation of one of the stated purposes of British involvement in the war, and it effectively delayed black enfranchisement for almost a century.

➤ 1914–1948: The revival of Afrikaner nationalism

The Boers had fought the South African War with desperation, especially in its latter months, and defeat had left them deeply angered. However, the bitter struggle had welded the disparate and sometimes quarrelsome elements of the Boer republics into a strongly united society with a common purpose: to retrieve their lost independence. They came to regard themselves less as immigrant Boers (farmers) and more as a cohesive Afrikaner nation to whom southern Africa was home.

In 1910 the four self-governing colonies – the Cape, Natal, the Transvaal and the Orange River Colony – were united in the Union of South Africa. British attempts to entice English-speaking immigrants had been unsuccessful, and Louis Botha's largely Afrikaner party held an overwhelming majority in parliament. His policy was to build an Afrikaner nation within the world power of the British Empire. For a small number of republican diehards, however, the lenient terms

of the Treaty of Vereeniging and the recovery of Afrikaner political dominance in the Union parliament did little to assuage their anger. Botha's conciliatory approach was regarded as appeasing an unpardonable enemy.

The Cradle-Magaliesberg was a stronghold of Afrikaner resentment. In 1912 Afrikaner inhabitants of the region heard General J.B.M. Hertzog address a gathering at De Wildt on the slopes of the Magaliesberg. Although he was a member of Botha's cabinet, his concept of unity differed from that of the government. He spoke of English and Afrikaans South Africans not as a united population, but as 'two separate streams' flowing side by side towards the same destination. His aim was to loosen ties with Britain, and his rallying cry was 'South Africa first'.[23] He was dropped from the cabinet, and soon afterwards he founded the National Party that would one day lead the country into the era of apartheid and worldwide condemnation.

23 See Union of South Africa (1916: 39)

Author Gustav Preller's home at Pelindaba overlooking the Crocodile River. His writings promoted the rise of Afrikaner nationalism.

In 1914 South Africa joined Britain in its war against Germany, and the Union government voted overwhelmingly (94 to 12) to invade German South West Africa. Many Afrikaners, mindful of their experiences in the South African War, refused to accept that decision, and about 15,000 of them took up arms against the Union government. The rebellion was strongest in the Orange Free State and northern Cape, but it soon spread through the Cradle region and into the Magaliesberg. General Christiaan Beyers, who had recently resigned as Commandant General of the Union Defence Force, established a rebel camp at Damhoek in the mountains due north of the Cradle. He rejected overtures of peace from his old South African War colleagues, Jan Smuts and Prime Minister Louis Botha, and moved his rebel army to Olifantsnek near Rustenburg. There they were confronted by the Union Defence Force led by Botha himself. Beyers fled, and later drowned while crossing the Vaal River. The rebellion was eventually put down and most of its leaders served light gaol sentences for sedition. An exception was Joseph (Jopie) Fourie, who had been appointed by Beyers to lead the rebellion in the Crocodile River ward. On the grounds that he had remained an enlisted officer

in the Union Defence Force while fighting with the rebels, he was court-marshalled and executed by firing squad in spite of nationwide pleas for clemency. Dr D.F. Malan (later a prime minister of South Africa) tried unsuccessfully to arrange a stay of execution. The circumstances of Fourie's execution – he died singing a hymn while facing his executioners unblindfolded – aroused widespread public sympathy. He was revered as a martyr, and his death played a significant role in strengthening the Afrikaner nationalist cause.

Afrikaner nationalism continued to grow after World War I, and found expression in the writings of Gustav Preller and his friend and colleague

Monument to the Crocodile River ward rebellion leader Jopie Fourie in the Magaliesberg.

Almost 250,000 people gathered for the inauguration of the Voortrekker Monument on 16 December 1949.

Die Burger

Eugène Marais. From Preller's farm Pelindaba in the Magaliesberg (now the home of the Nuclear Energy Corporation of South Africa (NECSA)) they promoted the formal use of the Afrikaans language and Afrikaner national identity. Their political writings and historical works contributed significantly to the replacement of Dutch with Afrikaans as South Africa's second official language in 1925.

Marais, who committed suicide at Pelindaba in 1936, is best remembered as a perceptive amateur naturalist whose work on mammal and insect behaviour is still cited by biologists today. But he was better known in the early twentieth century as an incisive political journalist with a wide and influential readership. However, it was Preller, the historian, who had the greater influence on Afrikaner nationalism.

Making use of every available medium to promote nationalistic concepts – newspapers, pamphlets, posters, film and public platforms – he wrote extravagant, heroic accounts in which Boer righteousness, British injustice, and black deceit and barbarism were persistent themes. His work became the epitome of Afrikaner nationalism, and reached its zenith when he scripted the centennial re-enactment of the Great Trek in 1938. In response to his concept of the idealised Voortrekker, men cultivated grey beards for the occasion, women stitched long dresses and *kappies* (protective sun-hoods), and people joined convoys of ox wagons rolling towards Pretoria from all over the country. There they met on 16 December 1938 to lay the foundation stone of the Voortrekker Monument (completed a decade later) and to celebrate the new awakening of the Afrikaner nation.

11 | SCIENCE AND ENGINEERING

This final chapter deals with the technological developments in the Cradle-Magaliesberg after the South African War. Some, like those relating to astronomy and nuclear energy, were located in the region late in the twentieth century because of its remoteness. Hartbeespoort Dam, on the other hand, was part of a much earlier attempt by the government of the day to respond to rural communities' need for economic development and poverty relief.

The completion of the Hartbeespoort Dam brought thousands of hectares of arable country under irrigation so that indigent white famers could be set up on plots of productive land, and was thus partially successful in reducing poverty in the area. However, real prosperity only began to revive after the discovery of platinum and the opening of some of the richest mines in the world in the Bushveld Complex, immediately north of the dam.

Construction of better roads and the increase in private car ownership after World War II brought visitors from the neighbouring cities into the region, and gradually the lives of people who had once been an impoverished rural community began to improve.

Peter Delmar

Evening tranquillity at Hartbeespoort Dam conceals the many troubles that beset its origins.

The manner in which the Hartbeespoort Dam wall was integrated into the geology of the river bed was a major technical accomplishment in the 1920s.

At the time of its construction, the dam (originally named Hartebeestpoort) was the largest project of its kind in South Africa, and a century later it remains the most conspicuous man-made feature in the Cradle-Magaliesberg. From the outset it was more than an irrigation scheme alone; it was planned by the government to serve as a poverty relief programme, a rural reconstruction project after the South African War, and a symbol of national prestige in the new Union of South Africa.

Early planning

Impounding of the Crocodile River has a long history. In 1898 General Hendrik Schoeman, a prominent local landowner and hero of the Transvaal War of 1880–1881, dammed the river on his farm Hartebeestpoort near the present township of Meerhof. He named the new dam Sophia Dam, after his wife, and declared his intention to develop a much larger project to support farming and recreation. This never came to fruition, however; he died in an explosion in his home shortly before the end of the South African War, which some say was an act of reprisal by Boer sympathisers who condemned his efforts to negotiate a peaceful end to the war. For decades after the war many Afrikaners ostracised those who had been reluctant to fight to the bitter end.

Sophia Dam was destroyed by floods in 1909, by which time the Transvaal had become a British colony, and the colonial government was planning an ambitious venture along the lines of Schoeman's larger vision for developing the area. The river was professionally surveyed in 1903 and a 43m gravity wall was designed, but implementation of the plan for the dam was repeatedly delayed as the Transvaal lurched from military occupation in 1902 to colonial administration in 1903, self-government in 1907, and finally becoming a province of the

This historical photograph shows the early construction of Hartbeespoort Dam which was fraught with difficulties and delays.

Union of South Africa in 1910. It was not until the Hartebeestpoort Irrigation Scheme (Crocodile River) Act No. 32 of 1914 was passed by the Union parliament that the building of the massive dam was finally authorised. The cost of its construction was estimated to be £605,000.

Further delays

The outbreak of World War I and the 1914 Rebellion against South Africa's participation in that war led to further delays in starting the construction work, and in 1915 the original planned location of the dam wall was moved. The plan for the structure of the wall was also altered in an unusual manner: it would now be a 60m-high concrete wall anchored to the rock on one side and to an angled spillway on the other.

Construction of the main dam wall finally began in 1921 and was completed in 1923.

The new site fell on a neighbouring farm, Hartebeestfontein, owned by Adriaan van Maarseveen, who was unwilling to have his land expropriated. This led to lengthy litigation which was only resolved in 1919 with the passing of the Hartebeestpoort Irrigation Scheme (Acquisition of Land) Act No. 23 of 1918, which provided for the expropriation of property necessary for building of the dam wall and spillway. At the same time the government expropriated about 12,500ha of land under the jurisdiction of three Tswana chiefs, Kgosi Jacobus Mamogale, Kgosi Johannes Mogale and Kgosi Darius Mogale, to provide farmland on which to settle white farmers as part of its 'poor white' poverty relief scheme. The African communities now dispossessed of this land were moved to land near the Bethanie mission station, but disputes over their compensation for the expropriated land persisted for decades.

White poverty relief

In the aftermath of the South African War the Cradle-Magaliesberg landscape was ruined, and its recovery was slow. The terms of the peace treaty provided for compensation for farmers whose properties had been destroyed, but the amounts awarded were barely adequate to support the long struggle of each farmer back to agricultural viability. Particularly hard hit were the non-landowning *bywoners* on the farms, who returned from the war or the concentration camps to find that there was no place for them on the farms where they had previously been tenants, and on which the farm owners themselves could now hardly survive. Thousands of them were left destitute, and they flooded into the cities in search of employment. What soon came to be dubbed the 'poor white' problem escalated rapidly in the early decades of the twentieth century, and became a major political issue facing the government.

Hartbeespoort Dam was one of several state projects intended to address the problem by providing employment for indigent whites. From 1916 labour recruitment for the construction of the dam began. The Department of Labour insisted that the entire labour force should be white, while the Department of Irrigation argued that, in order to save costs, a force of mixed black and white labour should be used. Ultimately the view of the Department of Labour prevailed, and the Department of Irrigation was compensated for the higher wage bill incurred by employing only white people. Single white men were paid 3s and 6d (about R85.00 today) and 6s and 6d (about R160.00) per day. Black workers would customarily have been paid about half that sum.

While war and legal disputes delayed construction of the main dam, a temporary narrow-gauge track was laid from a railway siding on the farm of Gert Brits, about 16km away. Over the next five years, cocopans drawn by mules and oxen carried thousands of tons of building material along the track, and the farm siding grew into the industrial town of Brits.

During construction of the dam, labourers lived with their families under wretched conditions in two camps, one in what is now the village of Schoemansville, and the other below the dam wall on the north. In 1918 the deadly Spanish influenza epidemic spread throughout the world, including to South Africa. In the overcrowded and unhealthy conditions of the labourers' camps it was particularly devastating, and many workers and their families died of the disease. The dead were buried in cemeteries in Schoemansville and Kommando Nek, with simple scrap iron and slate headstones to commemorate them.

Headstones made from building scrap testify to the poverty of those who died in the Hartbeespoort Dam labour camps.

The 'jam-tin pipe' was made using containers from a local fruit-canning factory.

During construction, the water of the Crocodile River became contaminated and unsuitable for human consumption, so a pipeline was built to bring potable water into the workers' camps from a mountain spring. The pipe was made out of tin cans from a fruit-canning factory, laid end-to-end and then covered in concrete cladding. The pipe was nicknamed the 'jam-tin pipe', and remnants of it can still be seen on the mountainside above the current property belonging to the Department of Water and Sanitation.

Construction

Once the infrastructure was in place and the postponements had been resolved, construction of the dam itself began in 1920. However, in March 1921 extreme floods destroyed the coffer dams that were deflecting the river from the main works, and the project was delayed yet again. When construction resumed, it was under the direction

of a new, and young, head engineer, Frederick Scott, whose name is now the one most closely associated with the building of the dam. Economic depression, drought and rising construction costs put Scott under growing pressure to complete the project quickly. The foundations were completed during the winter of 1921, and by 1923 the wall was complete. The cost, however, had escalated to £1,446,000 – more than double the 1914 estimate.

To avoid the 'poor white' construction workers remaining permanently dependent on state assistance after the dam had been completed, the National Party government of Prime Minister J.B.M. Hertzog initiated a scheme for re-skilling them, so that they could cultivate crops on the irrigated land below the dam at Losperfontein. A rigorous system of training and selection was implemented to determine how the plots should be allocated to suitable families on a probationary basis, and some farms are still owned by the descendants of those families who qualified for a plot.

The neo-classical arch on the dam wall celebrates a hydrological triumph and commemorates what was perceived as a victory over poverty. The inscription on the west side reads SINE AQUA ARIDA AC MISERA AGRI CULTURA (*Without water agriculture is withered and wretched*), quoted from the Roman writer Marcus Terentius Varro. The inscription on the east side is DEDI IN DESERTO AQUAS FLUMINA IN INVIO (*For I will pour water on the thirsty land, and streams on the dry ground* – Isaiah 44:3).

By 1930 a network of irrigation canals had been completed, bringing water to 16,000ha of potential farmland. A small hydroelectric power station at the base of the dam wall was also completed in that year, but seasonal fluctuations in the water level made it unreliable as a permanent electricity supply. Many years later, in 1970, sluice gates installed on top of the spillway effectively raised the height of the wall by 2.4m and increased the capacity of the dam to more than 200 million cubic metres.

Tourism

In 1925 the railway line from Pretoria to Magaliesburg was opened, crossing the upper waters of the dam close to the point where

A hydroelectric power plant provided electricity to the construction site but was decommissioned after completion of the dam.

A network of more than 700km of canals irrigates 16,200ha of farmland.

Schoeman had built Sophia Dam. Tourists were able to disembark at the Meerhof station and take a ferry across the dam to the hotel and resort at Schoemansville, on the northern bank. The venture failed financially, but after World War II and the growth in motor car ownership the dam became an increasingly popular tourism and recreation destination. Boating was a favourite activity, and ferries conveyed visitors across the dam to various picnic sites. By the 1980s, luxury holiday complexes were flourishing along the shoreline, and weekend traffic clogged the narrow roads.

However, urban growth upstream in Johannesburg and Pretoria has brought unexpected difficulties. The dam receives effluent from 12 wastewater treatment plants, and nutrients from the densely populated cities degrade the water quality and damage aquatic life. As a result, the dam has become one of the world's worst examples of eutrophication, a phenomenon in which the abundance of nutrients causes an explosive growth of algae and water hyacinth *Eichhornia crassipes*. This, in turn, depletes the oxygen in the water, killing fish and other aquatic life. The environmental state of the Hartbeespoort Dam today is an ignominious disappointment after the visions it embodied of redressing poverty,

benefitting agriculture and restoring national pride and economic growth a century ago. The water is still used for land irrigation but is too polluted for recreational and other purposes.

Remedial programmes have been attempted by the Department of Water and Sanitation but without success to date. A private initiative to extract the hyacinth and sell it commercially as fertiliser has been moderately successful and has

Uncontrollable growth of water hyacinth is threatening the recreational and commercial value of the dam today.

reduced the volume of hyacinth to manageable proportions. However, for the enterprise to continue permanently some weed must always be allowed to remain. Furthermore, the presence of a certain amount of hyacinth keeps the phosphate nutrients at a reasonable level and prevents excessive algal bloom. The ultimate solution lies not with the treatment of the polluted water in the dam, but rather in addressing uncontrolled urban development and mismanagement of effluent upstream.

➤ 1925: The mineral bonanza

Open-cast mining that abuts the northern boundary of the Magaliesberg Biosphere Reserve. The Magaliesberg ridge can be seen in the distance. Only the N4 highway, known as the Platinum Road, separates the environmental degradation of the mine from the Biosphere Reserve.

Viable mineral deposits

On the northern edge of the Magaliesberg lies the Bushveld Complex, with some of the richest mineral deposits in the world. Mining activity extends up to the boundaries of the Magaliesberg Biosphere Reserve. It has brought prosperity and employment to some of the local communities, but the ecological price of this activity has been high. Open-cast mines have radically transformed the natural landscape, and air pollution from smelters is bad enough to obscure the Sun on winter mornings. Mining companies are required by law to rehabilitate the land surface once they have extracted the mineral deposits, but the complex natural ecosystems of the region can never be restored to their pre-mining state.

Emissions from this and other chrome and platinum smelters are the cause of serious atmospheric pollution in the region.

Platinum and chrome

The extent of the chromium deposits in the Bushveld Complex began to be realised when they were exposed near Brits during the construction of the irrigation canals below Hartbeespoort Dam. Several mines came into operation in 1925, and today this region is one of the main producers of chromium in the world.

The presence of platinum along the edge of the Complex was revealed by the famous geologist Hans Merensky, who was born in Middelburg to missionary parents and had studied mining geology in Germany. In 1922 he was shown a sample of platinum ore that had been discovered by Andries Lombard near Lydenburg, and from there Merensky traced what was later to be called the Merensky Reef that extends around the whole perimeter of the Bushveld Complex as far as Rustenburg. In 1925 the Rustenburg Platinum Mine opened, and it soon became the world's largest platinum producer. Over the next 40 years, changes in global demand for platinum disrupted the fortunes of the industry, but in 1966 a worldwide need by the vehicle manufacturing industry for platinum catalysts to reduce toxic motor vehicle exhaust fumes produced a boom that lasted until the 1990s. A second giant mine, Impala Platinum, was developed during this time, and other investors from around the world have now opened mines in the region.

The Royal Bafokeng Nation had traditionally lived in this area, and for many decades there were acrimonious legal disputes between them and the owners of Impala Platinum. At first the battle was linked to political conflict between the royal house of the Fokeng and Lucas Mangope, who was the president of the apartheid-era bantustan, Bophuthatswana; after the end of apartheid the dispute focused on questions of mining rights and royalties that might be earned by the local communities. Eventually, in 2002, the complex matter was resolved with agreements being reached between the Fokeng and the mining houses.

The Star

The platinum miners' strike in 2012 at Marikana escalated into violence and death and became a political rallying point.

This has led to a profitable joint venture between the Royal Bafokeng Nation and Anglo American Platinum, and the income from mining has brought considerable prosperity to the people of the region.

While the mining industry has provided employment for many thousands of workers over the years, tougher international markets have led to declining employment and labour disputes. In 2012 striking miners murdered security staff and non-strikers, and this led to a clash between the police and strikers at Marikana in the course of which police officers shot and killed 34 strikers. The incident became a focal point of subsequent labour disputes and political posturing.

Dimension stone extraction from the granite deposits in the Bushveld Complex eventually consumes entire koppies.

Granite

The Bushveld Complex comprises a variety of igneous rocks. Some of the most widespread of these are norite and gabbro, which are quarried just north of the Magaliesberg for dimension stone (granite cladding for buildings, kitchen work-surfaces, tombstones and similar uses). The mining of granite to provide decorative kitchen tops and floor covering has transformed the landscape and entire hills have been quarried away in the process.

Glass

The silicon in the quartzite ridges of the Magaliesberg is exceptionally pure and suitable for the manufacture of glass. Environmentally damaging quarries were started in the 1970s and vehemently opposed by members of the Mountain Club of South Africa and other environmental activists. They succeeded in preventing quarrying at Castle Gorge, but mining persists at Kommando Nek where the post-extraction rehabilitation undertaken by the mining companies is only partially successful. The confrontation between environmentalists and mining companies led to the formation of the Magaliesberg Protection Association, and indirectly to the declaration of the Magaliesberg Biosphere Reserve four decades later.

➤ 1954: The Leiden telescopes

In the 1950s, an observatory was built in the Cradle-Magaliesberg on the banks of Hartbeespoort Dam, near Broederstroom. In 1923 the self-taught Scottish astronomer Robert Innes, the first Union Astronomer and founding director of the Union Observatory in Johannesburg, had entered into an agreement with Leiden University in the Netherlands for astronomers to visit and make use of the telescopes and equipment in Johannesburg. By 1954, however, observations in the city were compromised by the increasing light pollution, and three telescopes were moved to the new facility at Broederstroom where skies were dark.

Part of the historical Franklin Adams telescope at the Leiden Southern Station at Broederstroom, now under the care of the Tshwane University of Technology.

The Rockefeller 16-inch twin astrograph telescope at Broederstroom was a state-of-the-art photographic telescope when it was installed in the 1950s.

The first telescope to be moved was a 10-inch photographic refracting telescope originally donated by a wealthy amateur astronomer, John Franklin Adams, to the Government Meteorological Observatory (soon to become the Union Observatory) in 1909. It is a fine historical piece, now well over a century old.

A second telescope relocated to Broederstroom was a Rockefeller dual 16-inch astrograph telescope suitable for astronomic photography. In 1957, a 36-inch reflector telescope was installed to make it possible for astronomers to carry out stellar spectroscopy – the study of the chemical and physical properties of stars, measured in terms of the frequencies of radiation they emit. The new telescope was called a flux-collector telescope and its technology was the most advanced at the time. It was able to locate stars through an automated process, and it transmitted starlight via photomultipliers to generate an electronic spectrographic image.

The Union Observatory in Johannesburg was closed in 1964, but observations continued at Broederstroom until Leiden University cut ties with South Africa in the 1970s and the site was sold to the Pretoria Technikon (today the Tshwane University of Technology). The optical telescopes are still in place, but the great 36-inch flux-collector telescope was sent to the European Southern Observatory in La Silla in the remote Chilean Atacama Desert, where the air is very dry and the skies are among the darkest on Earth.

➤ 1961: Hartebeesthoek Radio Astronomy Observatory

In an isolated valley in the Magaliesberg, shielded from the interference of cell phones and other digital devices, the great radio telescopes of Hartebeesthoek Radio Astronomy Observatory (HartRAO) monitor radiation from stars in deep space, and gather data on the dynamics of the Universe. The science at HartRAO is sometimes eclipsed by the publicity surrounding the fossil discoveries in the Cradle of Humankind, but geophysics and astronomy throw light on the titanic phenomena that, over many billions of years, have laid the foundations for a living planet and established the unique set of conditions necessary for the emergence of life on Earth. By monitoring radio wave transmissions from deep space, astronomers at the observatory observe signals of the birth, life and death of stars, and help to develop our understanding of the dynamics of the Universe.

The original radio telescope at HartRAO was built in 1961 by the US National Aeronautics and Space Administration (NASA) to receive data and send commands to satellites and space missions. Its unique position in the southern hemisphere meant that the telescope could watch and monitor space probes during critical manoeuvres soon after rocket launching, when observations from other stations were obscured. The first ever colour photographs of Mars were received at HartRAO from the Mariner VI mission that operated from February to October 1969, and HartRAO was actively involved in the highly successful Apollo 15 mission of mid-1971 that was the fourth to land on the Moon.

HartRAO was one of the first completely automated observatories in the world; all the observations are computer-controlled. The largest

The 200-ton HartRAO telescope monitors faint radio signals from the extreme limits of space.

radio telescope at HartRAO has a reflecting surface 26m in diameter, and the moving part weighs 200 tons. For maximum sensitivity, its radio receivers are cooled to -257°C (16° above absolute zero).

In 1975 NASA handed the facility over to the South African Council for Scientific and Industrial Research (CSIR) and it was converted into a radio astronomy observatory. The following year the CSIR established the Satellite Remote Sensing Centre (SRSC) on the hill adjacent to HartRAO, and some years later the tracking station of the French National Space Agency was moved from Hammanskraal to HartRAO. Since 1988 HartRAO has operated under the management of the Foundation for Research Development (now renamed the National Research Foundation) and in 2010 some of the SRSC satellite tracking functions were taken on by the newly formed South African National Space Agency.

A group of physics students from North West University stand on the 26m antenna to study the microwave receivers of the radio telescope at HartRAO.

Marion West

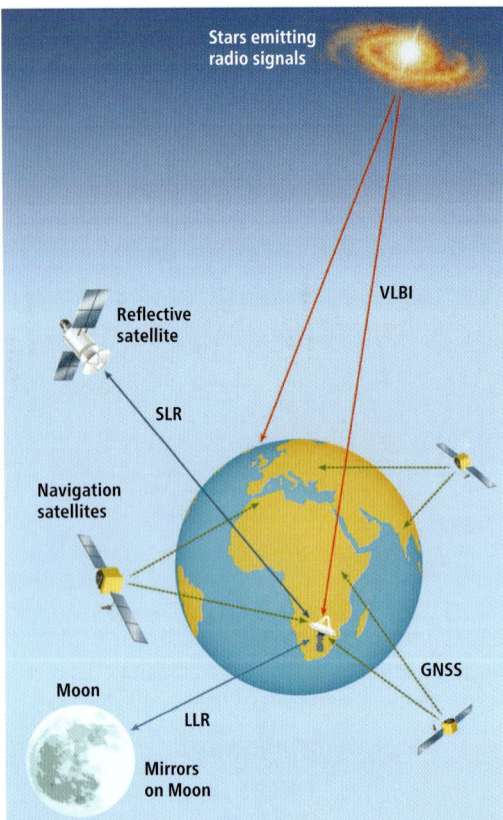

Stars emitting radio signals

VLBI

Reflective satellite

SLR

Navigation satellites

GNSS

Moon

LLR

Mirrors on Moon

Four of the many geodesy programmes being carried out or being developed at HartRAO are Very Long Baseline Interferometry (VLBI), Satellite and Lunar Laser Ranging (SLR and LLR), and Global Navigation Satellite Systems (GNSS).

Today, university students and staff carry out projects and research at HartRAO, and schools and public groups are able to visit the observatory and increase their awareness and understanding of astronomy, science and technology. The original function of the post-NASA observatory at HartRAO was to allow astronomers to pursue their research using radio astronomy, but the radio telescopes are now used for both astronomy and the many geodesy programmes (studies of the precise measurement of the Earth) being carried out at HartRAO.

Using Very Long Baseline Interferometry (VLBI), the observatory collaborates with a network of radio telescopes around the world to measure both continental drift and the Earth's rotation. The widely separated observatories receive radio wave emissions from deep space at slightly different times, and even the slightest movements in the Earth's crust can be detected by monitoring that time difference.

Satellite Laser Ranging (SLR) was installed at HartRAO in 2000 in collaboration with NASA. This programme accurately determines the position and orbit of a satellite by measuring the time taken for an intense pulse of laser light from the SLR instrument to be returned from special mirrors on the satellite.

Lunar laser ranging (LLR) monitors variations in the distance between the Earth and the Moon. Using a technique similar to SLR, laser pulses are reflected off specialised mirrors that were positioned on the Moon during the Apollo and Lunokhod space missions of the 1970s. The Moon's gravity affects land surfaces on Earth in the same way that it affects marine tidal movement: ground level at the Cradle rises and falls by about 23cm each day because of this, and HartRAO scientists have to adjust their extremely precise instruments to allow for the 'tidal' movement of the land.

A network of Global Navigation Satellite System (GNSS) receivers has been installed. These receivers contribute to widely used navigation systems including the Global Positioning System (GPS) used in the USA, the Global Orbiting Navigating Satellite System in Russia, Galileo in the European Union and the BeiDou Navigation Satellite System in China. HartRAO scientists have placed specialised instruments in Antarctica and on Marion and Gough islands, and the data from these instruments are fed to the HartRAO base in the Cradle. Variations in sea level have become critically important data for monitoring the impact of climate change, and the data from the GNSS receivers are combined with data obtained from tide gauges to allow oceanographers and other researchers to measure variations in ocean levels.

At a more everyday level, GPS information from HartRAO is coordinated with data from other systems around the world to create the mobile navigation systems used in cars, aircraft and mobile digital devices such as cell phones.

A laser beam from this instrument at HartRAO measures the orbits of satellites and the Moon with extreme precision.

The Square Kilometre Array (SKA) is an enormous astronomical project jointly located in Australia and South Africa; it will eventually result in the largest radio telescope ever built. HartRAO is being integrated into the SKA project, and in 2007 a 15m radio telescope was constructed at HartRAO as the first step towards developing suitable technologies for the SKA. This telescope has since been repurposed, mainly for geodetic VLBI. This entails the cooperative use of radio telescopes on other continents to form a virtual telescope nearly the size of the Earth.

Scientists at HartRAO have notched up many research successes. These have included the detection of a star-quake – a 'glitch' in the rotation – of the Vela Pulsar (or Pulsating Star), and 40 years of monitoring what astronomers first thought was a black hole, Circinus X-1, but which they have now identified as a neutron star.

HartRAO is the Cradle's link with the cosmos. The work that astronomers are doing there closes the loop between the present and the deep past of the Universe, as described in the first chapters of this book.

➤ 1965: Nuclear energy (Pelindaba)

Nothing epitomises human accomplishment more than mastery of nuclear power, the fundamental energy source of the Universe. It is the subject of considerable controversy worldwide, and Pelindaba, the Magaliesberg home of the Nuclear Energy Corporation of South Africa (NECSA), is no exception. Pelindaba lies at the geographic heart of the Cradle-Magaliesberg region, between the Cradle and Hartbeespoort Dam, but it is not included in the Magaliesberg Biosphere Reserve.

Because of widespread condemnation of nuclear facilities of any sort by those concerned about their potential danger and the damage they could cause to the environment, UNESCO prohibits their inclusion in Biosphere Reserves anywhere in the world, and insisted that NECSA be excised from the boundaries of the Magaliesberg Biosphere Reserve before it would grant registration. The extraordinary history of Pelindaba is nevertheless well worth relating.

View of the NECSA complex at Pelindaba from the grave site of Gustav Preller.

In the 1960s the US government agreed to help South Africa develop the capacity to generate electricity using nuclear power. A research reactor named SAFARI-1 was installed at Pelindaba in 1965 to advance the process of enriching uranium, which would be needed to fuel nuclear power stations such as the one that was eventually built at Koeberg in the Western Cape in 1984.

The project progressed well, and enriched uranium was produced during the 1970s. But as South Africa moved deeper into the apartheid era and international hostility towards the country became more intense, the government secretly extended research work at Pelindaba to include the development of nuclear weapons. In 1977 Soviet spy planes detected preparations for what appeared to be a South African nuclear weapons test site in the Kalahari Desert. At the time, France was negotiating possible involvement in the construction of the Koeberg power station and, to avert a potential Cold War incident, France and the USA brought pressure to bear on the South African government to end the testing programme.

However, the programme to develop atomic weapons did not stop at that point. In even greater secrecy, and supervised by the state-owned arms manufacturer Armscor, at least six fully functional TV-guided nuclear glide-bombs were eventually built at Pelindaba. In 1988 a US surveillance satellite detected a double flash over the Southern Ocean. The Americans suspected that South Africa might be testing weapons in collaboration with Israel and an investigation by the Massachusetts Institute of Technology was initiated, but no proof of this has ever emerged.

The following year, F.W. de Klerk became president of South Africa and, with the prospect of opening negotiations to end apartheid, the government agreed that all six bombs and their manufacturing plant would be dismantled under the supervision of the International Atomic Energy Agency. This was the only occasion on which a sovereign country and established manufacturer of nuclear power has voluntarily dismantled its nuclear weapons capability. In 1996, South Africa's new stand against nuclear weapons was further enhanced when states from all over Africa met at Pelindaba to sign the African Nuclear-Weapon-Free Zone Treaty, thereafter referred to as the 'Treaty of Pelindaba'. Almost all African countries have ratified this treaty and agreed not to develop, manufacture or possess nuclear weapons, and to prohibit the dumping of radioactive waste on their territory.

Under the direction of NECSA, Pelindaba is today one of the four world leaders in the production of molybdenum-99 (99Mo) and other medical isotopes that are used for the diagnostic scanning and therapeutic treatment of cancer. The Pelindaba complex also produces nuclear products used in the petrochemical industries, as well as equipment for handling and transporting radioactive materials. Millions of people around the world have received the benefits of medical isotopes originating from Pelindaba, the plant that once produced the most lethal types of weapons known.

➤ 1963–1994: Anti-apartheid activity in the Cradle-Magaliesberg area

The National Party election victory in 1948 initiated the apartheid era in South Africa. The new government's dual ideologies of republican isolation and rigorous segregation of races led the country into growing conflict with world opinion and the majority of its own people. Growing resistance from liberation movements and their supporters was met with vigorous oppression by the state, and anti-apartheid activity within the country was forced to become increasingly clandestine. The semi-rural isolation of the Cradle-Magaliesberg suited both pro- and anti-apartheid activists, and several incidents took place in the region during this dark period of South African history.

Bram Fischer

In 1963 Advocate Bram Fischer, a Rhodes Scholar, the son of a judge and grandson of the prime minister of the Orange River Colony, was one of the leading lawyers of his time. He helped to defend the Rivonia treason trialists Nelson Mandela, Ahmed Kathrada and Walter Sisulu, but in 1964 was himself arrested for his membership of the then-banned South African Communist Party. Realising the futility of trying to defend himself against the iniquities of apartheid legislation, he failed to appear in court one day during his trial and went into hiding on a farm in the Magaliesberg. Under a false identity he evaded his pursuers for some time, but eventually returned to Johannesburg where he was again arrested and sentenced to life imprisonment. Ten years later, in the final stages of terminal cancer, he was released under rigorous restrictions and died at his brother's home in Bloemfontein in 1975.

The Hanekoms

During the 1980s Derek and Trish Hanekom, a young couple farming near Magaliesburg village, joined the then-banned African National Congress (ANC). For some time they conducted covert activity from their farm, feeding confidential information to the ANC. This included secret information they obtained from Roland Hunter, the personal assistant to a South African Defence Force colonel, which they passed on to the government of Mozambique: it concerned the South African government's support for Renamo rebels in that country, and attempts by the South African government to destabilise its neighbouring states.

They were arrested in 1983 and sentenced to prison terms. Derek served three years and Trish almost four years before they were released and deported to Zimbabwe, where they remained in exile. In 1990 they returned to South Africa and participated in the ANC's preparations for a democratically elected government. After the election of the ANC to lead the government in 1994, both Hanekoms played influential roles in the development of the Cradle of Humankind. Derek has served in the cabinet as minister of three national departments – Agriculture and Land

Affairs, Science and Technology, and Tourism. Trish became the head of the Gauteng Department of Agriculture, Conservation, Environment and Land, from where she led the initiative to have the Cradle area proclaimed a World Heritage Site. For many years she remained in charge of the Cradle of Humankind until the management structure and staff had been fully established.

The Broederstroom cell

From a house in Broederstroom on the northern edge of the Cradle, four members of the ANC's military wing, Umkhonto we Sizwe, operated an armed insurgency cell during the closing years of the apartheid era. Their task was to bomb targets such as army personnel buses, and to sabotage electricity installations and other infrastructure. In May 1988 security police burst into their house in the early morning and arrested three of the four – Damian de Lange, Susan Donnelly and Iain Robertson. They had been betrayed by the fourth member of the cell, Hugh Lugg, who had crept away in the night while supposedly on guard duty and reported the group's activities at the nearby Pelindaba nuclear facility. A cache of assault rifles, mines, mortars and a surface-to-air missile was captured. The three prisoners were interrogated and tortured for more than a year before being tried and sentenced to long prison terms in 1989. But apartheid was beginning to crumble, and in April 1991 they were released. De Lange joined the new South African National Defence Force, rising to the rank of brigadier-general, while Donnelly, now his wife, worked in adult education, and Iain Robertson became part of the Gauteng Provincial Administration.

The Broederstroom encounter

The year 1988 was one of the darkest moments in South African history. The National Party government, led by an intransigent P.W. Botha, retained an immovable defence of its apartheid policies in the face of international condemnation and mounting internal defiance. Opposition was met with vigorous and often inhumane suppression. Most resistance movements were banned or infiltrated by police informers, their members were in disarray and their leaders in exile or detained without trial. Frustrations often found expression in violence. Many township streets were 'no-go' areas in the hands of rebellious gangs, fuelling dismay in the media and further polarising opinions. The prospect of peace seemed exceedingly remote.

At this time of terrible despair a secret meeting took place in the Magaliesberg that sowed seeds of hope and demonstrated the possibility of a negotiated reconciliation. The 77 delegates came together in the Gencor training centre (now the Alpha Conference Centre) near Broederstroom. Half of them were leaders in business or the academic world and they styled themselves the 'Creative Minority'.

The other half were leaders of resistance movements such as the Congress of South African Trade Unions (Cosatu) and the United Democratic Front (UDF), and they called themselves the 'Representatives of the Majority'. Many of the delegates, such as Azhar Cachalia (UDF), Jay Naidoo (Cosatu) Frederick van Zyl Slabbert (Institute for Democratic Alternatives in South Africa), Stuart Saunders (Vice-Chancellor of the University of Cape Town), Beyers Naudé (South African Communist Party), Andrew Boraine (UDF) and others had already played prominent roles in South African politics during the apartheid period and some would continue to do so after the first democratic elections in 1994. The ANC, the Pan African Congress (PAC) and the South African Communist Party were banned at the time, and their leaders were imprisoned or under such tight restriction orders that they could not attend, but many of them, including Govan Mbeki, Albertina Sisulu, Cheryl Carolus and Cyril Ramaphosa, sent messages of encouragement to the Magaliesberg meeting.

Although some of the Creative Minority group had met exiled members of the ANC in Dakar two months previously, this was the first time that such a gathering was to take place on South African soil. Delegates arrived on Friday, 6 August in dribs and drabs, and exchanged polite, superficial greetings. It had taken 18 months of clandestine planning and persuasion by Chris Ball of First National Bank, Chris Nel of Gencor and Zach de Beer of Anglo American to bring the group together, and suspicion and mistrust still prevailed on the first night – everyone was conscious of the threat of betrayal or a police raid.

The following morning the mood lightened, and participants began to trust and respect one another. Differences were thrashed out between 'reformers' (those who wished to change the existing political order to allow a more equitable dispensation of rights to all racially defined population groups) and 'transformers' (those who sought a fully democratic, non-racial society). Points of agreement were reached, and points of divergence were identified and exposed. By Sunday afternoon both groups had acquired a much better understanding of each other's positions and difficulties. The Creative Minority group formed themselves into a formal organisation called the Consultative Business Movement (CBM), and the following year, when the new president, F.W. de Klerk, steered the National Party in a different direction and opened the way for a negotiated peace, the CBM was ready to play a significant role.

The Broederstroom encounter was a historically important event at a critical time in South African history. It did not resolve the overwhelming problems facing the country at the time, but it pioneered the road to the negotiations between political parties and liberation organisations that eventually led to a democratic South Africa. Most importantly, it demonstrated that negotiations between polarised groups were possible, at a time when many believed that there was no hope of this ever happening in South Africa.

Daisy Farm

Underground activists of the anti-apartheid movement were not the only ones to find the rural isolation of the region convenient; the secret agents of apartheid also made use of it. In a lonely farmhouse on Daisy Farm in the Rhenosterspruit Conservancy, members of the counter-intelligence Special Branch of the South African Police imprisoned and interrogated opponents of the apartheid regime.

The scars of the past are still visible in South African society. The remoteness of the Cradle-Magaliesberg region, combined with its proximity to major urban areas, attracted activists into the area, and those who took part in the struggle against the apartheid system are a part of the story that defines what the region is today.

The partially demolished cell at Daisy Farm where political prisoners were held and interrogated by apartheid operatives.

CONCLUSION | THE ANTHROPOCENE

The chapters of this book have told the story of life on Earth as it has been recorded in the landscape of the Cradle-Magaliesberg and interpreted through the work of scientists and historians. The viewpoint in this long chronology has narrowed progressively as each event moved from deep time to the present, channelling the narrative towards the story of our own species, *Homo sapiens*. From the infinite breadth of the Universe it closed in on planet Earth, then more specifically on our first mini-continent and the early development of life. From there, it narrowed further to the Magaliesberg topography and the remarkable assemblage of fossil evidence of human evolution that has been found there. Finally, it focused on the history and development of people in this particular region.

An exhibition of 100 statues at Maropeng honours those who helped to shape our past and present. Future leaders will need to guide us through the Anthropocene.

Geologists and palaeoscientists measure this sequence of events on the Geological Time Scale (GTS) which is calibrated in a series of periods, grouped into eras, and subdivided into epochs (see pages 238–239). Each period is characterised by a particular assemblage of plant and animal life that flourished at that time. The transition from one period to the next is punctuated by cataclysmic events that accelerated the processes of extinction and evolution of species, and gave rise to a new group of living organisms in each case. We know that at least five of these transitions involved catastrophes that brought about mass extinctions of substantial proportions of all life that existed on Earth at the time. Meteor

impacts exterminated the dinosaurs at the end of the Cretaceous, mammal-like reptiles at the end of the Triassic and marine life at the end of the Devonian. The Ordovician and Permian periods ended with sudden climate and atmospheric changes.

Where do we stand now in this vast panorama of time, life and landscape?

The age of the Anthropocene

During the twentieth century, it became evident to environmentalists and other scientists that the rate of extinction of species was accelerating rapidly and that industrialisation and exponential population growth were the principal causes of this. The very species whose evolution is celebrated in this book was itself the catastrophe threatening a sixth mass extinction.

Since the industrial revolution that began in the mid-nineteenth century, humans have been altering environmental conditions faster than adaptation and natural selection can keep pace. Many scientists now believe that this era of significant human impact should be recognised as a new epoch on the geological time scale. They refer to it as the Anthropocene. It replaces the Holocene, named in 1885, which marks the 12,000 years that have passed since the last glacial 'ice age'. Recognising the epoch in which we are living now as the Anthropocene acknowledges the fact that there is obvious, visible and widespread evidence of the ways in which human activity is actually altering many of the evolutionary processes of the planet, including climate, atmospheric conditions, ecosystems and the hydrosphere. We have no means of stopping a meteor from colliding with the Earth, but we can, if we choose, restrict our own impact on the mass extinctions taking place. One of the most important implications of the

Anthropocene may be that the current global crisis summarised by that word has the power to bring together thinking from many disciplines to attempt to control what may otherwise become an unstoppable human-induced catastrophe.

The Cradle-Magaliesberg is surrounded by evidence of human impact. To the south and east lie the sprawling urban areas of Mogale City/ Krugersdorp, Johannesburg and Tshwane/Pretoria. To the north, platinum, chrome and manganese mines strip away the Bushveld substrate and pollute the atmosphere, while the Rustenburg urban complex expands to the west. In the midst of this, however, the Cradle-Magaliesberg still retains much of its rural character and unspoilt natural environment. Almost all the land is privately owned by people who protect the ecological integrity of their properties, while universities, state conservation departments and tourist associations collaborate to enhance knowledge and benefit local communities. In many respects, the region is a model to be emulated elsewhere because of its combination of scientific endeavour, sustainable economic enterprise, environmental responsibility and community development.

Views of the Johannesburg skyline are a reminder of the proximity of human impact on the Cradle-Magaliesberg.

The semi-rural tranquillity of the Cradle-Magaliesberg provides an oasis from which to reflect on the long history of our planet, but it is much more than a mere museum of evolution and history. The historical, ecological and scientific importance of the region has been given world recognition by UNESCO through its two separate designations as the Cradle of Humankind World Heritage Site and the Magaliesberg Biosphere Reserve. Formal international recognition is a practical way to acknowledge the significance of the region and safeguard its future. It also

The splendour of the Magaliesberg sunset is, unfortunately, coloured by atmospheric pollution from the mines. Increasing demands for energy, monocultural food production, industrial water use, waste disposal and contamination are disrupting ecosystems and depleting natural resources.

John Wesson

increases awareness of this priceless heritage, helping to promote it as a tourist and recreational destination, and providing unparalleled educational opportunities for learners at every level and in a wide range of natural and social sciences. The fact that a South African landscape is valued and appreciated throughout the international community is important in a country that is rebuilding national unity and a shared pride in its extraordinary past. For researchers, scholars, visitors and residents, this is a place of extraordinary wonder.

THE CRADLE OF LIFE ON THE GEOLOGICAL TIME SCALE

Era	Period	Epoch	Years ago	Timeline of chapters and events
CENOZOIC	Quaternary	Anthropocene	0–150	**11 │ SCIENCE AND ENGINEERING** Nuclear energy – Astronomy – Mining – Hartbeespoort Dam
		Holocene	150–10,000	**10 │ BOERS AND BRITISH** South African War – Guano, lime, gold – Annexation
		Pleistocene	10,000–1.8 million	**9 │ THE NINETEENTH CENTURY** Boer republics – Mogale – Mzilikazi
	Tertiary	Pliocene	1.8– 5.3 million	**8 │ THE FIRST PEOPLE** Migrations – Tswana cattle economy – Hunter-gatherers – Middle and Early Iron Ages – Later and Middle Stone Ages
		Miocene	5.3– 23.7 million	**7 │ THE HUMAN GENUS** *Homo sapiens – Homo naledi – Homo ergaster – Homo habilis*
		Oligocene	23.7– 33.7 million	**6 │ THE CRADLE HOMININS** *Paranthropus – Australopithecus*
		Eocene	33.7– 54.8 million	**5 │ THE HUMAN EVOLUTIONARY LINE** Adaptation to complex environments – Bipedalism – Upright posture
		Palaeocene	54.8– 65.5 million	

Era	Period	Years ago	Timeline of chapters and events
MESOZOIC	Cretaceous	65.5–144 million	
MESOZOIC	Jurassic	144–206 million	
MESOZOIC	Triassic	206–245 million	**4 | AFRICA** Caves and the karst landscape – Climate change – Primate evolution – Fragmentation of Gondwana
PALAEOZOIC	Permian	245–286 million	
PALAEOZOIC	Carboniferous	286–360 million	
PALAEOZOIC	Devonian	360–408 million	**3 | EVOLUTION AND EXTINCTION** Cradle-Magaliesberg in Gondwana – Cradle-Magaliesberg at the South Pole – Pilanesberg volcano – Eukaryotic cells – Vredefort Dome – Atmospheric oxygen
PALAEOZOIC	Silurian	408–428 million	
PALAEOZOIC	Ordovician	428–505 million	
PALAEOZOIC	Cambrian	505–570 million	
PRE-CAMBRIAN		570–2,500 million	**2 | THE FIRST LANDMASS AND EARLY LIFE** Earliest life forms – Cyanobacteria – Black Reef – First continent
ARCHAEAN		2,500–3,800 million	
HADEAN		3,800–4,600 million	**1 | THE BIRTH OF THE PLANET** Hydrosphere – Atmosphere – Magnetic field – Moon and climate change – Planet Earth – Universe
		4,600–18,000 million	

GLOSSARY

Accrete – Increase the size of an area or body by the accumulation and fusion of other similar entities. For example, the fusion of tectonic plates into a continent or the consolidation of inter-stellar debris into planets.

Acheulean tools – Early stone tools made by human ancestors, probably *Homo ergaster*. They are usually in the form of pear-shaped hand axes or scrapers. The name is derived from St Acheul in northern France, where tools of this type were first discovered.

Adit – A horizontal or shallowly sloping shaft into a mine.

Anaerobic – Being able to exist without oxygen.

Andesitic lava – A particular type of volcanic lava that is more viscous than others because of a high silicon content.

Anthropocene – The current period of time during which human activity has had a significant impact on the planet and its ecosystems. It follows and replaces the Holocene. (Greek: *anthropos* = human; *kainos* = contemporary.)

Anthropogenic – Caused by human activity.

Arboreal – Associated with trees, and physiologically adapted to inhabiting trees and forests.

Archaea – Primitive microorganisms, some of which evolved the ability to utilise oxygen to burn nutrients and create energy. Anaerobic archaea continue to exist today.

Astrophysics – The science and study of astronomical objects, their position in the Universe and their relationship with one another.

Atmosphere – The mixture of gases and water vapour that envelopes the Earth.

Aven – A narrow passage or chimney from the roof of a cave to the surface, providing an inlet shaft into the cave system.

Basalt – Igneous rock solidified from volcanic lava.

Binary fission – Asexual reproduction by dividing the body into two identical bodies with the same genetic inheritance.

Biome – A broad biological region characterised by a particular biodiversity and climate, such as grassland, forest or desert.

Biosphere – The envelope of land, water and air around the Earth's surface in which all living organisms exist or have existed. The biosphere comprises the lithosphere (land), hydrosphere (water) and atmosphere (air).

Biosphere Reserve – A region designated by the UNESCO Man and the Biosphere programme (MAB) where research, monitoring and education are used to explore ways of combining the conservation of natural and cultural assets with improved livelihoods, income and employment for the people of the region.

Bipedalism – The natural practice of walking on two legs (as opposed to four or more).

Bovid – Member of the family of large mammals that includes cattle, buffalo and antelope.

Breccia – Sedimentary rock composed of large fragments of material cemented together in a finer-grained medium. In the context of the Cradle, breccia refers specifically to the calcium carbonate matrix in which fossils have been encased.

Burgher – A citizen of the Boer republics, the Zuid Afrikaansche Republiek (Transvaal) and the Oranje Vrystaat. The term is conventionally used to describe the men who served in the Boer commandos during the South African War.

Calciferous – Containing calcium compounds such as calcium carbonate (limestone).

Chromosome – Pairs of tightly folded strings of DNA located in the nucleus of a cell that carry the genes that determine the characteristics of an organism inherited from its parents. A human body cell contains 46 chromosomes arranged in 23 pairs.

Chronospecies – A species that has evolved from an earlier species over time.

Clade – A group of organisms descended from a common ancestor and representing one branch on the evolutionary tree.

Cladistics – A genetic approach to biological classification in which a group of organisms are categorised according to shared characteristics that have evolved genetically from their most recent common ancestor and are not present in more distant ancestors.

Collagen – The most abundant protein in mammals and the main component of connective tissue and bone.

Computed tomography (CT) scan – A technique that uses multiple cross-sectional X-ray images to depict the interior of solid bodies.

Cosmogenic nuclides – Various isotopes of a mineral such as quartzite created by cosmic radiation.

Cosmology – The scientific study of the origin and structure of stars, galaxies and the Universe.

Cytoplasm – The chemical matrix within a living cell, excluding the complex structure of the nucleus.

Dark energy – A force that seems to oppose the attractive force of gravity, and causes stellar bodies in the Universe to separate from each other at an accelerating rate.

Dark matter – Invisible matter that is observed only because it appears to have a gravitational effect on the movement of other bodies in the Universe. It seems to make up a substantial part of the total mass of the Universe.

Denisovan – An extinct species of the genus *Homo* believed to have existed in Siberia about 40,000 years ago.

Divergent adaptation – The process by which two separated populations of the same species become more and more different from each other as they evolve.

DNA (deoxyribonucleic acid) – One of the two organic nucleic acid molecules that perpetuate the conditions for the life of an organism (the other is RNA). It takes the form of a twisted double strand that reproduces itself, and is the means by which hereditary characteristics pass from one generation to the next. It compacts into chromosomes that carry the genetic information.

Ecological niche – The combination of environmental factors that make a habitat suitable for a particular organism. These include the physical territory, climatic conditions, vegetation cover, food resources, competitive species, predators and other conditions that may affect the life and wellbeing of the organism.

Ecology – The study of the interaction and relationship between living organisms and their environment.

Ecotone – A transition area between two biomes or ecosystems.

Endocast – An internal cast formed within a hollow object, often the impression of the brain moulded within the cranial vault of an animal.

Eukaryotes – Cells that contain DNA in their nucleus as well as mtDNA in their cytoplasm.

Exaptation – Alteration in the functioning or purpose of an evolved adaptation, for example in feathers that evolved initially as insulation and were subsequently adapted for flight.

Facultative bipedalism – The ability to walk on two legs, but not as a normal or habitual way of moving.

Genetics – The study of genes, genetic variation and heredity in living organisms.

Geodesy – The study of the precise measurement of the Earth including its size and shape, movement in its tectonic plates and polar motion, gravitation and tides. In the Cradle, geodesy techniques used include the measurement of radio waves reaching the Earth from space and satellite transmissions.

Geomorphology – The branch of geology concerned with the structure, origin and development of the topographical features of the Earth's surface.

Geophysics – The study of the physical processes and properties of the Earth and space. It can include aspects of geology, geodesy, seismology and other related disciplines.

Glossopteris – A genus of extinct woody seed ferns with tongue-shaped leaves. They existed about 300 to 200 million years ago.

Histoplasmosis – A serious and sometimes fatal lung infection transmitted by airborne fungal spores that accumulate in bat guano.

Hominid – A member of the primate family Hominidae that includes the great apes, i.e. orangutans, gorillas, chimpanzees, humans and their extinct relatives.

Hominin – A member of the subfamily Hominini that includes humans and their ancestral relatives since their evolutionary divergence from apes.

Hornfels – Metamorphic rock derived from shale or mudstone and transformed by heat and pressure through contact with hot igneous lava.

Hydrosphere – The total amount of liquid water found on and below the surface of the Earth. Water vapour is often included but is here considered to be part of the atmosphere.

Isochronic – Pertaining to the level of difference between the proportion of decayed (secondary) isotopes resulting from cosmic radiation in two different samples of rock, one of which was exposed and the other buried. This difference is used when dating ancient fossil material.

Isotopes – Different forms of a chemical element with the same number of protons and electrons but different numbers of neutrons. Isotopes are often unstable and subject to radioactive decay.

Karst topography – Landscape formed from the dissolution of soluble rocks such as limestone and dolomite, and characterised by underground drainage systems with sinkholes and caves.

Kloof – Afrikaans term for a canyon or ravine, commonly used in South African English.

Knap – To use sharp blows to strike off or shape a flake from a core stone to make a stone tool.

Ligation – The joining of two nucleic acid fragments, such as two sections of RNA, to form a new RNA molecule.

Light year – The distance travelled in one year at the speed of light (about 945.7 billion kilometres).

Lime – The mineral calcium hydroxide $Ca(OH)_2$ (slaked lime) or calcium oxide CaO (quicklime), derived by burning limestone in kilns.

Lithosphere – The solid shell of the Earth's crust, made up of terrestrial and submarine rocks and their derivatives such as sand and soil.

Lopolith – A large convex intrusion of igneous material forming a single, unbroken block.

Magma – Molten rock originating from the mantle of the Earth and erupting to solidify into igneous rock within the crust or at the surface.

Magnetite – One of the iron ores, Fe_3O_4, from which iron is extracted. It is strongly attracted to a magnetic source and can be permanently magnetised to act as a magnet itself.

Matrix – The surrounding substance within which objects are enclosed, embedded or dissolved.

Megafauna – An ecological term referring to large wild animals. The determination of what makes an animal 'large' is imprecise, but scientists usually take it to mean 'larger than humans'.

Meiosis – Cell division during sexual reproduction in which the DNA of each parent divides and recombines with a similar division from the other parent.

Members (in fossil-bearing caves) – Sedimentary layers of rock that have been deposited at different times. Members in a cave system are usually numbered in chronological order of their deposition. The date of a fossil-bearing member can be an indication of the age of the fossils associated with it.

Metabolism – The series of chemical reactions in living organisms that sustain life. It includes processes such as food conversion to energy, blood circulation, neurological transmission, growth and reproduction.

Metabolites – Molecular structures responsible for metabolic processes.

Metapopulation – The total population of all members of a species that may be dispersed or separated geographically.

Microlith – A small stone tool from the Later Stone Age, usually made of fine-grained stone. Microliths were sometimes fastened to shafts as arrow-heads.

Milankovitch cycles – The combined long-term fluctuations in orbit, axial tilt and polar rotation of the Earth that give rise to climate change.

Mitosis – Division of a cell into two daughter cells, each of which has the same genetic composition as the original cell.

Morphology – The physical form and structure of an organism.

Neanderthal – An extinct species of the genus *Homo* widespread in Europe and central Asia from about 100,000 to 40,000 years ago.

Nebula – A cloud of gas and other inter-stellar debris, composed mainly of hydrogen and helium, drawn together in space by gravity. With continuing gravitational contraction, a nebula may become dense enough to form stars and planets.

Nuclear fission – Splitting of the nucleus of a heavy atom, such as uranium, into smaller nuclei through bombardment by subatomic particles or gamma rays. Energy is released, and neutrons are emitted triggering a chain reaction of further fission, which can be controlled as a source of heat, or detonated in a nuclear weapon.

Nuclear fusion – Combination of two atomic nuclei to form the nucleus of a heavier element. Fusion occurs under extreme heat and pressure, where the force of nuclear attraction exceeds the repellent electrostatic force.

Nucleic acids – Chemical compounds that make up the main information-carrying molecules that direct the process of protein synthesis, and determine the inherited characteristics of living organisms. The two main classes of nucleic acids are deoxyribonucleic acid (DNA, see page 241) and ribonucleic acid (RNA, see page 243).

Nuclide – An atom with a standard number of protons and neutrons.

Obligate bipedalism – Habitually walking upright on hind legs in normal perambulation.

Oldowan tools – The oldest and most primitive stone tools found in the Cradle. They are typically made by chipping a flake off a stone to give it a sharp edge for chopping or scraping. The name comes from the Olduvai Gorge in Tanzania where tools of this type were first found by scientists.

Oncolite – A small spherical stromatolite.

Osteodontokeratic culture – The hypothesis proposed by Raymond Dart, but no longer accepted by palaeontologists, that human evolution was determined by the development of predatory and aggressive use of lethal tools made from animal bone, teeth and claws to kill wild prey and other hominins.

Palaeoanthropology – The scientific study of the fossil remains of early humans or hominins.

Palaeontology – The scientific study of prehistoric life, usually through the fossil record but also drawing on methods from other scientific disciplines.

Paramagnetic centres – Locations where material has been weakly magnetised as a result of unpaired electrons in the atoms, creating a minute magnetic field.

Pathogen – Any biological cause of disease such as bacteria, viruses or other microorganisms.

Phreatic zone – The subterranean region below the water table or natural level of groundwater (see also Vadose zone).

Phylogeny – The evolutionary development of a species of organisms. The term also refers to the evolutionary development of a particular organ or part of an organism.

Plate tectonics (continental drift) – The gradual movement of large continental plates that make up the Earth's crust or lithosphere. The plates 'float' on the fluid base of the Earth's mantle and 'drift' as they diverge from each other at the margins and converge elsewhere, as one plate is subducted under its neighbour. Seismic and volcanic activity accompanies both divergence and subduction (see also Subduction).

Precipitation – The separation of a solid substance from a solution (the opposite of dissolving). The term is also used to describe the formation of rain, snow or ice from water vapour.

Preparator – A specialist who extracts and prepares fossils for scientific investigation.

Prognathic face – Ape-like prominence of the lower face and jaw.

Prokaryote – A simple, single-celled organism that lacks a nucleus and consists of a single open space not divided internally by membrane walls.

Pulsars – Highly magnetised, rotating neutron stars or white dwarfs that emit a beam of electromagnetic radiation which appears to pulsate as the pulsars rotate.

Red giant – A dying star in which nuclear fusion has exhausted the hydrogen supply and there is no counter-energy to offset the force of gravity. The star collapses, creating heat from compression. This heat re-ignites the gas shell, which expands to hundreds of times its original size, engulfing and incinerating orbiting planets.

Remanence magnetism – Magnetisation that is retained in material such as igneous rock after the discontinuation of the source of magnetism.

Rhizome – The modified stem of a plant that grows horizontally underground, producing vertical roots and shoots and causing the plant to exhibit a creeping form of growth.

Rhyolite lava – Viscous lava that erupts and flows slowly from volcanic pipes; it tends to solidify into sheer-sided, block-shaped piles of rock called lava domes.

Rifting (geological) – The pulling apart of the Earth's crust, caused by upwelling magma stretching the overlying lithosphere so that it ruptures.

RNA (ribonucleic acid) – One of the two organic nucleic acid molecules essential to life (the other is DNA). It is assembled as a chain, but unlike DNA, it occurs as a single strand folded onto itself, rather than a paired double strand. Messenger RNA (mRNA) is a particular form of RNA that directs the synthesis of proteins.

Ruminant – An animal with multiple stomach chambers. Its digestion of fibrous material (such as grass) is improved by regurgitating the partly digested food (cud) from one chamber and re-ingesting it into another chamber for further extraction of nutrients.

Rupturing (geological) – Cracking of the Earth's crust by earthquakes or other seismic activity.

Sagittal crest – The elevated bone ridge along the midline across the top of the cranium.

The commemorative bust of Robert Broom at Sterkfontein, a pioneer of South African palaeoanthropology (defined on page 243).

Seismology – The study of earthquakes and other disturbances in the Earth's crust.

Serial site – Part of a World Heritage Site that is geographically separated from the main site but considered to be integral to its overall significance. Taung in North West Province and Makopane in Limpopo Province are serial sites of the Cradle of Humankind in Gauteng, because they are also hominin fossil sites.

Silicon – One of the most common chemical elements on Earth. Most rocks and sand consist of silicon.

Solar wind – A stream of electrons, protons and other subatomic particles released from the corona of the Sun.

Speciation – Evolution of new species through divergent adaptation, usually as a result of the geographic, physiological or behavioural separation of populations that prevents them from interbreeding.

Spectroscopy – The study and identification of a substance by observing the frequency of the light waves emitted or reflected from it.

Speleothem – A calciferous cave formation such as flowstone, stalagmites and stalactites.

Stellar nucleosynthesis – The creation of new, heavier chemical elements in stars as a result of the fusion of lighter elements such as hydrogen and helium.

Stellar spectroscopy – The study of the frequencies of light waves and other radiation emitted from stars to establish their physical and chemical properties.

Stolon – A stem growing from a plant and producing buds or shoots where it is in contact with the ground; also known as a runner.

Stromatolite – A layered calciferous dome formed by the growth of cyanobacteria as it progressively creates alternating layers of bacterial growth and calciferous deposit in the form of a dome.

Subduction – The thrusting of one tectonic plate below another plate at their point of contact, forcing the lower plate to move into the molten mantle of the Earth.

Substrate – A platform or floor that supports a substance or process above it.

Supernova – Explosion of a star, creating exceptionally large waves of energy and light and dispersing the substance of the star into space.

Sustainability – Use of resources in a manner and at a rate that allows them to be perpetually renewed, and never irreplaceably consumed or irreparably damaged.

Taphonomy – The study of the processes that occur from the moment of an organism's death to its fossilisation.

Taxon – A defined category of organisms such as a species, genus, family, phylum, etc.

Taxonomy – The science of classifying and naming organisms in an ordered system that indicates their natural evolutionary relationships.

Therapsids – Mammal-like reptiles from which mammals evolved.

Turnover pulse hypothesis – Determination of the rate of evolutionary change of organisms (adaptation, speciation and extinction) based on their responses to changes in ecological factors such as climate and habitat. The hypothesis was developed by Elisabeth Vrba based on research she conducted in the Cradle.

Type specimen – A particular specimen of an organism selected to be representative of a species as a whole, and to exhibit the defining features of that species.

Ungulates – Herbivorous mammals that have hooves. The group of ungulates includes antelopes, horses, cattle, pigs, giraffes, rhinoceros and hippopotami.

Vadose zone – The subterranean region above the water table or natural level of groundwater and below the surface (see also Phreatic zone).

Valgus knee – The slightly 'knock-kneed' anatomy of the human leg that brings the legs in from the hips and places the body weight vertically above the lower leg.

Dolomitic water gushes from the karst topography (defined on page 242), keeping the underground caverns above the phreatic zone (defined on page 243).

SOURCES

Anderson, J.M. (ed.) (1999) *Towards Gondwana Alive: Promoting Biodiversity and Stemming the Sixth Extinction*. Gondwana Alive Society, Pretoria.

Anhaesser, C.R., Viljoen, M.J. & Viljoen, R.P. (eds) (2016) *Africa's Top Geological Sites*. Struik Nature, Cape Town.

Atkins, P. (2003) *Galileo's Finger*. Oxford University Press, Oxford.

Berger, L. & Hawks, J. (2017) *Almost Human: The Astonishing Tale of* Homo naledi. Jonathan Ball & National Geographic, Johannesburg & Washington DC.

Bonner, P., Esterhuysen, A. & Jenkins, T. (eds) (2007) *The Search for Origins: Science, History and South Africa's Cradle of Humankind*. Witwatersrand University Press, Johannesburg.

Brain, C.K. (1981) *The Hunters or the Hunted?* University of Chicago Press, Chicago.

Breutz, P.-L. (1953) *The Tribes of Rustenburg and Pilansberg Districts*. Ethnological Publications No. 28. Department of Native Affairs, Pretoria.

Bruxelles, L., Clarke, R.J., Maire, R., Ortega, R. & Stratford, D. (2014) 'Stratigraphic analysis of the Sterkfontein StW 573 *Australopithecus* skeleton and implications for its age'. *Journal of Human Evolution* 70: 36–48.

Burchell, W. (1967) *Travels in the Interior of Southern Africa*. Longman, Hurst, London (1824). Facsimile Reprint. Struik, Cape Town.

Carruthers, V. (2014) *The Magaliesberg: Biosphere Edition*. 3rd edition. Protea Books, Pretoria.

Carruthers, V. (2015) *Mountains of Wonder: A Celebration of the Magaliesberg Biosphere*. Hartbeespoort Tourism Association, Hartbeespoort.

Clarke, R.J. & Partridge, T.C. (2010) *Caves of the Ape-Men*. S.E. Publications, Pretoria.

Compton, J.S. (2016) *Human Origins: How Diet, Climate and Landscape Shaped Us*. Earthspun Books, Cape Town.

Creswicke, L. (1901) *South Africa and the Transvaal War*. Volume 6. T.C. & E.C. Jack, Edinburgh; D.E. McDonnell & Co, Cape Town & Johannesburg.

Dawkins, R. (2005) *The Ancestor's Tale: A Pilgrimage to the Dawn of Life*. Phoenix, London.

Dawson, E.B. & Robertson, T.C. (eds) (1940) *Greater South Africa: Plans for a Better World. The Speeches of General the Right Honourable J.C. Smuts P.C., C.H., K.C., D.T.D*. The Truth Legion, Johannesburg.

Delmar, P. (2013) *The Platinum Road*. Parkview Press, Johannesburg.

Du Preez, M., Evans, G. & Grealy, R. (1988) *The Broederstroom Encounter.* Consultative Business Movement, Johannesburg.

Eales, H. (2007) *Riddles in Stone: Controversies, Theories and Myths about Southern Africa's Geological Past*. Witwatersrand University Press, Johannesburg.

Elliott, MC & Berger L.R., A Handbook to the Cradle of Humankind. Johannesburg: Reach Publishers, 2018.

Some of the sources of information used in the compilation of this book.

The granite cross overlooking Hartbeespoort Dam commemorating General Hendrik Schoeman whose complex life is recorded in *The Magaliesberg* by Carruthers.

Fig, D. (2004) *Uranium Road: Questioning South Africa's Nuclear Direction*. Heinrich Böll Foundation, Johannesburg.

Friede, H.M. (1977) 'Iron Age metal working in the Magaliesberg area'. *Journal of the South African Institute of Mining and Metallurgy* 77: 224–232.

Granger, D.E., Gibbon, R.J., Kuman, K., Clarke, R.J., Bruxelles, L. & Caffee, M.W. (2015) 'New cosmogenic burial ages for Sterkfontein Member 2, *Australopithecus* and Member 5, Oldowan'. *Nature* 522: 85–86.

Griffiths, B. (2018) *Deep Time Dreaming: Uncovering Ancient Australia*. Black Inc., Melbourne.

Hamilton, C. (ed.) (1995) *The Mfecane Aftermath: Reconstructive Debates in Southern African History*. Witwatersrand University Press & University of Natal Press, Johannesburg & Pietermaritzburg.

Harris, P. (2010) *Birth: The Conspiracy to Stop the '94 Election*. Umuzi, Cape Town.

Harris, W.C. (1986) *Portraits of the Game and Wild Animals of Southern Africa*. The Proprietor, London (1840). Reprinted by Sable Publishers, Cape Town.

Hilton-Barber, B. & Berger, L.R. (2004) *Field Guide to the Cradle of Humankind*. Revised edition. Struik, Cape Town.

Hilton-Barber, B. & Berger, L.R. (2006) *A Guide to Sterkfontein: The Cradle of Humankind*. Struik, Cape Town.

Hofmeyr, I. (1988) 'Popularising history: the case of Gustav Preller'. *Journal of African Studies* 29(3): 521–535.

Huffman, T.N. (1993) 'Broederstroom and the central cattle pattern'. *South African Journal of Science* 89: 220–226.

Huffman, T.N. (2007) *Handbook to the Iron Age*. University of KwaZulu-Natal Press, Pietermaritzburg.

Huffman, T.N. (2009) 'A cultural proxy for drought: ritual burning in the Iron age of Southern Africa'. *Journal of Archaeological Science* 36: 991–1005.

Huffman, T.N. (2010) 'Intensive El Niño and the Iron Age of South-eastern Africa'. *Journal of Archaeological Science* 37: 2572–2586.

Huffman, T.N. & Murimbika, M. (2003) 'Shona ethnography and Iron Age burials'. *Journal of African Archaeology* 1(2): 237–246.

James, H. (2000) 'The rock engravings of several portions of the farm Doornkloof 393 JQ along the Magaliesberg range'. Unpublished MA dissertation, Department of Archaeology, University of Pretoria.

Jha, A. (2016) *The Water Book*. Headline, London.

Johanson, D. & Edgar, B. (2006) *From Lucy to Language*. Simon & Schuster, New York.

Johnson, M.R., Anhaeusser, C.R. & Thomas, R.J. (eds) (2006) *The Geology of South Africa*. Geological Society of South Africa & Council for Geoscience, Pretoria.

Kuljian, C. (2016) *Darwin's Hunch: Science, Race and the Search for Human Origins*. Jacana Media, Johannesburg.

Letcher, O. (1936) *The Gold Mines of Southern Africa*. Waterlow & Sons, London.

Lewis-Williams, D. & Dowson, T. (2000) *Images of Power: Understanding San Rock Art*. Struik, Cape Town.

Lewis-Williams, J.D. (1983) *The Rock Art of Southern Africa*. Cambridge University Press, Cambridge.

MacRae, C. (1999) *Life Etched in Stone: Fossils of South Africa*. Geological Society of South Africa, Johannesburg.

Mason, R. (1969) *Prehistory of the Transvaal*. Witwatersrand University Press, Johannesburg.

Mason, R. (1986) *Origins of Black People of Johannesburg and the Southern Western Central Transvaal AD 350–1880*. Occasional Paper No. 16. Archaeological Research Unit, University of the Witwatersrand, Johannesburg.

Mason, R. (1988) *Kruger Cave Magaliesberg, Transvaal*. Occasional Paper No. 17. Archaeological Research Unit, University of the Witwatersrand, Johannesburg.

Mason, R.J. (1968) 'Transvaal and Natal Iron Age settlement revealed by aerial photography and excavation'. *African Studies* 27(4): 1–16.

Mason, R.J. (1974) 'Background to the Transvaal Iron Age: new discoveries at Olifantspoort and Broederstroom'. *Journal of the South African Institute of Mining and Metallurgy* 74: 211–216.

Mason, R.J. (1989) *South African Archaeology 1922–1988*. Occasional Paper No. 22. Archaeological Research Unit, University of the Witwatersrand, Johannesburg.

Mason, R.J. & Van der Merwe, N.J. (1964) 'Radiocarbon dating of Iron Age sites in the southern Transvaal: Melville Koppies and Uitkomst Cave'. *South African Journal of Science* 60(5): 142.

McCarthy, T. & Rubidge, B. (2005) *The Story of Earth & Life*. Struik, Cape Town.

Meredith, M. (2011) *Born in Africa: The Quest for the Origins of Human Life*. Jonathan Ball & Simon & Schuster, Johannesburg & London.

Miller, D., Boeyens, J. & Küsel, M. (1995) 'Metallurgical analyses of slags, ores, and metal artefacts from archaeological sites in North West Province and Northern Transvaal'. *The South African Archaeological Bulletin* 50(161): 39–54.

Mitchell, P. (2002) *The Archaeology of Southern Africa*. Cambridge University Press, Cambridge.

Morton, F. (2009) *When Rustling Became an Art: Pilane's Kgatla and the Transvaal Frontier*. David Philip, Cape Town.

An old bridge over the Magalies River from the days of the construction of Hartbeespoort Dam, described in Van Vuuren's *In the Footsteps of Giants*.

Mucina, L. & Rutherford, M.C. (eds) (2006) *The Vegetation of South Africa, Lesotho and Swaziland. Strelitzia* 19. SANBI, Pretoria.

Nhaura, G. (2010) 'Characterization of the elemental deposits in fossils from the Cradle of Humankind in South Africa and modern bones from the same geological area'. Unpublished MSc dissertation, University of the Witwatersrand.

Nield, T. (2007) *Supercontinent: Ten Billion Years in the Life of our Planet*. Granta, London.

Oppenheimer, S. (2003) *Out of Africa's Eden: The Peopling of the World*. Jonathan Ball, Johannesburg & Cape Town.

Palmer, D. (2007) *The Origins of Man*. New Holland, London.

Partridge, T.C. (ed.) (1999) *Tswaing: Investigations into the Origin, Age and Palaeoenvironments of the Pretoria Saltpan*. Memoir 85, Council for Geoscience, Geological Survey of South Africa, Pretoria.

Partridge, T.C. & Maud, R.R. (eds) (2000) *The Cenozoic of Southern Africa*. Oxford University Press, New York.

Pickering, T.R., Clarke, R.J. & Heaton, J.L. (2004) 'The context of Stw 573, an early hominid skull and skeleton from Sterkfontein Member 2: taphonomy and paleoenvironment'. *Journal of Human Evolution* 46: 279–297.

Rasmussen, R.K. (1978) *Migrant Kingdom: Mzilikazi's Ndebele in South Africa*. Rex Collings & David Philip, London & Cape Town.

Reimold, W.U. & Gibson, R.L. (2005) *Meteorite Impact! The Danger from Space and South Africa's Mega-impact: The Vredefort Structure*. Chris van Rensburg, Johannesburg.

Sanders, M. (1973) 'Glimpses of the Past'. Unpublished manuscript.

Soodyall, H. (ed.) (2006) *The Prehistory of Africa: Tracing the Lineage of Modern Man*. Jonathan Ball, Johannesburg.

Swanepoel, N., Esterhuysen, A. & Bonner, P. (eds) (2008) *500 Years Rediscovered: Southern African Precedents and Prospects.* Witwatersrand University Press, Johannesburg.

Swart, S. (2015) 'An African contribution to the nuclear weapons debate'. *International Review of the Red Cross* 97(899): 753–773.

Sykes, B. (2001) *The Seven Daughters of Eve*. Corgi Books, London.

One of the many waterfalls in the beautiful Magaliesberg geology, explained in Viljoen & Viljoen's *Geological Excursion Guide.*

Union of South Africa. *Report of the Judicial Commission of Inquiry into the Causes and Circumstances Relating to the Recent Rebellion in South Africa, December 1916*. UG46'16.

Van As, J., Du Preez, J., Brown, L. & Smit, N. (2012) *The Story of Life & the Environment: An African Perspective*. Struik Nature, Cape Town.

Van Vuuren, L. (2012) *In the Footsteps of Giants: Exploring the History of South Africa's Large Dams*. Water Research Commission, Pretoria.

Viljoen, M.J. & Viljoen R.P. (2019) *Geological Excursion Guide to the Magaliesberg Cableway at Hartbeespoort Dam*. Council for Geoscience, 35th International Geological Congress, Legacy Publication.

Wadley, L. (1996) 'Changes in the social relations of pre-colonial hunter-gatherers after agropastoralist contact: an example from the Magaliesberg, South Africa'. *Journal of Anthropological Archaeology* 15(2): 205–217.

Wilson, H.W. (1902) *After Pretoria: The Guerrilla War*. Volume 1. The Amalgamated Press, London.

INDEX